Mental Health Services in Criminal Justice System Settings

Recent Titles in
Research and Bibliographical Guides in Criminal Justice

Criminal Activity in the Deep South, 1700–1930: An Annotated Bibliography
A. J. Wright, compiler

Criminal Justice Ethics: Research and Bibliographical Guide
Frank Schmalleger, compiler, with the assistance of Robert McKenrick

Comparative Criminology: An Annotated Bibliography
Piers Beirne and Joan Hill, compilers

Criminal Justice in Israel: An Annotated Bibliography of English Language
Publications, 1948–1993
Robert J. Friedmann

Female Offenders: An Annotated Bibliography
Kathleen A. O'Shea and Beverly R. Fletcher, compilers

Mental Health Services in Criminal Justice System Settings

A Selectively Annotated Bibliography, 1970–1997

Compiled by
Rodney Van Whitlock
and Bernard Lubin

Foreword by Stanley L. Brodsky

Published in cooperation with NTL Institute
for Applied Behavioral Science

Research and Bibliographical Guides in Criminal Justice, Number 6

Greenwood Press
Westport, Connecticut • London

RC
451.4
.P68
V34
1999

Library of Congress Cataloging-in-Publication Data

Van Whitlock, Rodney.
   Mental health services in criminal justice system settings : a
selectively annotated bibliography, 1970–1997 / compiled by Rodney
Van Whitlock and Bernard Lubin ; foreword by Stanley L. Brodsky.
     p.   cm.—(Research and bibliographical guides in criminal
justice, ISSN 1042–4636 ; no. 6)
  Includes bibliographical references and indexes.
  ISBN 0–313–30186–7 (alk. paper)
   1. Prisoners—Mental health services—Bibliography. 2. Prisoners—
Mental health—Bibliography. I. Lubin, Bernard, 1923– .
II. Title. III. Series.
Z5703.4.P75V34 1999
[RC451.4.P68]
016.3622'086'927—dc21   98–29678

British Library Cataloguing in Publication Data is available.

Copyright © 1999 by Rodney Van Whitlock and Bernard Lubin

All rights reserved. No portion of this book may be
reproduced, by any process or technique, without the
express written consent of the publisher.

Library of Congress Catalog Card Number: 98–29678
ISBN: 0–313–30186–7
ISSN: 1042–4636

First published in 1999

Greenwood Press, 88 Post Road West, Westport, CT 06881
An imprint of Greenwood Publishing Group, Inc.

Printed in the United States of America

The paper used in this book complies with the
Permanent Paper Standard issued by the National
Information Standards Organization (Z39.48–1984).

10 9 8 7 6 5 4 3 2 1

DISCARDED
WIDENER UNIVERSITY

WIDENER UNIVERSITY
WOLFGRAM
LIBRARY
CHESTER, PA

Contents

Foreword by Stanley L. Brodsky   vii

Preface   ix

1.   Mental Disorders (Axis I)   1

2.   Antisocial and Other Personality Disorders   15

3.   Assessment and Classification of Offenders   23

4.   Institution-Based Programs and Services   37

5.   Community-Based Programs and Services   53

6.   Local Justice System Issues   65

7.   Individual Psychotherapy   81

8.   Group, Marital, and Family Therapy   85

9.   Jail and Prison Suicide   91

10.   Violence and Aggression   99

11.   Sex Offenders   115

12.   Adolescent Offenders   131

13.   Female Mentally Ill Offenders   141

14.   Professional and Ethical Issues   149

15.   Education and Training   161

Author Index   165

Subject Index   183

Foreword

One of the great deficits in planning treatment of psychologically disturbed offenders has been the process of beginning from point zero. Practitioners and planners alike start by drawing on their training and their experience. The trouble is that little training exists in graduate education and continuing education workshops for dealing with mentally disturbed offenders and that research suggests that clinicians do not learn well from experience. The responsible alternative is to draw on the existing scholarly and professional literature.

Those of us who regularly scour the literature find it a daunting task. The published articles are scattered in a half-dozen databases, and even these are sketchy and incomplete. Some of my graduate students recently searched databases and libraries for articles on specific psychological treatments in prisons, unearthing only a handful of useful publications.

It is exactly for the two reasons of planning treatment of offenders and conducting research that this annotated bibliography is so important. Van Whitlock and Lubin have taken on the encyclopedic task of gathering in one source the citations to 1264 articles, chapters, and books, and annotations of many of them. The cited journals cover an impressive range, from well-established and known journals to discontinued journals like *Issues in Criminological and Legal Psychology* and *Forensic Reports*, among others, and journals new to me, such as the *Journal for Specialists in Group Work* and *Confrontation Psychologique*. One of the outcomes of using this bibliography is the need for an excellent reference librarian or unusual perseverance to search out the little known and discontinued journals. I would hope that Van Whitlock and Lubin would consider placing their articles in an archive which could allow access by interested scholars and practitioners.

This annotated bibliography covers a period of 27 years. During this time psychological treatments in criminal justice settings have evolved substantially. In the early 1970s, one common working assumption was that effective psychotherapy cured criminals. Another assumption was that indeterminate sentences were desirable because they allowed treatment until readiness for release. A third assumption was that psychodynamically based therapies were the treatments of choice, an assumption that has given way to problem-focused, eclectic and cognitive-behavioral therapies as typical treatments of choice. Although the citations in this book are organized by topic (and properly so) rather than over time, the articles cited reflect the ways in which these three assumptions have been discarded in part and reshaped since 1971.

The work of book editors is often difficult to sort out from the individual contributions. In the case of compilers of bibliographies, their work is nearly invisible. It is only through a four year project annotating 1500 articles on sexual assault and victims that I became aware of the magnitude of the work. Van Whitlock and Lubin have given us a product of enormous effort and scholarship. This book is an important addition to our resources for understanding and planning mental health treatments for offenders. Samuel Johnson once wrote that "Knowledge is of two kinds. We know a subject ourselves or we know where we can find information upon it." It is the latter form of knowledge that Van Whitlock and Lubin have so thoughtfully shared with us.

Stanley L. Brodsky
Tuscaloosa, Alabama
April 27, 1998

Preface

It is perhaps inevitable that U.S. legal and correctional system policies as well as cultural tendencies to exclude more and more people for longer and longer periods of time should contribute to the increase in numbers and severity of major mental health problems in our jails and prisons. As yet, federal, state, and municipal budgets have not shown awareness of the growing problems by funding an increasing number of mental health professionals in the correctional system.

The need to increase the number of mental health professionals trained in matters important to the legal and correctional systems can be seen also in the increasing number of situations for which such skills are required. Advising judicial decision-makers by assessing pre-trial competency, insanity and dangerousness, assisting in jury selection, conducting parent evaluations in child custody cases, and evaluating psychological injury in civil damage cases, are only a few of such situations.

Several professions make important contributions to mental health practice and research in the legal-correctional system. It was our purpose to collect a comprehensive sample of the corrections-related literature from several of these professions, including psychology, psychiatry, nursing, education, social work, and related empirical, and practice-related issues that mental health researchers and practitioners encounter in providing services to mentally ill and substance abusing offenders in criminal justice system settings.

The 1264 citations listed in this bibliography are presented in 15 sections. Both an author index and a subject index are provided in order to facilitate access to these resources. Of the citations listed, 150 are books, and 542 of the citations are annotated. Letters, comments, and other non-empirical articles were annotated only if they were of considerable theoretical or practical value. Most empirically based citations were annotated.

The citations are divided into the following fifteen sections: (1) Mental Disorders (Axis I), (2) Antisocial and Other Personality Disorders, (3) Assessment and Classification of Offenders, (4) Institution-Based Programs and Services, (5) Community-Based Programs and Services, (6) Local Justice System Issues, (7) Individual Psychotherapy, (8) Group,

Marital and Family Therapy, (9) Jail and Prison Suicide, (10) Violence and Aggression, (11) Sex Offenders, (12) Adolescent Offenders, (13) Female Mentally Ill Offenders, (14) Professional and Ethical Issues, and (15) Education and Training.

It is our hope that this bibliography will encourage and, perhaps, facilitate additional research and publication in the area of mental health services within correctional systems.

R.V.W.
B.L.

Mental Health Services in Criminal Justice System Settings

1

Mental Disorders (Axis I)

1. Abram, K.M., & Teplin, L.A. (1990). Drug disorder, mental illness, and violence. National Institute on Drug Abuse Research Monograph Series, Monograph 103, 222-238.

2. Baldwin, L.J., Beck, N.C., Menditto, A.A., Arms, T.S., et al. (1992). Decreasing excessive water drinking by chronically mentally ill forensic patients. Hospital and Community Psychiatry, 43, 507-509.
   Studied the use of operant learning procedures in reducing polydipsia among 5 inpatients with diagnoses of schizophrenia or schizoaffective disorder. The procedures were designed to reduce psychotic and aggressive behavior and increase basic life skills. Using 3 measures of water consumption (weight gain, urine specific gravity, and serum sodium level), results indicate that the subjects were able to curb excessive water consumption during treatment.

3. Beckerman, A., & Fontana, L. (1989). Vietnam veterans and the criminal justice system: A selected review. Criminal Justice and Behavior, 16, 412-428.
   This review of published and unpublished studies of the criminal activities and incarceration of Vietnam era veterans found that the majority of incarcerated veterans are Vietnam era veterans. Although Vietnam era veterans do not have higher arrest rates than do non-veterans, those who actually served in Vietnam do, although they are primarily for non-violent offenses. Further, the authors suggest that future research should focus on the prevalence of Post Traumatic Stress Syndrome (PTSD) in incarcerated Vietnam veteran offenders and the relation of PTSD to criminal activity.

4. Bradford, J.M. (1983). The forensic psychiatric aspects of schizophrenia. Psychiatric Journal of the University of Ottawa, 8, 96-103.

5.   Chiles, J.A., von-Cleve, E., Jemelka, R.P, & Trupin, E.W. (1993). Substance abuse and psychiatric disorders in prison inmates. In Dual diagnosis of mental illness and substance abuse: Collected articles from Hospital and Community Psychiatry. Washington, DC: American Psychiatric Association.

6.   Chiles, J.A., von-Cleve, E., Jemelka, R.P., & Trupin, E.W. (1990). Substance abuse and psychiatric disorders in prison inmates. Hospital and Community Psychiatry, 41, 1132-1134.
      In a study of 109 male mentally ill offenders, 92% of those diagnosed with antisocial personality demonstrated symptoms of drug abuse/dependence, while 82% of those diagnosed with depression.   All offenders diagnosed with schizophrenia, schizophreneform disorder, dysthymia, or mania also were diagnosed substance abuse/dependent.

7.   Cohen, J.M. (1986). Rhythm and tempo in mania. Music Therapy, 6A, 13-29.

8.   Cornell, D.G., & Hawk, G.L. (1989). Clinical presentation of malingerers diagnosed by experienced forensic psychologists. Law and Human Behavior, 13, 375-383.

9.   Denkowski, G.C., & Denkowski, K.M. (1985). The mentally retarded offender in the state prison system: Identification, prevalence adjustment, and rehabilitation. Criminal Justice and Behavior, 12, 55-70.
      A survey of prison administrators in 48 states found that about 2% of inmates nationwide could be diagnosed as mentally retarded.   The relatively low rate was attributed to increasing efforts at diverting mentally retarded offenders from the criminal justice system.   Other survey findings indicate that mentally retarded persons do not adjust well to prison life and that few supplemental rehabilitation services are provided for such offenders in correctional settings.

10.   Dorman, A., O'Connor, A., Hardiman, E., Freyne, A., & O'Neill, H. (1993). Psychiatric morbidity in sentenced segregated HIV-positive prisoners. British Journal of Psychiatry, 163, 802-805.

11.   Eisenman, R. (1992). Creativity in prisoners: Conduct disorders and psychotics. Creativity Research Journal, 5, 175-181.

12.   Eyestone, L.L., & Howell, R.J. (1994). An epidemiological study of attention-deficit hyperactivity disorder and major depression in a male prison population. Bulletin of the American Academy of Psychiatry and the Law, 22, 181-193.
      A study of 102 inmates was conducted to determine the prevalence of both attention-deficit hyperactivity disorder and major depression in a prison population. Both ADHD and depression were found in 25.5% of the sample. Combined with the significant association of ADHD and depression, the findings lead the authors to argue for further research on the association between these two disorders.

13.   Faulk, M. (1976). A psychiatric study of men serving a sentence in Winchester prison. Medicine, Science and the Law, 16, 244-251.

14.   Fido, A.A., & al-Jabally, M. (1993). Presence of psychiatric morbidity in prison population in Kuwait. Annals of Clinical Psychiatry, 5, 107-110.

15.   Fine, E.W. (1983). Alcoholism and forensic psychiatry. American Journal of Forensic Psychiatry, 4, 113-118.
       Discusses the relationship between alcoholism and antisocial and criminal behavior, the aggravation of other psychiatric illnesses and personality disorders by alcoholism, and problems in diagnosis due to alcohol-related complications (e.g., withdrawal symptoms, hallucinations, paranoid states, head injuries, impaired judgement and memory, etc.) and the heterogeneity of the alcoholic population.

16.   Glancy, G.D., & Regehr, C. (1992). The forensic psychiatric aspects of schizophrenia. Psychiatric Clinics of North America, 15, 575-589.
       After reviewing the literature on schizophrenia and crime, the authors conclude that the relationship between the two is complex and may be related to social and personality disorganization among schizophrenics. This relationship may be further exacerbated by the effects of deinstitutionalization on length of hospital stays and stricter admission criteria, leaving the schizophrenic extremely vulnerable to a number of crimes.

17.   Good, M.I. (1978). Primary affective disorder, aggression, and criminality: A review and clinical study. Archives of General Psychiatry, 35, 954-960.
       Reviews the literature on relations between bipolar and unipolar depressive disorders and aggression and criminality and presents findings of a study of the prevalence of primary affective disorders among 100 prisoners referred for psychiatric evaluation. Approximately one in ten prisoners was diagnosed with a primary affective disorder.

18.   Griffiths, A.W. (1988). Previous psychiatric illness and addiction amongst prisoners in 1973 and 1986. British Journal of Criminology, 28, 402-403.
       A study of 200 male prison inmates in the United Kingdom from 1973 and 1986 found a substantial, and increasing incidence of previous drug abuse and psychiatric illness over the period of the study. Psychiatric Ss were more seriously addicted to drugs than nonpsychiatric controls.

19.   Gross, M., DeJong, W., Lamb, D., Enos, T., Mason, T., & Weitzman E. (1994). "Drugs and AIDS--reaching for help": A videotape on AIDS and drug abuse for criminal justice populations. Journal of Drug Education, 24, 1-20.

20.   Gunn, J., Maden, A., & Swinton, M. (1991). Treatment needs of prisoners with psychiatric disorders. British Medical Journal, 303(6798), 338-341.

21.   Herrman, H., Mills, J., Doidge, G., McGorry, P., & Singh, B. (1994). The use of psychiatric services before imprisonment: a survey and case register linkage of sentenced prisoners in Melbourne. Psychological Medicine, 24, 63-68.

22.   Hodgins, S., & Gaston, L. (1989). Patterns of recidivism and relapse among groups of mentally disordered offenders. Behavioral Sciences and the Law, 7, 551-558.
       Identified 5 groups of male, mentally disordered offenders with respect to treatment needs: (1) career criminals, (2) chronic schizophrenics, (3) violent psychotics, (4)

violent middle-class individuals, and (5) intellectually handicapped Ss. The 5 groups were differentiated by 3 variables relating to criminal recidivism: length of sentences, number, and severity of violent crimes. The groups were not distinguished by patterns of clinical relapse. Less than half of those studied were correctly classified by discriminant function analyses.

23.   Holcomb, W.R., & Ahr, P.R. (1988). Arrest rates among young adult psychiatric patients treated in inpatient and outpatient settings. Hospital and Community Psychiatry, 39, 52-57.
Analyses of young adult psychiatric patients in 5 psychiatric diagnostic categories showed that those with primary diagnoses of drug or alcohol abuse had the greatest overall frequency of arrests and the highest frequency of arrests for burglary, peace disturbance and probation and parole violations. The best predictors of arrest following mental health treatment were greater number of lifetime arrests for felonies, younger age, racial minority status, and greater number of years since first public mental health services.

24.   Jackson, M. (1988). The mentally ill offender: A Maori perspective. Community Mental Health in New Zealand, 4, 45-51.
Argues that in New Zealand, analyses of causes of criminal offending and definitions of mental illness have been imposed on Maori offenders, creating a monocultural approach in a bicultural setting. It is suggested that criminologists and health experts should recognize the distinct manifestations of mental illness in Maori offenders.

25.   James, J.F., Gregory, D., Jones, R.K., & Rundell, O.H. (1980). Psychiatric morbidity in prisons. Hospital and Community Psychiatry, 31, 674-677.
Presents findings and recommendations from a statewide assessment of mental health treatment needs in the Oklahoma prison population. Over three-quarters of inmates were diagnosable, covering a wide range of mental disorders. Over a third of the population were found to be in need of treatment other than brief interventions, with about ten percent considered seriously mentally ill. Finally, about one-fifth were rated as resistant, possibly requiring involuntary treatment.

26.   Jones, B.E., & Katz, N.D. (1992). Madness and addiction: Treating the mentally ill chemical abuser. Journal of Health Care for the Poor and Underserved, 3, 39-45.
Individuals with dual diagnoses of mental disorder and substance abuse have increasingly become the population served in the public sector, having multiple contacts with law enforcement and correctional agencies, as well as social service agencies, community mental health centers, and public sector substance abuse facilities. Further, most of these individuals are also impoverished and come from racial and ethnic minorities, primarily in urban areas. The shunting of this multi-problem population into correctional systems reflects the unwillingness of communities' and society's unwillingness to devote resources other than correctional institutionalization to the lowest of the underclass. The authors argue for the need of broad-based, multi-agency interventions for dual diagnosed individuals.

27.   Joukamaa, M. (1995). Psychiatric morbidity among Finnish prisoners with special reference to socio-demographic factors: results of the Health Survey of Finnish Prisoners (Wattu Project). Forensic Sciences International, 73, 85-91.

28.   Kassebaum, G., & Chandler, S.M. (1994). Polydrug use and self control among men and women in prisons. Journal of Drug Education, 24, 333-350.

29.   Kearns, A., & O'Connor, A. (1988). The mentally handicapped criminal offender. A 10-year study of two hospitals. British Journal of Psychiatry, 152, 848-851. Compared 92 mentally handicapped offenders to the general criminal population and found that the mentally handicapped offenders were older and more likely to be single rather than married. Although most fell into the normal and mildly mentally handicapped range on intelligence, those with lower intelligence were more likely to have been arrested for property or public order offenses, suggesting that factors other than intelligence, such as social skills, must have affected their hospital admissions.

30.   Kindred, M., & Sales, B. (1986). Developmentally disabled persons in the criminal justice system. In W.J. Curran, A.L. Garry, & S.A. Shah (Eds.), Modern forensic psychiatry and psychology. Philadelphia, PA: F.A. Davis.

31.   Kokkevi, A., & Stefanis, C. (1995). Drug abuse and psychiatric comorbidity. Comprehensive Psychiatry, 36, 329-337. A study of 176 opiate-dependent males from prisons and treatment facilities found the prevalence of lifetime diagnoses of non-substance abuse disorders to be 90 and 66 percent respectively. The most common axis I disorders were anxiety (32%) and affective (25%) disorders. Antisocial personality disorder (ASP) had a lifetime prevalence of 69.3%. Higher rates of affective and anxiety disorders were diagnosed in the treatment sample than in the imprisoned sample. On the other hand ASP was most diagnosed in the prison sample. Psychiatric disorders seem to precede drug dependence in the majority of cases.

32.   Kopelman, M.D. (1987). Crime and amnesia: A review. Behavioral Sciences and the Law, 5, 323-342.

33.   Kunjukrishnan, R., & Bradford, J.M. (1988). Schizophrenia and major affective disorder: Forensic psychiatric issues. Canadian Journal of Psychiatry, 33, 723-733.

34.   Kunjukrishnan, R., & Bradford, J.M. (1990). The profile of a major affective disorder offender. Psychiatric Journal of the University of Ottawa, 15, 11-14. Noting that the incidence of major mental illnesses in general and of major affect disorders in particular in criminal populations is relatively small, the authors describe a profile of major affective disorder offender based on data collected from 46 consecutive patients referred to a psychiatric hospital.

35.   Kunjukrishnan, R., & Varan, L.R. (1992). Major affective disorders and forensic psychiatry. Psychiatric Clinics of North America, 15, 569-574. Reviews studies that examine the relationship between major affective disorders and crime, especially serious violent crime. Many such offenders are found not guilty by reason of insanity and are sent to psychiatric hospitals for treatment. Issues of fitness and criminal responsibility are also discussed.

36.   Larkin, E.P. (1991). Food refusal in prison. Medicine, Science and the Law, 31, 41-44.
The prevalence of mental disorder among food refusers in prison was studied and found that the prevalence of psychiatric disorder among these prisoners was extremely high. The authors state, however, that the majority respond well to counseling and observation.

37.   Lau, B.W. (1981). The medical recommendation for psychiatric remands into prison: The Hong Kong scene. Medicine, Science and the Law, 21, 57-65.

38.   Lee, S.R. (1984). Aftercare for the psychotic offender. Psychiatric Forum, 12, 59-65.

39.   Lees-Haley, P.R. (1984). Detecting the psychological malingerer. American Journal of Forensic Psychology, 2, 165-169.

40.   Lees-Haley, P.R. (1989). Malingering post-traumatic stress disorder on the MMPI. Forensic Reports, 2, 89-91.

41.   Lees-Haley, P.R. (1989). The MMPI F and F-K scales: Questionable indices of malingering. American Journal of Forensic Psychology, 7, 81-84.

42.   Leuchter, A.F. (1981). The responsibilities of the state for the prevention and treatment of mental illness among prisoners. Journal of Forensic Sciences, 26, 134-141.
Argues that imprisonment may be regarded as a source of severe stress which may lead to profound psychophysiological disturbances lasting for years. Since the prison population already has a high baseline incidence of mental illness, the stress of imprisonment may also greatly exacerbate existing psychoses or trigger initial psychotic episodes in certain prisoners. The authors further stress that there is a lack of clarity in the responsibilities of the state in preventing and treating mental disorder in the prison population, and failure to take reasonable steps to prevent and treat mental illness among prisoners may constitute cruel and unusual punishment under the Eighth amendment.

43.   Leukefeld, C.G. (1991). Chronic mental illness. Health and Social Work, 16, 7-10.
Outlines three issues associated with the chronically ill population that have received public attention: 1) the connection between chronic mental illness and homelessness, 2) the complications of chemical abuse or dual diagnosis, and 3) the role that jails play in treating mentally ill people. These issues highlight dilemmas facing the general public, policymakers, and social work practitioners. Guiding principles for psychiatric services in jails are discussed.

44.   Levine, D. (1970). Criminal behavior and mental institutionalization. Journal of Clinical Psychology, 26, 279-289.

45.   Lewis, D.O., & Bard, J.S. (1991). Multiple personality and forensic issues. Psychiatric Clinics of North America, 14, 741-756.

This discussion of multiple personality disorder in forensic settings focusses on issues involving competency, insanity, diminished capacity, and mitigation, as well as, problems with diagnosis in forensic settings, evidentiary issues, malingering, and misdiagnosis with antisocial personality disorder.

46.   Lindqvist, P., & Allebeck, P. (1990). Schizophrenia and crime: A longitudinal follow-up of 644 schizophrenics in Stockholm. British Journal of Psychiatry, 157, 345-350.
A fifteen year study of 644 schizophrenics found that the crime rate for male schizophrenics was no different than that of the male general population, while the crime rate for female schizophrenics was twice that of the general female populations. Overall, the rate of violent crime among schizophrenics was four times higher than that of the general population, with assault, unlawful threat, and threat or violence against officials accounting for 95 percent of violent offenses among schizophrenics.

47.   Maden, A., & Gunn, J. (1993). When does a prisoner become a patient? Criminal Behaviour and Mental Health, 3, iii-viii.

48.   Maden, A., Swinton, M., & Gunn, J. (1992). A survey of pre-arrest drug use in sentenced prisoners. British Journal of the Addictions, 87, 27-33.

49.   Marciniak, R.D. (1986). Implications to forensic psychiatry of Post-Traumatic Stress Disorder: A review. Military Medicine, 151, 434-437.
Reviews the legal problems of Vietnam War veterans, the incidence prevalence, and diagnostic criteria for PTSD. Case histories involving veterans with PTSD in the legal system are discussed and a general framework for understanding the relationship between PTSD and criminal behavior is presented.

50.   Martell, D.A. (1992). Estimating the prevalence of organic brain dysfunction in maximum-security forensic psychiatric patients. Journal of Forensic Sciences, 37, 878-893.
Studied the prevalence of organic brain dysfunction in a sample of 50 prison inmates and found multiple indicators of OBS in 64% of the sample and at least one indicator in 84% of the sample.

51.   McFarland, B.H., Faulkner, L.R., Bloom, J.D., Hallaux, R.J., et al. (1989). Chronic mental illness and the criminal justice system. Hospital and Community Psychiatry, 40, 718-723.

52.   McGrath, P.G. (1973). The mentally abnormal offender. Medico Legal Journal, 41, 4-13.

53.   Meloy, J.R. (1986). Rapid classification of the functionally psychotic individual in custody. Criminal Justice and Behavior, 13, 185-195.

54.   Melville, C., & Brown, C. (1987). The use of patient education in a prison mental health treatment program. Journal of Offender Counseling, Services and Rehabilitation, 12, 131-140.

55.   Mitchison, S., Rix, K.J., Renvoize, E.B., & Schweiger, M. (1994). Recorded psychiatric morbidity in a large prison for male remanded and sentenced prisoners. Medicine, Science and the Law, 34, 324-330.

56.   Moffitt, T.E. (1987). Parental mental disorder and offspring criminal behavior: An adoption study. Psychiatry, 50, 346-360.
       Multiple convictions for nonviolent criminal behavior were found for adoptees whose biologic parents were characterized by the presence of mental disorder and criminal involvement. A similar, but non-significant association was noted for violent crimes. Biologic parental diagnostic types associated with son's later criminal behavior were alcohol/drug abuse and personality disorders. Psychotic disorders were not associated with later criminality of sons.

57.   Monahan, J., & Steadman, H. (1982). Crime and mental disorders: An epidemiological approach. In N. Morris & M. Tonry (Eds). Review of research in crime and justice. Chicago, IL: University of Chicago Press.

58.   Monahan, J., & Steadman, H. (1983). Mentally disordered offenders. New York: Plenum.

59.   Monahan, J., & Steadman, H.J. (1983). Crime and mental disorder: An epidemiological approach. In Crime and Justice: An annual review of research, 4, 145-189.

60.   Morgan, D.W., Edwards, A.C., & Faulkner, L.R. (1993). The adaptation to prison by individuals with schizophrenia. Bulletin of the American Academy of Psychiatry and the Law, 21, 427-433.
       Compared the adaptation to prison of schizophrenics and a group of matched non-schizophrenic controls and found that the schizophrenics had more disciplinary infractions, a higher number of lock-ups, longer periods of lock-up and had poorer post-release adjustment than the non-schizophrenic controls.

61.   Mortimer, D.B. (1993). History and treatment efforts for a prison special management unit: II. The psychiatrist's role in the special management unit. International Journal of Offender Therapy and Comparative Criminology, 37, 117-130.

62.   Mullen, P.E. (1993). Care and containment in forensic psychiatry. Criminal Behaviour and Mental Health, 3, 212-225.

63.   Neighbors, H.W. (1987). The prevalence of mental disorder in Michigan prisons. DIS Newsletter, 4, 8-11.

64.   Palermo, G.B., Gumz, E.J., & Liska, F.J. (1992). Mental illness and criminal behavior revisited. International Journal of Offender Therapy and Comparative Criminology, 36, 53-61.
       Compares research concerning the relationships between mental illness and criminal behavior from before and after deinstitutionalization. The literature seems to support the view that since deinstitutionalization the number of mentally ill persons in U.S.

jails is consistently increasing. However, the offenses for which they are jailed are most commonly misdemeanors. Schizophrenia and antisocial personality disorder are the most common diagnoses.

65.   Palermo, G.B., Gumz, E.J., Smith, M.B., & Liska, F.J. (1992). Escape from psychiatrization: A statistical analysis of referrals to a forensic unit. International Journal of Offender Therapy and Comparative Criminology, 36, 89-102.

66.   Palsson, A. (1992). Sentenced to treatment: Treated in residential psychiatric care. Nordic Journal of Psychiatry, 46, 257-260.

67.   Panton, J.H. (1976-77). Personality characteristics of aged inmates within a state prison. Offender Rehabilitation, 1, 203-208.
       Compared the MMPI profiles of 120 offenders aged 60 or older to MMPI profiles of 2251 randomly selected state prison inmates and found fewer psychopathic but more neurotic responses among the aged inmates. Further, the older inmates showed greater anxiety, despondency, apprehension, and concern with physical functioning.

68.   Panton, J.H. (1979). MMPI profiles associated with outcomes of intensive psychotherapeutic counseling with youthful first offender prison inmates. Research Communications in Psychology, Psychiatry and Behavior, 4, 383-395.
       Results of pre- and post-test comparisons of MMPI profiles of 50 prisoners (aged 16 to 20) participating in an intensive psychotherapy program and a control group of similar prisoners not participating showed that pre-post-test changes in MMPI scales were found for only the experimental group. The experimental group showed significant pre- to post-test differences on 10 of the 15 scales analyzed, suggesting improvements in anxiety, depression, social alienation, and antisocial behavior.

69.   Perr, I.N. (1991). Crime and multiple personality disorder: A case history and discussion. Bulletin of the American Academy of Psychiatry and the Law, 19, 203-214.

70.   Pols, J. (1989). Mental illness and rationality: A critique. International Journal of Law and Psychiatry, 12, 71-79.

71.   Porporino, F.J., & Motiuk, L.L. (1995). The prison careers of mentally disordered offenders. International Journal of Law and Psychiatry, 18, 29-44.

72.   Quinsey, V.L. (1981). The long term management of the mentally ill offender. In S.J. Hucker, C.D. Webster, & M. Ben-aron (Eds.), Mental disorder and criminal responsibility (pp. 137-155). Toronto: Buttersworth.

73.   Quinsey, V.L., Cyr, M., & Lavallee, Y.J. (1988). Treatment opportunities in a maximum security psychiatric hospital: A problem survey. International Journal of Law and Psychiatry, 11, 179-194.

74.   Resnick, P.J. (1984). The detection of malingered mental illness. Behavioral Sciences and the Law, 1, 21-38.

75. Richman, B.J., Convit, A., & Martell, D.A. (1992). Homelessness and the mentally ill offender. Journal of Forensic Sciences, 37, 932-937.
Studied 69 mentally ill offenders released from a psychiatric hospital and found significant relationships between variables of homelessness at the time of arrest, prior offense history, and substance abuse.

76. Rideau, W., & Sinclair, B. (1983). The mentally retarded offender. Journal of Prison and Jail Health, 3, 101-111.

77. Robertson, G., Dell, S., James, K., & Grounds, A. (1994). Psychotic men remanded in custody to Brixton Prison. British Journal of Psychiatry, 164, 55-61.

78. Robertson, G., Grounds, A., Dell, S., & James, K. (1994). A follow-up of remanded mentally ill offenders given court hospital orders. Medicine, Science and the Law, 34, 61-66.

79. Rodenhauser, P., & Khamis, H.J. (1988). Predictors of improvement in maximum security forensic hospital patients. Behavioral Sciences and the Law, 6, 531-542.
In a study of 376 maximum security forensic patients conducted to determine the best predictors of treatment effectiveness and restoration to competency, schizophrenia, previous hospitalizations, felony charges, drug treatment refusal, involuntary medication, physical restraint, and absence of personality disorders were associated with increased length of hospitalization, while, nonschizophrenic diagnosis without histories of previous incarceration was associated with greater success in competency restoration.

80. Roesch, R., Ogloff, J.R.P., & Eaves, D. (1995). Mental health research in the criminal justice system: The need for common approaches and international perspectives. International Journal of Law and Psychiatry, 18, 1-14.
Provides an overview of research concerning mental disorders among prison inmates. Six specific topics are discussed: (1) the prevalence of mental disorders among prison inmates, (2) methods or models of detecting mental disorders in jails and prisons, (3) specific assessments that may be performed during jail incarceration, (4) intervention in jails and prisons, (5) diversion or transfer out of jails and prisons to mental health facilities, and (6) gradual release programs and community management of offenders with mental disorders. Also discussed are some specific procedural aspects of working with the processing of people with mental disorders in the criminal justice system.

81. Rogers, R. (1992). Treatability of mentally disordered offenders: A commentary on Heilbrun et al. Forensic Reports, 5, 97-101.
Comments on the problem of generalizing from research conducted under optimal conditions to typical forensic practice.

82. Rogers, R., Gillis, J.R., & Dickens, S.E. (1988). Treatment recommendations for mentally disordered offenders: More than roulette? Canadian Journal of Behavioural Science, 20, 192-200.

83.   Roman, D.D., & Gerbing, D.W. (1989). The mentally disordered criminal offender:
A description based on demographic, clinical, and MMPI data. Journal of Clinical
Psychology, 45, 983-990.

84.   Sadoff, R.L. (1971). Criminal behavior masking mental illness. Corrective Psychiatry
and Journal of Social Therapy, 17, 41-47.

85.   Schanda, H., Foldes, P., Topitz, A., Fliedl, R., et al. (1992). Premorbid adjustment
of schizophrenic criminal offenders. Acta Psychiatrica Scandinavica, 86, 121-126.

86.   Schulte, J.L. (1985). Treatment of the mentally disordered offender. American
Journal of Forensic Psychiatry, 6, 29-36.
Discusses several issues concerning the treatment of the mentally disordered criminal
offender. Guidelines are presented for a realistic assessment of rehabilitation time
needed; recruitment of top professionals; research, evaluation, and training in mental
health facilities; vocational rehabilitation; establishment of a statewide forensic
system; and statistical studies of the magnitude of mental disorder in the prison
populations.

87.   Schultz-Ross, R.A. (1993). Theoretical difficulties in the treatment of mentally ill
prisoners. Journal of Forensic Sciences, 38, 426-431.

88.   Shah, S.A. (1989). Mental disorder and the criminal justice system: Some
overarching issues. Special Issue: Mental disorder and the criminal justice system.
International Journal of Law and Psychiatry, 12, 231-244.

89.   Shaw, D.M., Churchill, C.M., Noyes, R., Loeffelholz, P.L. (1987). Criminal
behavior and post-traumatic stress disorder in Vietnam veterans. Comprehensive
Psychiatry, 28, 403-411.
A comparison of 34 incarcerated Vietnam veterans with 31 Vietnam veterans in the
community revealed relatively equal proportions of veterans suffering from post-
traumatic stress disorder (PTSD; 39% incarcerated, 37% community). However a
greater proportion of the incarcerated veterans had antisocial personality disorder
with onset prior to military service. Also alcohol and drug abuse were significantly
higher among the incarcerated group, particularly among those with PTSD. No
relationship between PTSD and crimes leading to incarceration was found.

90.   Shore, D., Filson, C.R., & Johnson, W.E. (1988). Violent crime arrests and paranoid
schizophrenia: The White House case studies. Schizophrenia Bulletin, 14, 279-281.
Studied the arrest records of schizophrenic patients who had attempted to see the
US President or other political figures based on hallucinations or delusional beliefs
and found that over the 9 to 12 year period after their release, 31 of the 217 men
had murder or assault arrests.

91.   Sprull, J., & May, J. (1988). The mentally retarded offender: Prevalence rates based
on individual versus group intelligence tests. Criminal Justice and Behavior, 15, 484-
491.

A study comparing individually and group administered intelligence found that the prevalence of mental retardation found that group testing over estimated the prevalence of mental retardation in a prison sample by four to one.

92.   Steadman, H.J., & Halton, A. (1971). The Baxstrom patients: Backgrounds and outcome. Seminars in Psychiatry, 3, 376-386.

93.   Steadman, H.J., & Keveles, C. (1972). The community adjustment and criminal activity of Baxstrom patients: 1966-1970. American Journal of Psychiatry, 129, 304-310.

94.   Steadman, H.J., Rosenstein, M.J., MacAskill, R.L., & Manderscheid, R.W. (1988). A profile of mentally disordered offenders admitted to inpatient psychiatric services in the United States. Law and Human Behavior, 12(1), 91-99.
Reanalysis of 1980 admission surveys conducted by the National Institute of Mental Health found that of over 31,000 admissions of mentally disordered offenders treated in inpatient psychiatric facilities, 85% went to state or county hospitals. The largest group were those found to be incompetent to stand trial (58%), followed by mentally disordered prisoners (32%), those not guilty by reason of insanity (8%), and mentally disordered sex offenders (3%). Women and whites were over represented in the mentally disordered offender population and clear diagnostic differences be legal status were found. Schizophrenia was predominant among those not guilty by reason of insanity, while alcohol and substance abuse disorders were most common among those judged incompetent to stand trial.

95.   Steinbock, E.A. (1976). A definitional framework: Who is the retarded offender? In P.L. Browning (Ed.), Rehabilitation and the retarded offender. Springfield, IL: Thomas.

96.   Swinton, M., Maden, A., & Gunn, J. (1994). Psychiatric disorder in life-sentenced prisoners. Criminal Behaviour and Mental Health, 4, 10-20.
In a study comparing rates of psychiatric morbidity between a group of male life-sentenced prisoners and 1630 males from the general prison population, it was found that rates of psychiatric morbidity were quite similar between the two groups, but the life-sentenced prisoners were significantly more likely to report episodes of self harm before and after their index offense and after sentence, even when data was adjusted for time in prison.

97.   Taylor, P.J., & Parrott, J.M. (1988). Elderly offenders: A study of age-related factors among custodially remanded prisoners. British Journal of Psychiatry, 152, 340-346.

98.   Templer, D.I., Kaiser, G., & Siscoe, K. (1993). Correlates of pathological gambling propensity in prison inmates. Comprehensive Psychiatry, 34, 347-351.

99.   Teplin, L.A. (1990). The prevalence of severe mental disorder among male urban jail detainees: Comparison with the Epidemiological Catchment Area program. American Journal of Public Health, 80, 663-669.

Using the NIMH Diagnostic Interview Schedule, the prevalence of severe mental disorder (e.g., Schizophrenia, Major Affective Disorders) among jail detainees in Chicago was compared to that of the general population. Prevalence rates were 2 to 3 times higher for the jail sample (N = 728) than that of the general population after controlling for differences in age and race were controlled.

100. Teplin, L.A., McClelland, G.M., & Abram, K.M. (1993). The role of mental disorder and substance abuse in predicting violent crime among released offenders. In S. Hodgins (Ed.), Mental disorder and crime. Newbury Park, CA: Sage.

101. Toch, H., Adams, K., & Greene, R. (1987). Ethnicity, disruptiveness, and emotional disorder among prison inmates. Criminal Justice and Behavior, 14, 93-109.

102. Walters, G.D., Mann, M.F., Miller, M.P., & Hemphill, L., et al. (1988). Emotional disorder among offenders: Inter- and intra-setting comparisons. Criminal Justice and Behavior, 15, 433-453.
Found that the prevalence of severe emotional disorder, based on the Psychiatric Diagnostic interview ranged from 7 to 10 percent in populations of state, federal, and military prisoners. Severely emotionally disturbed military offenders were more likely than those from state or federal settings to satisfy criteria for primary affective disorder, while emotionally disturbed state offenders were more likely than the other groups to satisfy criteria for schizophrenic disorders. Although there were significant demographic differences between emotionally disturbed prisoners in the three settings, there were no differences on MMPI scales. Emotionally disturbed prisoners in each setting were significantly more likely to have serious problems with adjustment to prison life than did non-emotionally disturbed prisoners.

103. Walters, G.D., Scrapansky, T.A., & Marlow, G.A. (1986). The emotionally disturbed military criminal offender: Identification, background, and institutional adjustment. Criminal Justice and Behavior, 13, 261-285.
Compared the personality characteristics and institutional adjustment of 43 emotionally disturbed military criminal offenders with 43 non-emotionally disturbed military offenders matched for age, confining offense and length of sentence. Emotionally disturbed offenders had committed more crimes against persons, but fewer drug offenses than controls. Further, the emotionally disturbed group was more likely to have been divorced, to have elevated MMPI scale profiles, and had a more extensive history of family and personal psychiatric difficulty and had poorer institutional adjustment than controls.

104. World Health Organization (1990). Drug abusers in prisons: Managing their health problems. Copenhagen: World Health Organization.

105. Wulach, J.S. (1983). Mania and crime: A study of 100 manic defendants. Bulletin of the American Academy of Psychiatry and the Law, 11, 69-75.

106. Yang, H.K., Brown, G.C., & Magargal, L.E. (1981). Self-inflicted occular mutilation. American Journal of Ophthalmology, 91, 658-663.
Discusses the characteristics of patients with self-inflicted mutilation of the eyes. Typically, patients are young males who have criminal records, and a history of drug

abuse and/or schizophrenia. Further, such patients suffer from castration fears, oedipal conflicts, repressed homosexual impulses, severe guilt and need for punishment. Two cases studies are presented.

107.   Yarvis, R.M. (1972). Psychiatric pathology and social deviance in 25 incarcerated offenders. Archives of General Psychiatry, 26, 79-84.

2

Antisocial and Other
Personality Disorders

108. Appleby, L., & Joseph, P. (1991). Management of personality disorder. International Review of Psychiatry, 3, 59-70.
Personality disorders may be conceptually flawed diagnoses applied to individuals whose cognitive style and behavior is distressful to the individual and others. Cognitive behavioral therapies may hold the most promise for treatment and management, while drug therapy for symptoms of depression, anxiety and paranoia is a useful adjunct. The possibility that such offenders may develop other mental disorders and are prone to suicidal behaviors requires careful clinical supervision.

109. Barbour-McMullen, J., Coid, J., Howard, R. (1988). The psychometric identification of psychopathy in mentally abnormal offenders. Personality and Individual Differences, 9, 817-823.
Compared the European and American concepts of psychopathy in a study using scales from the MMPI and the California Personality Inventory (CPI). Only the Socialization scale of the CPI differentiated between offenders diagnosed with antisocial personality disorder from other groups of offenders and a control group of psychiatric nurses. The authors contend that this finding supports the American concept of psychopathy.

110. Blackburn, R. (1982). On the relevance of the concept of the psychopath. Issues in Criminological and Legal Psychology, 2, 12-25.
Argues that the concept of psychopathic personality is both meaningful and necessary to understand antisocial behavior and rehabilitate offenders. Psychopaths are unaffected by verbal therapies, social skills training procedures, influence via social reinforcers, but are more responsive to both positive and negative material reinforcers, access to stimulating activities, and sociodrama.

111.   Blackburn R., & Lee-Evans, J.M. (1985). Reactions of primary and secondary psychopaths to anger-evoking situations. British Journal of Clinical Psychology, 24(Pt 2), 93-100.

112.   Blanchard, E.B., Bassett, J.E., & Koshland, E. (1977). Psychopathy and delay of gratification. Criminal Justice and Behavior, 4, 265-271.

113.   Bradford, J., & Dimock, J. (1986). A comparative study of adolescents and adults who willfully set fires. Psychiatric Journal of the University of Ottawa, 11, 228-234. A comparison of 57 adult and 45 juvenile arsonists found that mental retardation was diagnosable in about 10% of cases in both groups. Conduct disorders were common among juveniles, while alcoholism, personality disorders, and schizophrenia were common among adults. About 40% of adolescents came from single parent homes and adult psychopathology and physical abuse were common in the homes of juvenile adolescents.

114.   Brett, T.R. (1992). The Woodstock approach: One ward in Broadmoor Hospital for the treatment of personality disorder. Criminal Behaviour and Mental Health, 2, 152-158.

115.   Bruce-Jones, W.D., & Coid, J. (1992). Identity diffusion presenting as multiple personality disorder in a female psychopath. British Journal of Psychiatry, 160, 541-544.

116.   Carson, D. (1992). Holding the patient to account at the gate-keeping stage. Criminal Behaviour and Mental Health, 2, 224-233.

117.   Cleckley, H. (1976). The mask of sanity. (4th Ed.). St. Louis, MO: Mosby.

118.   Coid, J.W. (1992). DSM-III diagnosis in criminal psychopaths: A way forward. Criminal Behaviour and Mental Health, 2, 78-94. Using DSM-III classification, 86 male and 93 female psychopaths were assessed and found to have multiple Axis-II personality disorder categories and multiple Axis-I clinical syndromes over their lifetime. Borderline and antisocial personality disorder were the most prevalent diagnoses, often in combination

119.   Collins, J.J., Schlenger, W.E., & Jordan, B.K. (1988). Antisocial personality and substance abuse disorders. Bulletin of the American Academy of Psychiatry and the Law, 16, 187-198. Results of a study of 1,149 male prison inmates indicated that whites are more likely than nonwhites to receive a diagnosis of antisocial personality disorder with a co-occurring substance abuse diagnosis than a diagnosis of antisocial personality disorder alone. Further, a co-occurring substance abuse disorder diagnosis magnified antisocial personality symptoms.

120.   Davies, W., & Feldman, P. (1981). The diagnosis of psychopathy by forensic specialists. British Journal of Psychiatry, 138, 329-331.

121. Devonshire, P.A., Howard, R.C., & Sellars, C. (1988). Frontal lobe functions and personality in mentally abnormal offenders. Personality and Individual Differences, 9, 339-344.

122. Dinitz, S. (1978). Chronically antisocial offenders. In J. Conrad, & S. Dinitz (Eds.), In fear of each other: Studies of dangerousness in America. Lexington, MA: Lexington Books.

123. Feldbrugge, J.T. (1992). Rehabilitation of patients with personality disorders: Patient-staff collaboration used as a working model and a tool. Criminal Behaviour and Mental Health, 2, 169-177.

124. Gunn, J. (1992). Personality disorders and forensic psychiatry. Criminal Behaviour and Mental Health, 2, 202-211.
Discusses the inadequate use of both voluntary and involuntary inpatient services with forensic clients diagnosed with severe personality disorders. Imprisonment of inmates with personality disorders has a role to play in their management, but prison management should not be the mainstay of treatment. An important goal for forensic psychiatry is to conduct research into personality disorders in order to reduce the negativity associated with this term.

125. Hare, R.D. (1980). A research scale for the assessment of psychopathy in criminal populations. Personality and Individual Differences, 1, 111-117.

126. Hare, R.D. (1983). Diagnosis of antisocial personality in two prison populations. American Journal of Psychiatry, 7, 887-889.

127. Hare, R.D., & McPherson, L.M. (1984). Violent and aggressive behavior by criminal psychopaths. International Journal of Law and Psychiatry, 7, 35-50.

128. Hare, R.D., Forth, A.E., & Strachan, K.E. (1992). Psychopathy and crime across the life span. In R.D. Peters, R.J. McMahon, & V.L. Quinsey (Eds.), Aggression and violence throughout the life span. Newbury Park, CA: Sage.

129. Hare, R.D., Harpur, T.J., Hakstian, A.R., Forth, A.E., et al. (1990). The revised Psychopathy Checklist: Reliability and factor structure. Psychological Assessment, 2, 338-341.
Reports on the psychometric properties of the revised Psychopathy Checklist. Data from 5 prison samples (N=925) and 3 forensic psychiatric samples (N=356) indicate that the revised checklist resembles its predecessor most respects. The authors conclude that the revised scale measures the same construct as the original and that it is a reliable and valid instrument for the assessment of psychopathy in male forensic populations.

130. Hare, R.D., McPherson, L.M., & Forth, A.E. (1988). Male psychopaths and their criminal careers. Journal of Consulting and Clinical Psychology, 56, 741-747.

131. Harpur, T.J., & Hare, R.D. (1994). Assessment of psychopathy as a function of age. Journal of Abnormal Psychology, 103, 604-609.

Assessed psychopathy as a function of age in 889 male prison inmates using the Psychopathy Checklist. Factor 1, which describes a cluster of affective-interpersonal traits central to psychopathy appears to be stable across the age-span, while Factor 2, which describes traits and behaviors associated with an unstable, unsocialized lifestyle, or social deviance, declined with age.

132.   Harris, G.T., Rice, M.E., & Cormier, C.A. (1991). Psychopathology and violent recidivism. Law and Human Behavior, 15, 625-637.
Studied recidivism among 169 male mentally disordered offenders over a 10 year period. Using the Psychopathy Checklist, offenders were classified as either psychopathic (N = 52) or non-psychopathic (N = 117). Psychopaths recidivated at a higher rate that non-psychopaths even beyond the age of 40, with 77% of the psychopaths rearrested for violent offenses, while only 21% of the non-psychopathic offenders were rearrested for violent offenses. The authors conclude that the Psychopathy Checklist was a reliable and valid instrument for predicting recidivism when compared to the predictive performance of a combination of indices including childhood history, adult history, index offense, and program variables.

133.   Harris, G.T., Rice, M.E., & Cormier, C.A. (1994). Psychopaths: Is a therapeutic community therapeutic? International Journal for Therapeutic and Supportive Organizations, 15, 283-289.

134.   Harris, G.T., Rice, M.E., & Quinsey, V.L. (1994). Psychotherapy as a taxon: Evidence that psychopaths are a discrete class. Journal of Consulting and Clinical Psychology, 62, 387-397.

135.   Hart, S.D., Kropp, P.R., & Hare, R.D. (1988). Performance of male psychopaths following conditional release from prison. Journal of Consulting and Clinical Psychology, 56, 226-232.

136.   Heilbrun, A.B., Jr., & Heilbrun, M.R. (1985). Psychopathy and dangerousness: Comparison, integration, and extension of two psychopathic typologies. British Journal of Clinical Psychology, 24, 181-195.
Studied the relationship of psychopathy, intelligence, and social withdrawal to violence and found that the highest dangerousness for prison and parole samples combined was found for psychopaths who were low in intelligence, were socially withdrawn, and who had a history of violence.

137.   Hemphill, J.F., Hart, S.D., & Hare, R.D. (1994). Psychopathy and substance use. Journal of Personality Disorders, 8, 169-180.

138.   Henderson, M.C., & Kalichman, S.C. (1990). Sexually deviant behavior and schizotypy: A theoretical perspective with supporting data. Psychiatric Quarterly, 61, 273-284.

139.   Hivert, P. (1980). Behavior and care of psychopathic patients in prison. Confrontation Psychologique, 18, 161-174.

140.   Howard, R.C. (1984). The clinical EEG and personality in mentally abnormal offenders. Psychological Medicine, 14, 569-580.

141.   Howard, R.C. (1990). Psychopathy Checklist scores in mentally abnormal offenders: A re-examination. Personality and Individual Differences, 11, 1087-1091.

142.   Jordan, B.K., Schlenger, W.E., Fairbank, J.A., & Caddell, J.M. (1996). Prevalence of psychiatric disorders among incarcerated women. II. Convicted women entering prison. Archives of General Psychiatry, 53, 513-519.
        A study of 805 women felons entering prison found that women inmates had higher rates of substance abuse disorders, anti-social personality, borderline personality, and mood disorders, but lower rates of anxiety disorders than women in community epidemiological studies. Lifetime rates of exposure to traumatic events were also elevated while Euro-American women were more likely than African-American women to have diagnosable mental disorders.

143.   Joseph, P.L. (1992). Non-custodial treatment: Can psychopaths be treated in the community? Criminal Behaviour and Mental Health, 2, 192-200.
        Argues mental health care provided in community settings does not provide the structure needed by psychopathic patients. Based on clinical experience with homeless psychopaths, the author states that psychopaths receiving clinic care do not engage in treatment except under duress, and others attend therapy only sporadically. Other difficulties include arranging short-term hospitalization and inadequacy of case management interventions with this population.

144.   Lidberg, L. (1985). Platelet monoamin oxidase activity and psychopathy. Psychiatry Research, 16, 339-343.
        Compared 37 male offenders hospitalized for forensic psychiatric assessment and 2 control groups to asses the correlation between platelet MAO activity and criminal psychopathology.   Findings indicate that offenders who were diagnosed as psychopaths according to the H. Cleckley criteria (1976) had significantly lower platelet MAO activity than did controls.

145.   Link, N.F., Scherer, S.E., & Byrne, P.H. (1977). Moral judgement and moral conduct in the psychopath. Canadian Psychiatric Association Journal, 22, 341-346.

146.   Norton, K. (1992). Personality disordered individuals: The Henderson Hospital model of treatment. Criminal Behaviour and Mental Health, 2, 180-191.
        Describes a therapeutic community for 29 adults with personality disorders, most of whom are criminal offenders and the components of the model which are most salient to patient progress.

147.   Oldroyd, R.J. (1975). A principal components analysis of the BPI and MMPI. Criminal Justice and Behavior, 2, 85-90.
        A comparative study of the Bipolar Psychological Inventory (BPI), developed for use in correctional settings, and the MMPI found that the BPI more adequately identified personality disorders, which are common among prison inmates, than the MMPI, which was more adequate at identifying psychotic disorders, which are evident among only about ten percent of the prison population.

148.   Parker, N. (1991). The Garry David case. Australian and New Zealand Journal of Psychiatry, 25, 371-374.

149.   Pavelka, F.L. (1986). Psychosocial characteristics of parolees in forensic social work. Journal of Psychiatry and Law, 14, 217-223.
Parolees administered the MMPI were found to have personality characteristics of long-term pathological behavior recognizable in early adolescence. Recidivism correlated significantly with unemployment, substance use, and antisocial personality characteristics.

150.   Peay, J. (1988). Offenders suffering from psychopathic disorder: The rise and demise of a consultation document. British Journal of Criminology, 28, 67-81.

151.   Raine, A. (1985). A psychometric assessment of Hare's checklist for psychopathy on an English prison population. British Journal of Clinical Psychology, 24, 247-258.
Results of factor analysis of Hare's psychopathy checklist showed substantial correspondence between English and Canadian samples and that four primary trait clusters (emotional detachment, superficial relationships, egocentricity, and impulsivity) were central in the identification of psychopathy.

152.   Raine, A. (1988). Psychopathy: A single or dual concept? Personality and Individual Differences, 9, 825-827.
Argues that there is little support for the notion that European and American concepts of psychopathy are distinct. Evidence that the two conceptions of psychopathy are related at an empirical level and that psychiatrists in both continents adopt the same concept of psychopathy in making a diagnosis is presented.

153.   Reich, J., & Thompson, W.D. (1987). DSM-III personality disorder clusters in three populations. British Journal of Psychiatry, 150, 471-475.

154.   Rogers, R., Gillis, J.R., & Dickens, S.E. (1989). A research note on the MMPI Pd Scale and sociopathy. International Journal of Offender Therapy and Comparative Criminology, 33, 21-25.
Investigated the distribution of the MMPI Pd and non-Pd 2-point codes and ICD diagnoses for 470 court-referred patients. Pd 2-point codes were not useful in identifying antisocial personality disorders and were often present in individuals with either major psychiatric disorders or no disorders at all.

155.   Serin, R.C. (1992). The clinical application of the Psychopathy Checklist-Revised (PCL-R) in a prison population. Journal of Clinical Psychology, 48, 637-642.

156.   Steadman, H.J., & Cocozza, J.J. (1974). Careers of the criminally insane. Lexington, MA: Lexington Books.

157.   Thornberry, T., & Jacoby, J. (1979). The criminally insane: A community followup of mentally ill offenders. Chicago, IL: University of Chicago Press.

158. Virkkunen, M. (1976). Self-mutilation in antisocial personality disorder. Acta Psychiatrica Scandinavica, 54, 347-352.

159. Walters, G.D. (1985). Scale 4 (Pd) of the MMPI and the diagnosis Antisocial Personality. Journal of Personality Assessment, 49, 474-476.
Investigated the relationship of the MMPI Pd scale to diagnosis of antisocial personality disorder in 225 military offenders and found that offenders diagnosed with antisocial personality disorder scored higher on the Pd scale than did non-diagnosed offenders regardless of whether K or non-K corrected T scores were used.

160. Walters, G.D. (1986). Correlates of the Megargee criminal classification system: A military correctional setting. Criminal Justice and Behavior, 13, 19-32.
Studied the MMPI profiles of over 400 offenders in a maximum security military prison using the Megargee classification system and found support for the validity of the system with military offenders.

161. Walters, G.D., & Chlumsky, M.L. (1993). The Lifestyle Criminality Screening Form and antisocial personality disorder: Predicting release outcome in a state prison sample. Behavioral Sciences and the Law, 11, 111-115.
Compared the Lifestyle Criminality Screening Form (LCSF) with a DSM-III-R diagnosis of antisocial personality disorder in predicting the release outcome of 100 medium security state prisoners. An 18-month follow-up revealed that high LCSF scores and diagnoses of antisocial personality disorder identified inmates who were eventually reincarcerated for a parole violation or new offense. Because of overlap between the 2 predictors, partial correlations were calculated and results showed that only the LCSF displayed a robust relationship with release outcome independent of diagnosis.

162. Wulach, J.S. (1983). August Aichorn's legacy: The treatment of narcissism in criminals. International Journal of Offender Therapy and Comparative Criminology, 27, 226-234.

163. Zarrella, K.L., Schuerger, J.M., & Ritz, G.H. (1990). Estimation of MCMI DSM-III Axis II constructs from MMPI scales and subscales. Journal of Personality Assessment, 55, 195-201.

3

Assessment and Classification of Offenders

164. Aadland, R.L., & Schag, D.S. (1984). The assessment of continued threat to the community in a mentally ill offender program. Journal of Criminal Justice, 12, 81-86. Studied the charts of 36 offenders from a mentally ill offender program to investigate how mental health evaluators determine whether an offender is or is not a threat to the community when evaluating offenders for possible release. The final decision to release or retain in the program was related to three variables identified by program staff: (1) initial psychiatric diagnosis, (2) presence of supportive relationships in the community, and (3) improvement during therapy.

165. Amoureus, M.P.S.R., van den Hurk, A.A., Schippers, G.M., Breteler, M.H.M. (1994). The Addiction Severity Index in penitentiaries. International Journal of Offender Therapy and Comparative Criminology, 38, 309-318. Assessed the utility of the Addiction Severity Index (ASI) with prisoners. Reliability and validity of the ASI was tested with 128 drug-abusing prisoners, with information collected on the amount, duration, and intensity of the symptoms during Ss' lifetime, specifically in the 30 days prior to assessment. Results indicated that the internal consistency was good, that the ASI problem areas were independent, that the ASI produced valid severity ratings, and that the validity of its psychiatric subscale was moderately good.

166. Andrews, D.A., Bonta, J., & Hoge, R.D. (1990). Classification for effective rehabilitation: Rediscovering psychology. Criminal Justice and Behavior, 17, 19-52.

167. Annis, H.M., & Chan, D. (1983). The differential treatment model: Empirical evidence from a personality typology of adult offenders. Criminal Justice and Behavior, 10, 159-173.

Randomly assigned 100 adult male offenders with alcohol and drug problems to either an intensive 8-week group therapy program or to routine institutional care. For each group, 2 types of offenders (positive or negative self image) were identified via an empirical clustering procedure. Although neither treatment or offender type had significant effects on measures of recidivism 1 year after release, a significant interaction of treatment x offender type was found indicating that offenders with positive self-image showed significant improvement in recidivism (e.g., fewer reconvictions and lower reconviction offense severity), while those with negative self image fared worse in the group therapy condition than in traditional institutional care.

168.   Apter, A., Ratzoni, G., Iancu, I., Weizman, R., & Tyano, S. (1993). The Ganser syndrome in two adolescent brothers. Journal of the American Academy of Child and Adolescent Psychiatry, 32, 582-584.
Considers the case of two adolescent brothers diagnosed with Ganser syndrome after incarceration who later developed signs and symptoms of affective disorder. Diagnosis and management of such cases are discussed.

169.   Austin, R.L. (1975). Construct validity of I-level classification. Criminal Justice and Behavior, 2, 113-129.

170.   Bonta, J., & Moituk, L.L. (1985). Utilization of an interview-based classification instrument: A study of correctional halfway houses. Criminal Justice and Behavior, 12, 333-352.
A study of the validation of the Level of Supervision Inventory (LSI) with 164 male prisoners placed in halfway houses found that the LSI successfully predicted in-program and post-program recidivism. Further, the scale demonstrated acceptable internal consistency and convergent reliability based on relationships to MMPI scales. The authors conclude that the LSI has utility, not only as a risk-assessment instrument, but also as a tool in selecting treatment goals and program evaluation.

171.   Borzecki, M., Wormith, J. S., & Black, W.H. (1988). An examination of differences between native and non-native psychiatric offenders on the MMPI. Canadian Journal of Behavioural Science, 20, 287-301.

172.   Boulet, J., & Boss, M.W. (1991). Reliability and validity of the Brief Symptom Inventory. Psychological Assessment, 3, 433-437.
Examined the reliability and validity of the Brief Symptom Inventory (BSI) in a sample of 501 forensic psychiatric inpatients and outpatients. Alpha coefficients for the 9 primary symptom dimensions were high. However, scores on the 9 BSI dimensions were found to correlate with both analogous and nonanalogous MMPI scales, indicating a limited convergent validity and a poor discriminant validity for the instrument. Reactivity to response bias was demonstrated by prominent correlations between the BSI dimensions and the MMPI validity scales. The findings may indicate the inappropriateness of BSI profile analysis in this sample. The BSI may hold some promise as a general indicator of psychopathology but further research is needed to justify its use as a clinical psychiatric screening tool.

173.   Carbonell, J.L. (1983). Inmate classification systems: A cross tabulation of two methods. Criminal Justice and Behavior, 10, 285-292.

174.   Carey, R.J., Garske, J.P., & Ginsberg, J. (1986). The prediction of adjustment to prison by means of an MMPI-based classification system. Criminal Justice and Behavior, 13, 347-365.
        The predictive validity of an MMPI based classification system was evaluated in a study of 495 state prison inmates. Results indicated that although over 90% of the inmates could be assigned to 1 or 10 categories and between-groups differences in prison adjustment were as expected, the applicability of the classification system with non-White inmates was questionable.

175.   Carroll, J.S. (1982). Evaluation, diagnosis, and prediction in parole decision making, Law and Society Review, 17, 199-228.
        Investigated parole release decision making in a study of case files and post-hearing questionnaires of 1,035 actual parole decisions in Pennsylvania. Results indicated that the Pennsylvania Parole Board based decisions on institutional behavior as well as predictions of future risk and rehabilitation. Predictions seemed to be based in part on identifying causes of crime such as personality traits, drug and alcohol use, income and post-release environment. A 1 year follow-up of 838 parolees showed that Parole Board predictions were unrelated to known post-release outcomes. An actuary prediction device developed by the authors was shown to be more predictive than the subjective conclusions of the parole board. The authors conclude that using decision guidelines such as those developed in their actuarial device may have great impact on the problem of discretionary decision making in the criminal justice system.

176.   Cavior, H.E., & Schmidt, A. (1978). A test of the effectiveness of a differential treatment strategy at the Robert F. Kennedy Center. Criminal Justice and Behavior, 5, 131-139.

177.   Cooke, G., & Thorwarth, C. (1978). Prediction of elopement of mentally ill offenders using the MMPI. Criminal Justice and Behavior, 5, 151-157.
        Compared 64 mentally ill elopers and 30 mentally ill non-elopers using the MMPI. When a prediction of elopement was made, it was correct 85% of the time. The utility of the prediction strategy is discussed as are issues involving the patient's right to a least restrictive environment are discussed.

178.   Cornell, D.G., & Hawk, G.L. (1989). Clinical presentation of malingerers diagnosed by experienced forensic psychologists. Law and Human Behavior, 13, 375-383.
        Compared clinical presentations of 39 criminal defendants diagnosed as malingering psychotic symptoms with those of 25 defendants diagnosed as genuinely psychotic to determine how the diagnosis of malingering is used in forensic clinical practice. Malingerers differed from psychotics on 14 of 24 clinical presentation variables, including measures of general presentation, affect, hallucinations, delusions, and formal thought disorder.

179.   Dahlstrom, W.G., Panton, J.H., Bain, K.P., & Dahlstrom, L.E. (1986). Utility of the Megargee-Bohn MMPI typological assignments: Study with a sample of death row inmates. Criminal Justice and Behavior, 13, 5-17.

180.   Davis, B.A., Durden, D.A., Pease, K., Yu, P.H., Green, C., Gordon, A., & Menzies, R., Templeman, R., & Boulton, A.A. (1993). A longitudinal study of the relationships between psychometric test scores, offence history and the plasma concentrations of phenylacetic and 5-hydroxyindoleacetic acids in seven inmates of a prison for the psychiatrically disturbed. Progress in Neuropsychopharmacology, Biology, and Psychiatry, 17, 619-635.

181.   Davis, B.A., Yu, P.H., Durden, D.A., Pease, K., Green, C., Menzies, R., Gordon, A., Templeman, R., & Boulton, A.A. (1991). Longitudinal study of inmates of a prison for the psychiatrically disturbed: plasma concentrations of biogenic amine metabolites and amino acids. Psychiatry Research, 36, 85-97.

182.   Davis, D.L. (1985). Treatment planning for the patient who is incompetent to stand trial. Hospital and Community Psychiatry, 36, 268-271.

183.   Davis, G.L., & Hoffman, R.G. (1991). MMPI and CPI scores of child molesters before and after incarceration-for-treatment. Journal of Offender Rehabilitation, 17, 77-85.

184.   Davis, R.W. (1983). Assessing offenders: Dying for reprieve. Journal of Personality Assessment, 49, 605-612.
Describes stages of the psychological adaptation to arrest, conviction, and imprisonment and argues that assessment and treatment should emphasize a developmental rather than static notion of the adaptation process.

185.   De Giosa, P., & Minervini, M.G. (1980). Pathology of neuropsychiatric importance among the inmates of a military prison: Its incidence in relation to the type of crime and length of detention. Rivista de Medicina Aeronautica e Spaziae, 43, 128-140.

186.   DiCataldo, F., Greer, A., & Profit, W.E. (1995). Screening inmates for mental disorder: An examination of the relationship between mental disorder and prison adjustment. Bulletin of the American Academy of Psychiatry and the Law, 23, 573-585.
The rapid growth of prison populations has severely limited the prison system's ability to effectively screen inmates for mental disorders and mental health service needs. This study describes a comprehensive mental health screening program which used a modified version of the Referral Decision Scale (RDS). Results indicate that the modified RDS may be an effective screening measure for use in correctional settings.

187.   DiFrancesca, K.R., & Meloy, J.R. (1989). A comparative clinical investigation of the "How" and "Charlie" MMPI subtypes. Journal of Personality Assessment, 53, 396-403.
Studied the thought and affective disturbances in the Megargee-Bohn typology's most psychopathological subtypes, the "How" and "Charlie" profiles. Results

indicate that both subtypes had mild formal thought disorder, with the former showing greater variance of thought disorder. Charlie subtypes, however, were more angry, less depressed, more vigorous, and more constricted and defensive than the How subtypes.

188. Drob, S.L., & Berger, R.H. (1987). The determination of malingering: A comprehensive clinical-forensic approach. Journal of Psychiatry and Law, 15, 519-538.
Describes a model for identifying malingerers based on three criteria: (1) presence of classic signs and symptoms of feigned mental illness, (2) determining a motive for malingering, and (3) ruling out true psychopathology.

189. Duthie, B., & French, A.P. (1990). Forensic utility of the MMPI contemporary norms. American Journal of Forensic Psychology, 8, 13-18.

190. Edinger, J.D., Reutefors, D., Logue, P.E. (1982). Cross-validation of the Megargee MMPI typology: A study of specialized inmate populations. Criminal Justice and Behavior, 9, 184-203.

191. Eysenck, H. (1977). Crime and personality. London: Routledge and Kegan Paul.

192. Friedt, L.R., & Gouvier, W.D. (1989). Bender Gestalt screening for brain dysfunction in a forensic population. Criminal Justice and Behavior, 16, 455-464.

193. Hankins, G.C., Barnard, G.W., & Robbins, L. (1993). The validity of the M Test in a residential forensic facility. Bulletin of the American Academy of Psychiatry and the Law, 21, 111-121.

194. Hiscock, C.K., Layman, L.B., & Hiscock, M. (1994). Cross-validation of two measures for assessing feigned mental incompetence in male prison inmates. Criminal Justice and Behavior, 21, 443-453.

195. Kanwischer, R.W., & Hundley, J. (1990). Screening for substance abuse in hospitalized psychiatric patients. Hospital and Community Psychiatry, 41, 795-797.

196. Keilitz, I. (1984). A model process for forensic mental health screening and evaluation. Law and Human Behavior, 8, 355-369.

197. Kennedy, T.D. (1986). Trends in inmate classification: A status report of two computerized psychometric approaches. Criminal Justice and Behavior, 13, 165-184.

198. Krefft, K.M., & Brittain, T.H., Jr. (1983). A prison assessment survey: Screening of a municipal prison population. Canadian Journal of Psychiatry, 28, 434-437.

199. Langevin, R., Ben-Aron, M., Wortzman, G., Dickey, R., & Handy, L. (1987). Brain damage, diagnosis, and substance abuse among violent offenders. Behavioral Sciences and the Law, 5, 77-94.

200.   LaWall, J.S. (1983). Profile of the older criminal. American Journal of Forensic Psychiatry, 3, 141-146.
Studied offenders 50+ years old seen at a court clinic during a 1-yr period. Each S underwent a clinical interview and psychometric testing. Data on the type of prior offense was obtained, and diagnosis was reached from S's clinical record as well as the relationship of drug or alcohol intoxication to the current offense. A wide range of criminal behavior, including violent crime, was observed. The prevalence of alcoholism as a primary diagnosis among the group of offenders was striking. A significant number of felons committed prior felonies, suggesting that the seriousness of crime does not necessarily decrease with age.

201.   Lawrence, S. (1984). Manual for the Lawrence psychological forensic examination. San Bernardino, CA: Associates in Forensic Psychology.

202.   Lilienfeld, S.O., Andrews, B.P., Stone-Romero, E.F., & Stone, D. (1994). The relations between a self-report honesty test and personality measures in prison and college samples. Journal of Research in Personality, 28, 154-169.

203.   Louscher, P.K., Hosford, R.E., Moss, C.S. (1983). Predicting dangerous behavior in a penitentiary using the Megargee typology. Criminal Justice and Behavior, 10, 269-284.

204.   Maden, A., & Gunn, J. (1993). When does a prisoner become a patient? Criminal Behaviour and Mental Health, 3, iii-viii.

205.   Mathias, R.E. (1988). Assessment of competency for execution: Assessment and dissonance on death row: The dilemma of consultation. Forensic Reports, 1, 125-132.

206.   McCartney, J.L. (1934). An intensive psychiatric study of prisoners: The receiving routine in the Classification Clinic Elmira Reformatory. American Journal of Psychiatry, 90, 1183-1203.

207.   McCormack, J.K., Barnett, R.W., & Wallbrown, F.H. (1989). Factor structure of the Millon Clinical Multiaxial Inventory with an offender sample. Journal of Personality Assessment, 53, 442-448.
A factor analysis of the Millon Clinical Multiaxial Inventory in a sample of 1200 inmates found four factors, three of which were similar to factors found in other populations (drug abusers, psychiatric patients, Vietnam veterans) and one factor which was unique to the offender sample.

208.   McMain, S., Webster, C.D., & Menzies, R.J. (1989). The post-assessment careers of mentally disordered offenders. Special Issue: Mental disorder and the criminal justice system. International Journal of Law and Psychiatry, 12, 189-201.
Studied the 6-year criminal and mental health careers of 195 mentally disordered offenders who were evaluated by a court forensic service. In the 6 yrs following their pretrial fitness assessment, 98% of the offenders had further contact with the criminal justice and/or mental health systems. Periods of hospital and prison confinement were highest during the 2 years subsequent to the assessment. Nearly

60% of the offenders continued to have contacts with psychiatric and correctional facilities following the 2nd year.

209.   McNeil, K., & Meyer, R.G. (1990). Detection of deception on the Millon Clinical Multiaxial Inventory (MCMI). Journal of Clinical Psychology, 46, 755-764.
       94 incarcerated males with no history of psychiatric treatment and 144 males from a forensic psychiatric inpatient setting were divided into distorted and nondistorted groups based on "fake bad" instructions and concurrent Minnesota Multiphasic Personality Inventory (MMPI) profiles. All Ss were administered the MCMI. Significant differences were found between groups for MCMI profile validity, weight factor scores, and total profile correction scores. MCMI profiles were consistent with expected symptomatology and test design. MCMI weight factor scores may be valuable indicators of symptom distortion in otherwise valid profiles in forensic settings. The diagnostic accuracy of MCMI reports may vary greatly in relation to clinical population, symptom prevalence, and diagnostic category.

210.   Megargee, E.I. (1984). A new classification system for criminal offenders: VI. Differences among the types on the Adjective Checklist. Criminal Justice and Behavior, 11, 349-376.
       Classified 1,164 male offenders according to an MMPI based classification developed by Megargee, Bohn, Meyer and Sink (1979) and compared the groups on the Gough and Heilbrun Adjective Check List Scales (ACL) and data from other sources. Results indicate that there are significant qualitative differences between the 10 types in terms of offender self description and descriptions made by others.

211.   Megargee, E.I. (1986). A psychometric study of incarcerated presidential threateners. Criminal Justice and Behavior, 13, 243-260.
       Compared MMPI scores of 45 presidential threateners and 48 nonthreateners evaluated at mental health facilities for federal prisoners and found that threateners' MMPI profiles and were more elevated and that classifications into Megargee's (1979) MMPI-based typology of offenders were significantly more deviant than in previously tested samples. Threateners tended to be more anti-social and prone to violence than had been previously suggested.

212.   Megargee, E.I. (1994). Using the Megargee MMPI-based classification system with MMPI-2s of male prison inmates. Psychological Assessment, 6, 337-344.

213.   Megargee, E.I. (1995). Assessment research in correctional settings: Methodological issues and practical problems. Psychological Assessment, 7, 359-356.

214.   Megargee, E.I., & Carbonell, J.L. (1985). Predicting prison adjustment with MMPI correctional scales. Journal of Consulting and Clinical Psychology, 53, 874-883.

215.   Meloy, J.R. (1986). Rapid classification of the functionally psychotic individual in custody. Criminal Justice and Behavior, 13, 185-195.

216.   Mendelson, E.F. (1992). A survey of practice at a regional forensic service: what do forensic psychiatrists do? Part I: Characteristics of cases and distribution of work. British Journal of Psychiatry, 160, 769-772.

217. Metzner, J.L., Miller, R.D., & Kleinsasser, D. (1994). Mental health screening and evaluation within prisons. Bulletin of the American Academy of Psychiatry and the Law, 22, 451-457.
      Describes the results of a study of the departments of corrections of all 50 state regarding mental health screening and evaluation in correctional mental health programs. The vast majority of states appear to have adopted some variation of the most recognized guidelines for screening and evaluation. Results are also provided information concerning the use of standardized psychological tests and informed consent issues.

218. Mikkelsen, E.J. (1980). The Bridgewater 100: An analysis of admissions to a hospital for the criminally insane. Psychiatric Quarterly, 52, 190-200.

219. Moss, C.S., Johnson, M.E., & Hosford, R.E. (1984). An assessment of the Megargee Typology in lifelong criminal violence. Criminal Justice and Behavior, 11, 225-234.

220. O'Sullivan, M.J., & Jemelka, R.P. (1993). The 3-4/4-3 MMPI code type in an offender population: An update on levels of hostility and violence. Psychological Assessment, 5, 493-498.
      Compared levels of hostility and type of crime committed between 94 male offenders with either 3-4 or 4-3 MMPI two point codes and in 94 offenders without these codes who were then matched for race with the 3-4/4-3 group. Except for higher scores on Megargee's Overcontrolled-Hostility scale, the 3-4/4-3 offenders either did not differ from or scored lower than the controls on type of crime and a number of self-report measures of hostility, anger, and violence.

221. Oldroyd, R.J. (1975). A principal components analysis of the BPI and MMPI. Criminal Justice and Behavior, 2, 85-90.
      A comparative study of the Bipolar Psychological Inventory (BPI), developed for use in correctional settings, and the MMPI found that the BPI more adequately identified personality disorders, which are common among prison inmates, than the MMPI, which was more adequate at identifying psychotic disorders, which are evident among only about ten percent of the prison population.

222. Ownby, R.L., Wallbrown, F.H., Carmin, C.N., & Barnett, R.W. (1990). A combined factor analysis of the Millon Clinical Multiaxial Inventory and the MMPI in an offender populations. Journal of Clinical Psychology, 46, 89-96.
      Results of a combined factor analysis of the Millon Clinical Multiaxial Inventory and the MMPI in a sample of 2,245 adjudicated offenders found that although some overlap between the two instruments exists, each instrument contains substantial unique variance. The authors argue that both instruments should be used as part of an objective assessment battery.

223. Page, R.C., & Myrick, R.D. (1978). The Public Offender Counseling Inventory: An instrument for assessing counseling outcomes in prisons. Criminal Justice and Behavior, 5, 141-150.

224.   Panton, J.H. (1974). Personality differences between male and female prison inmates measured by the MMPI. Criminal Justice and Behavior, 1, 332-339.
Compared the MMPI profiles of 128 male and 128 female prisoners and found that males had significantly higher means on the HS and D scales, while females had significantly higher means on the Si and Pa scales. Both groups had elevated Pd scores.

225.   Panton, J.H. (1976-77). Personality characteristics of aged inmates within a state prison. Offender Rehabilitation, 1, 203-208.
Compared the MMPI profiles of 120 offenders aged 60 or older to MMPI profiles of 2251 randomly selected state prison inmates and found fewer psychopathic but more neurotic responses among the aged inmates. Further, the older inmates showed greater anxiety, despondency, apprehension, and concern with physical functioning.

226.   Payne, C., McCabe, S., & Walker, N. (1974). Predicting offender-patient reconvictions. British Journal of Psychiatry, 125, 60-64.

227.   Posey, C.D., & Hess, A.K. (1985). Aggressive response sets and subtle-obvious MMPI scale distinctions in male offenders. Journal of Personality Assessment, 49, 235-239.
Studied the effects of aggressive versus non-aggressive response sets on subtle, neutral, and obvious items on MMPI clinical scales in a sample of 58 male prison inmates and found that inmates could significantly feign aggressiveness or nonaggressive on the obvious and neutral items, but not on those items judged to be subtle.

228.   Prandoni, J.R., & Swartz, C.P. (1978). Rorschach protocols for three diagnostic categories of adult offenders. Journal of Personality Assessment, 42, 115-120.
Developed norms for the Rorschach among 4 groups of adult offenders: (1) nonpsychotic/nonorganic, (2) organic/nonpsychotic, (3) psychotic/nonorganic, and (4) psychotic/organic. Comparisons of the three mentally disordered groups with the nonpsychotic/nonorganic group and an adult normative population are discussed.

229.   Pugh, D.N. (1994). Revision and further assessments of the Prison Locus of Control Scale. Psychological Reports, 74(3 Pt 1), 979-986.
Discusses the structure, reliability, and validity of the revised Prison Locus of Control Scale in several studies. Results demonstrate strong support for the reliability and validity of the revised scale.

230.   Quinsey, V.L. (1988). Assessments of the treatability of forensic patients. Behavioral Sciences and the Law, 6, 443-452.
The treatment of mentally disordered offenders (MDOs) receives very little attention in the literature and that the treatment concerns should be seen as a more central issue than the prediction of dangerousness. Assessments of treatability should be seen as more relevant to dispositional decisions than assessments of criminal responsibility, and improvements in the effectiveness of treatment a more useful approach to the problem of dangerousness than attempts to improve predictive methods.

231.   Quinsey, V.L., & Ambtman, R. (1979). Variables affecting psychiatrists' and teachers' assessments of the dangerousness of mentally ill offenders. Journal of Consulting and Clinical Psychology, 47, 353-362

232.   Reich, J., & Thompson, W.D. (1987). Comparison of psychiatric diagnoses in three populations. Hillside Journal of Clinical Psychiatry, 9, 36-46.

233.   Reinehr, R.C., Swartz, J.D., & Dudley, H.K. (1984). Ethnic differences in the measurement of hostility in forensic patients. Revista Interamericana de Psicologia, 18, 53-64.
        Studied the responses of 130 Anglo-American, 109 Black-American, and 34 Hispanic-American male forensic patients on the Buss-Durkee Hostility-Guilt Inventory (BDHI) and the Holtzman Inkblot Technique (HIT) and found no differences between Anglo-American and Hispanic-American patients. However, Black- and Hispanic-American patients and Anglo-and Black-American patients differed on some scales for both instruments.

234.   Reitsma-Street, M., & Leschied, A.W. (1988). The conceptual-level matching model in corrections. Criminal Justice and Behavior, 15, 92-108.

235.   Rice, M.E., & Harris, G.T. (1988). An empirical approach to the classification and treatment of maximum security psychiatric patients. Behavioral Sciences and the Law, 6, 497-514.

236.   Rodenhauser, P., Schwenkner, C.E., & Khamis, H.J. (1987). Factors related to drug treatment refusal in a forensic hospital. Hospital and Community Psychiatry, 38, 631-637.
        Used the hospital records of 421 adult patients in a maximum-security forensic hospital to study the relationship between clinical factors and receptiveness vs. refusal of drug treatments. Drug treatment refusal was significantly related to a psychotic diagnosis in the absence of a personality disorder. Psychotic patients with personality disorders were relatively receptive and compliant with drug treatment. Those who refused treatment had significantly longer lengths of hospitalization that were not reduced by medication.

237.   Rogers, R., & Nussbaum, D. (1991). Interpreting response styles of inconsistent Minnesota Multiphasic Personality Inventory profiles. Forensic Reports, 4, 361-366. Random or inconsistent responses on the Minnesota MMPI may reflect insufficient reading comprehension, disinterest or lack of motivation, hostility, disorganized thinking, or attempts to malinger. A guide for interpreting such protocols is presented and discussed.

238.   Rogers, R., & Webster, C.D. (1989). Assessing treatability in mentally disordered offenders. Law and Human Behavior, 13, 19-29.

239.   Rogers, R., Dolmetsch, R., & Cavanaugh, J.L. (1983). Identification of random responders on MMPI protocols. Journal of Personality Assessment, 47, 364-368.

240.   Rogers, R., Gillis, J.R., & Dickens, S.E. (1989). A research note on the MMPI Pd Scale and sociopathy. International Journal of Offender Therapy and Comparative Criminology, 33, 21-25.
Pd 2-point codes were not useful in identifying antisocial personality disorders in a study of 470 offenders and were often present in individuals with either major psychiatric disorders or no disorders at all.

241.   Rogers, R., Gillis, J.R., Dickens, S.E., & Webster, C.D. (1988). Treatment recommendations for mentally disordered offenders: More than roulette? Behavioral Sciences and the Law, 6, 487-495.

242.   Saltstone, R., Halliwell, S., & Hayslip, M.A. (1994). A multivariate evaluation of the Michigan Alcoholism Screening Test and the Drug Abuse Screening Test in a female offender population. Addictive Behavior, 19, 455-462.
Although principal components analysis of the Michigan Alcoholism Screening Test (MAST) and the Drug Abuse Screening Test (DAST) revealed factor structures similar to those found in studies of male offenders, both scales were basically unidimensional in this study of 615 women offenders.

243.   Scapinello, K.F., & Blanchard, R. (1987). Historical items in the MMPI: Note on evaluating treatment outcomes for a criminal population. Psychological Reports, 61, 775-778.
Based on the evaluation of 13 MMPI profiles of prison inmates before and after receiving individual psychotherapy, the authors conclude that the MMPI may be unsuitable as an treatment outcome measure due to large numbers of items that reflect irrevocable past events and are therefore insensitive to changes associated with psychotherapeutic intervention.

244.   Schmalz, B.J., Fehr, R.C., & Dalby, J.T. (1989). Distinguishing forensic, psychiatric and inmate groups with the MMPI. American Journal of Forensic Psychology, 7, 37-47.
Results of this study showed that forensic patients and inmates who had committed a severely assaultive crime scored significantly higher on the O-H Scale than did forensic patients and inmates who had committed mildly or moderately assaultive crimes. Further, severely assaultive forensic Ss and inmates also obtained significantly higher O-H scores than did a group of nonoffending psychiatric patients. The O-H scale contributed significantly to the discrimination of offenders and nonoffenders.

245.   Seamons, D.T., Howell, R.J., Carlisle, A.L., & Roe, A.V. (1981). Rorschach simulation of mental illness and normality by psychotic and nonpsychotic legal offenders. Journal of Personality Assessment, 45, 130-135.

246.   Sherman, L.G., & Morschauser, P.C. (1989). Screening for suicide risk in inmates. Psychiatric Quarterly, 60, 119-138.

247.   Smith, L.B., Silber, D.E., & Karp, S.A. (1988). Validity of the Megargee-Bohn MMPI typology with women incarcerated in a state prison. Psychological Reports, 62, 107-113.

248.   Steinberg, A. (1991). Issues in providing mental health services to hearing-impaired persons. Hospital and Community Psychiatry, 42, 380-389.

249.   Stewart, S.D. (1994). Community-based drug treatment in the Federal Bureau of Prisons. Federal Probation, 58, 24-28.

250.   Straus, M.A. (1993). Identifying offenders in criminal justice research on domestic assault. American Behavioral Scientist, 36, 587-600.
       Discusses the use of the Conflict Tactics Scales in the identification of high-risk domestic violence offenders based on whether the assaults are chronic and severe and whether there are other risk factors, such as alcohol or drug abuse, and prior arrest or conviction for violent crime.

251.   Sutker, P.B. (1973). A psychosocial description of penitentiary inmates. Archives of General Psychiatry, 29, 663-667.

252.   Swanson, S.C., Templer, D.I., Thomas-Dobson, S., Cannon, W.G., Streiner, D.L., Reynolds, R.M., & Miller, H.R. (1995). Development of a three-scale MMPI: the MMPI-TRI. Journal of Clinical Psychology, 51, 361-374.

253.   Swett, C. (1984). Use of the Michigan Alcohol Screening Test in a prison hospital. American Journal of Drug and Alcohol Abuse, 10, 563-569.

254.   Templer, D.I. (1992). Prison norms for Raven's Standard Progressive Matrices. Perceptual and Motor Skills, 74(3 Pt 2), 1193-1194.

255.   Templer, D.I., & Jackson, P.A. (1992). Jewish inmates: an atypical prison group. Psychological Reports, 71, 513-514.

256.   Tobey, L.H., & Bruhn, A.R. (1992). Early memories and the criminally dangerous. Journal of Personality Assessment, 59, 137-152.
       Using the Early Memory Aggressiveness Potential Score System (EMAPSS), 73% of criminally dangerous (N = 30) and nondangerous (N = 30) forensic patients were correctly classified with 15 of 16 (94%) classified as dangerous actually being dangerous.

257.   Traub, G.S., & Bohn, M.J., Jr. (1985). Note on the reliability of the MMPI with Spanish-speaking inmates in the federal prison system. Psychological Reports, 56, 371-374.

258.   VanVoorhis, P. (1988). A cross classification of five offender typologies: Issues in construct and predictive validity. Criminal Justice and Behavior, 15, 109-124.

259.   Villanueva, M.R., Roman, D., & Tuley, M.R. (1988). Determining forensic rehabilitation potential with the MMPI: Practical implications for residential treatment populations. American Journal of Forensic Psychology, 6, 27-35.
       Found that overcontrolled hostility, prison maladjustment and clinical scales 1 and 5 differentiated between forensic patients in a residential treatment program who were either successful or non-successful in the program.

260. Walters, G.D. (1986). Screening for psychopathology in groups of black and white prison inmates by means of the MMPI. Journal of Personality Assessment, 50, 257-264.

261. Walters, G.D. (1991). Predicting the disciplinary adjustment of maximum and minimum security prison inmates using the Lifestyle Criminality Screening Form. International Journal of Offender Therapy and Comparative Criminology, 35, 63-71.

262. Walters, G.D. (1995). The Psychological Inventory of Criminal Thinking Styles: I. Reliability and preliminary validity. Criminal Justice and Behavior, 22, 307-325.
Discusses the creation, standardization, and preliminary validation of the Psychological Inventory of Criminal Thinking Styles, designed to measure thinking styles believed to be associated with patterns of serious criminal conduct. Responses obtained from 450 prison inmates were used to establish norms, assess the reliability of the scales, and investigate preliminary validity issues. Results indicate that maximum-security inmates attained significantly higher scores on the scales than minimum- and medium-security inmates and that the inventory is of sufficient reliability and initial validity to warrant continued investigation.

263. Webster, C.D., et al. (1985). Psychoeducational assessment programmes for forensic psychiatric patients. Canadian Psychology, 26, 50-53.
Describes 2 Canadian programs which attempt to interrupt the revolving-door phenomenon between the criminal justice and the mental health systems. The first program offers forensic psychiatric patients information about both the legal and psychiatric systems that is relevant to their immediate situations as well as for the future. The 2nd program, a cognitive behavioral intervention for anger control, offers patients exposure to a short-term treatment.

264. Wright, K.N. (1988) The relationship of risk, needs, and personality classification systems and prison adjustment. Criminal Justice and Behavior, 15, 454-471.

265. Wrobel, N.H., Wrobel, T.A., & McIntosh, J.W. (1988). Application of the Megargee MMPI typology to a forensic psychiatric population. Criminal Justice and Behavior, 15, 247-254.

266. Yokelson, S. & Samenow, S. (1977). The criminal personality. New York: Aronson.

267. Zager, L.D. (1988). The MMPI-based Criminal Classification System: A review, current status, and future directions. Criminal Justice and Behavior, 15, 39-57.

268. Ziskin, J. (1984). Malingering of psychological disorders. Behavioral Sciences and the Law, 2, 39-49.

4

Institution-Based Programs and Services

269. Adams, K. (1986). The disciplinary experiences of mentally disordered inmates. Criminal Justice and Behavior, 13, 297-316.
Compared 373 male offenders referred to prison mental health units with 510 nonreferred inmates on rule violations and discipline. Findings indicate that referred inmates had higher infraction rates than nonreferred inmates and that these violations reflected symptomatic behavior. Although sanctions usually involved mental health staff assistance along with punishment, there were certain conditions under which punitive responses led to escalation of disruptive behavior. The author concludes that disruptive behavior and pathology are interrelated among emotionally disturbed inmates.

270. Adams, S. (1977). Evaluating correctional treatments: Toward a new perspective. Criminal Justice and Behavior, 4, 323-339.
Takes issue with reviews of correctional treatment which have concluded that rehabilitation of offenders does not occur and discusses conditions under which rehabilitative treatments can be successful.

271. Albrecht H., Chaplow, D., & Peters, J. (1992). Forensic psychiatry and prison liaison services in Auckland: The first twelve months. New Zealand Medical Journal, 105(940), 334-335.

272. Alexander, R. (1992). Determining appropriate criteria in the evaluation of correctional mental health treatment for inmates. Journal of Offender Rehabilitation, 18, 119-134.
Critiques the use of adjustment indicators such as within-institution adjustment or rates of recidivism is studies of the effectiveness of prison-based mental health treatment. Alternative indicators of treatment effectiveness are discussed.

273.   American Psychiatric Association (1989). Psychiatric Services in Jails and Prisons. Washington, DC: Author.

274.   Anno, B.J. (1991). Organizational structure of prison health care: Results of a national survey. Journal of Prison and Jail Health, 10, 59-74.
Surveyed the organizational structure of health services in the 50 state Departments of Corrections and found numerous models in use with organizational structures ranging from totally centralized to totally decentralized. Successful models integrate medical, mental health and other services and have division status within the department.

275.   Arboleda-Florez, J.E., & Chato, F. (1985). Issues regarding admissions from a correctional facility to a hospital forensic unit. International Journal of Offender Therapy and Comparative Criminology, 29, 43-62.

276.   Arboleda-Florez, J. (1981). Forensic psychiatry services in Canada: Strengths and weaknesses. International Journal of Law and Psychiatry, 4, 391-399.
This discussion of forensic psychiatry in Canada includes discussions of treatment for sex offenders and mentally ill offenders in prisons and after release.

277.   Atkinson, D.R. (1976). Effect of media training on inmate interpersonal relationship skills. Criminal Justice and Behavior, 3, 41-52.

278.   Banerjee, S., O'Neill B.K., Exworthy, T., & Parrott, J. (1995). The Belmarsh Scheme. A prospective study of the transfer of mentally disordered remand prisoners from prison to psychiatric units. British Journal of Psychiatry, 166, 802-805.

279.   Barker, E.T., & Buck, M.H. (1977). L.S.D. in a coercive milieu therapy program. Canadian Psychiatric Association Journal, 22, 311-314.

280.   Barte, H.N. (1989). L'isolement carceral. Perspectives Psychiatriques, 28, 252-255.
Discusses the pathogenic effects of solitary confinement. Prisoners remaining in solitary confinement for extended periods of time may become schizophrenic instead of becoming more receptive to social rehabilitation. The author concludes that solitary confinement is unjustifiable, counterproductive, and indistinguishable from torture.

281.   Barthwell, A.G., Bokos, P., Bailey, J., Nisenbaum, M., Devereux, J., & Senay, E.C. (1995). Interventions/Wilmer: A continuum of care for substance abusers in the criminal justice system. Journal of Psychoactive Drugs, 27, 39-47.
This article describes a collaboration between a private sector substance abuse treatment provider and a county judiciary and correctional department to provide comprehensive treatment and support services for substance abusers in jail. The program is individually tailored and includes a six-month inpatient program which, aside from traditional treatment, consists of education and job skills training, and extensive post-release follow-up and monitoring as well as support services such as transportation and child care services. No evaluation results have yet been reported.

282.   Belfrage, H. (1990). The crime-preventive effect of psychiatric treatment in special
       units or in county hospitals. Nordisk Psykiatrisk Tidsskrift, 44, 485-487.

283.   Belfrage, H. (1991). The crime preventive effect of psychiatric treatment on
       mentally disordered offenders in Sweden. International Journal of Law and
       Psychiatry, 14, 237-243.

284.   Benezech, M., Gerard, H., & Serin, N. (1993). Establishment of a criminal ward at
       a facility for dangerous patients in Cadillac: A new development in French
       psychiatric practice. Annales Medico Psychologiques, 151, 260-264.
       Discusses an innovative ward for the criminally insane at a community-based
       psychiatric hospital. The advantages of incorporating treatment for criminally insane
       patients into community-based psychiatric hospitals are discussed as is the
       importance of maintaining good communication legal and medical personnel and
       systems.

285.   Berlin, F.S., & Malin, H.M. (1991). Media distortion of the public's perception of
       recidivism and psychiatric rehabilitation. American Journal of Psychiatry, 148,
       1572-1576.
       Results of this study suggest that inaccurate media presentations concerning
       psychiatric rehabilitation that ignore treatment successes and focus only on alleged
       failures do a disservice to patients, mental health workers, and society at large.

286.   Bloom, J.D., Bradford, J.M., & Kofoed, L. (1988). An overview of psychiatric
       treatment approaches to three offender groups. Hospital and Community Psychiatry,
       39, 151-158.
       Discusses diagnosis and treatment of insanity acquittees, sexual offenders, and
       offenders with alcohol problems.

287.   Bloom, J.D., Faulkner, L.R., Shore, J.H., & Rogers, J.L. (1983). The young adult
       chronic patient and the legal system: A systems analysis. New Directions for Mental
       Health Services, 19, 37-50.
       In a discussion of many issues at the interface of law and mental health, the authors
       describe the Oregon prison system with on-site medical and psychiatric services and
       a voluntary correctional treatment program for mentally ill offenders, as well as
       community treatment for patients requiring concurrent psychiatric care and justice
       system monitoring.

288.   Bowden, P. (1977). The current management of the mentally disordered offender.
       Proceedings of the Royal Society of Medicine, 70, 881-884.

289.   Brodsky, S.L., & Scogin, F.R. (1988). Inmates in protective custody: First data on
       emotional effects. Forensic Reports, 1, 267-280.
       An interview study of 69 male mentally ill inmates in protective custody at 3 large,
       maximum-security institutions found psychopathological consequences in an
       estimated two-thirds of mentally ill offenders in protective custody at 2 institutions
       in which mentally ill offenders were excluded from program participation and were
       largely restricted to their cells. In the institution in which adequate cell space,
       program participation, and mobility were present, no adverse consequences were

found. Protective custody confinement is not necessarily harmful, but social isolation and restriction from participation have potential for negative psychological effects.

290.   Cohen, F., & Dvoskin, J. (1992). Inmates with mental disorders: A guide to law and practice. Mental and Physical Disability Law Reporter, 16, 462-470.
Proposes a community mental health model for mental health services in prison. The goals are to reduce the disabling effects of serious mental illness; to reduce human suffering; and to help keep the prison safer for staff, volunteers, and visitors. These goals provide a common ground for the many actors involved in the prison environment. The essential services of the community model are screening and triage, follow-up evaluations, crisis intervention services, acute care beds, intermediate care programs, clinic services, and consultation services.

291.   Conacher, G.N. (1993). Issues in psychiatric care within a prison service. Canada's Mental Health, 41, 11-15.

292.   Condelli, W.S., Dvoskin, J.A., & Holanchock, H. (1994). Intermediate care programs for inmates with psychiatric disorders. Bulletin of the American Academy of Psychiatry and the Law, 22, 63-70.
The New York State Intermediate Care Programs for mentally ill inmates were studied. Data from 209 inmates who had been in the program and prison for at least six months revealed significant reductions in serious rules infractions, suicide attempts, correctional discipline, and three mental health services: crisis care, seclusion, and hospitalization.

293.   Cooke, M.K., & Cooke, G. (1982). An integrated treatment program for mentally ill offenders: Description and evaluation. International Journal of Offender Therapy and Comparative Criminology, 26, 53-61.
Describes a collaborative treatment program involving both the criminal justice and mental health systems. Treatment occurred in a hospital rather than a prison and included psychological evaluations; psychotropic medication; group and individual psychotherapy; occupational, recreational, and music therapy; and vocational and/or academic counseling and training. The treatment modality was based on a therapeutic community model. Several case histories are provided to illustrate the program's effectiveness.

294.   Cormier, B.M. (1973). The practice of psychiatry in the prison society. Bulletin of the American Academy of Psychiatry and the Law, 1, 156-183.

295.   Corrigan, P.W. (1991). Social skills training in adult psychiatric populations: A meta-analysis. Journal of Behavior Therapy and Experimental Psychiatry, 22, 203-210.
Reviewed findings from studies of social skills training with 4 psychiatric populations: (1) developmentally disabled, (2) psychotic, (3) non-psychotic, and (4) mentally ill offenders. Generally, social skills training had the most impact on the developmentally disabled groups and the least with offender groups.

296.   Crossley, T., & Guzman, R. (1984). Management of a forensic psychiatric unit. American Journal of Forensic Psychiatry, 5, 159-172.

297.   Davis, D.L. (1985). Treatment planning for the patient who is incompetent to stand trial. Hospital and Community Psychiatry, 36, 268-271.

298.   Day, K. (1988). A hospital-based treatment programme for male mentally handicapped offenders. British Journal of Psychiatry, 153, 635-644.
Evaluated the effectiveness of a treatment program for male mentally ill offenders that included personal and practical skills training and a socialization program based on a token-economy and found that at a final follow-up (approximately 3 years) that although each participant continued to offend and to be judged as displaying significant psychosocial pathology, 85% had experienced at least a fair response to treatment. The best outcomes were associated with more than 2 years of inpatient care, a good response to the treatment program, stable residential placement, regular employment, and regular supervision and support in the community.

299.   Day, K. (1988). Services for psychiatrically disordered mentally handicapped adults: A U.K. perspective. Australia and New Zealand Journal of Developmental Disabilities, 14, 19-25.
Describes the increasing replacement of institutional care with community care, with discussion about services for psychiatrically and behaviorally disturbed mentally handicapped and mentally handicapped offenders.

300.   Eckerman, W.C. (1972). A nationwide survey of mental health and correctional institutions for adult mentally disordered offenders. National Institute of Mental Health. DHEW Pub. No. (HSM)73-9018. Washington, DC: U.S. Government Printing Office.

301.   Edinger, J.D. (1980). Treating psychiatrically repressed prison inmates in a therapeutic community. Hospital and Community Psychiatry, 31, 781-783.

302.   Edwards, A.C., Morgan, D.W., & Faulkner, L.R. (1994). Prison inmates with a history of inpatient psychiatric treatment. Hospital and Community Psychiatry, 45, 172-174.

303.   Evans, B., Souma, A., & Maier, G.J. (1989). A vocational assessment and training program for individuals in an inpatient forensic mental health center. Psychosocial Rehabilitation Journal, 13, 61-69.
Describes a program designed to provide vocational training and to obtain competitive employment for forensic psychiatry patients upon release from prison. Case examples presented suggest that the program was more successful for those diagnosed with personality disorders than for those diagnosed with schizophrenic disorders.

304.   Evans, A. (1985). Roles and functions of occupational therapy in mental health. American Journal of Occupational Therapy, 39, 799-802.
This discussion of the role of occupational therapy in a variety of mental health settings includes some discussion of occupational therapy in forensic psychiatric settings.

305. Falkin, G.P., Prendergast, M., Anglin, M.D. (1994). Drug treatment in the criminal
      justice system. Federal Probation, 58, 31-36.
      Based on data from the National Institute of Justice's 1992 Drug Use Forecasting
      program, 50-80% of arrestees in the 24 DUF cites tested positive for one or more
      drugs after arrest. Rates of drug use are especially high for minorities and women.
      The authors argue that the need for treatment is not being met and that drug
      treatment might be an effective government response. A review of case studies
      illustrates strategies for coordination approaches to drug treatment, and for treating
      jailed defendants, as well as probationers, and parolees.

306. Foster, D.V. (1988). Consideration of treatment issues with American Indians
      detained in the Federal Bureau of Prisons. Psychiatric Annals, 18, 698-701.

307. Fraley, S.E. (1991). From self-blame to self-acceptance: Benefits of learning
      psychology in a prison undergraduate program. Teaching of Psychology, 18, 234-
      235.
      The author, an inmate graduate psychology student, discusses how education in
      psychology aided in his own rehabilitation, focussing on the developmental themes
      of Freud, Piaget, and Erickson.

308. Fuller, J.R. (1985). Treatment environments in secure psychiatric settings: A case
      study. International Journal of Offender Therapy and Comparative Criminology, 29,
      63-76.

309. Geller, E.S., Johnson, D.F., Hamlin, P.H., & Kennedy, T.D. (1977). Behavior
      modification in a prison: Issues, problems, and compromises. Criminal Justice and
      Behavior, 4, 11-43.

310. Goldmeier, J., Patterson, E.F., & Sauer, R.H. (1972). Community mental health an
      the mentally ill offender. Maryland State Medical Journal, 21, 56-59.

311. Greene, R.T. (1988). A comprehensive mental health care system for prison inmates:
      Retrospective look at New York's ten year experience. Special Issue: Forensic
      administration. International Journal of Law and Psychiatry, 11, 381-389.
      Forensic mental health care for sentenced prisoners in New York State has been
      transformed due to increasing comprehensiveness due to having community mental
      health clinics in prisons, continuity of care for inmates transferred within the prison
      system, coordination of inmate access to all levels of mental health care, and
      cooperation with the Department of Correctional Services.

312. Groder, M.G. (1973). Butner: A clear blueprint: New hope for mentally ill federal
      offenders. Mental Health, 57, 5.

313. Gudjonsson, G.H. (1990). Psychological treatment for the mentally ill offender.
      Issues in Criminological and Legal Psychology, 16, 15-21.

314. Hamm, M.S., & Schrink, J.L. (1989). The conditions of effective implementation:
      A guide to achieving rehabilitative objectives in corrections. Criminal Justice and
      Behavior, 16, 166-182.

Results of a survey conducted by the authors and other research show that although public officials offer little opposition to rehabilitative goals, complex correctional bureaucracies hinder the implementation and overall success of rehabilitative interventions in correctional settings. The authors discuss an implementation plan that may be successful in less than optimal correctional settings.

315.   Harmon, R.B. (1989). Administration and management of an urban forensic psychiatry unit. In R. Rosner, & R.B. Harmon (Eds.), Criminal court consultation: Critical issues in American psychiatry and the law, vol. 5. New York: Plenum Press.

316.   Harris, G.T. (1989). The relationship between neuroleptic drug dose and the performance of psychiatric patients in a maximum security token economy program. Journal of Behavior Therapy and Experimental Psychiatry, 20, 57-67.

317.   Hartstone, E., Steadman, H.J., Robbins, P.C. (1984). Identifying and treating the mentally disordered prison inmate. In L.A. Teplin (Ed.), Mental health and criminal justice. Beverly Hills, CA: Sage Publications.

318.   Hayman, P.M. (1981). Medication acceptance and refusal among involuntary confined mentally ill criminal offenders. Corrective and Social Psychiatry and Journal of Behavior Technology, Methods and Therapy, 27, 88-92.
        A study of 118 male involuntarily confined mentally ill offenders found that participants had a similar rate of refusal and similar motives for refusal as other psychiatric patients. The two most prominent motives were side effects and perceived need for, and benefit from, medication.

319.   Heilbrun, K., Nunez, C.E., Deitchman, M.A., Gustafson, D., et al. (1992). The treatment of mentally disordered offenders: A national survey of psychiatrists. Bulletin of the American Academy of Psychiatry and the Law, 20, 475-480.
        Surveyed 115 public, inpatient mental health centers providing treatment to mentally ill offenders and found that patterns of treatment offered appeared to be clinically appropriate.   Behavioral and cognitive-behavioral treatments, however, were reported infrequently.

320.   Hilkey, J.H. (1988). A theoretical model for assessment of delivery of mental health services in the correctional facility. Psychiatric Annals, 18, 676-679.

321.   Hodgins, S. (1988). The organization of forensic services in Canada. International Journal of Law and Psychiatry, 11, 329-339.
        Describes the strengths and weaknesses associated with various organization and funding of Canadian mental health services for persons accused or convicted of criminal offenses, including those found not guilty by reason of insanity or incompetent to stand trial as well as residents of penal institutions.

322.   Hoyer, G. (1988). Management of mentally ill offenders in Scandinavia. International Journal of Law and Psychiatry, 11, 317-327.

323.   Hunter, G.C. (1994). Who's really in charge of my life, anyway? Locus of control
       and cognitive substance abuse treatment in a federal prison. Journal of Rational
       Emotive and Cognitive Behavior Therapy, 12, 219-227.
       Studied changes in locus of control for 19 federal prison inmates who were
       graduates of a 9-month residential cognitive substance abuse treatment program
       with 20 inmates on a waiting list. Results showed that the treatment group displayed
       significantly more general internal locus of control and vocational locus of control
       than controls.

324.   Ishikawa, Y. (1994). The treatment of mentally disordered offenders in Japanese
       medical prisons. Japanese Journal of Psychiatry and Neurology, 48(Supplement),
       85-95.

325.   James, J.F., & Gregory, D. (1980). Improving psychiatric care for prisoners.
       Hospital and Community Psychiatry, 31, 671-673.
       Based on a needs assessment of the mental health treatment needs of inmates in
       Oklahoma prisons, the authors argue that the prison is a community, requiring
       community mental health systems type services including partial hospitalization,
       outpatient services, acute inpatient treatment, and transitional living units. The
       authors further suggest that mental health professionals should work towards
       improving the prison living environment, drawing on their experiences in other
       institutional settings where therapeutic communities and patient governments have
       been used.

326.   Jemelka, R., Trupin, E., & Chiles, J.A. (1989). The mentally ill in prisons: A review.
       Hospital and Community Psychiatry, 40. 481-491.

327.   Johnson, S.C., Hoover, J.O. (1988). Mental health services within the Federal
       Bureau of Prisons. Psychiatric Annals, 18, 673-674.
       Discusses psychiatric treatments available to federal prison inmates and the
       challenges involved in this effort. The ramifications of the prison environment for
       individuals with schizophrenia, borderline disorder, and antisocial personality are
       discussed.

328.   Kaufman, E. (1973). Can comprehensive mental health care be provided in an
       overcrowded prison system? Journal of Psychiatry and Law, 1, 243-262.

329.   Kerr, C.A., Roth, J.A., Courtless, T.F., & Zenoff, E.H. (1987). Survey of facilities
       and programs for mentally disordered offenders. National Institute of Mental Health.
       DHHS Pub. No. (ADM)86-1493. Washington, DC: U.S. Government Printing
       Office.

330.   Kohlmeyer, W.A. (1979). The first year of operation under the new Patuxent Laws.
       Bulletin of the American Academy of Psychiatry and the Law, 7, 95-102.

331.   Kutch, J.M. (1987). The Federal Prisons' Mental Health Program: 1930-1985.
       Journal of Mental Health Administration, 14, 20-25.
       Examines changes in the Federal Bureau of Prisons Mental Health program through
       three stages of development: (1) concentration on severe mental conditions requiring

extensive psychiatric care; (2) recognition of the needs of milder forms of mental disorders; and (3) recognition of both mental health and mental illness as community responsibilities and a need to consider the prison population a community.

332.   Levinson, R. (1984). The system that cannot say no. American Psychologist, 39, 811-812.
        Discusses how the criminal justice system has dealt with deinstitutionalized psychiatric patients, and how it attempts to cope with the increasing influx of mentally disordered offenders.

333.   Lidberg, L., & Belfrage, H. (1991). Mentally disordered offenders in Sweden. Bulletin of the American Academy of Psychiatry and the Law, 19, 389-393.

334.   Lloyd, C. (1985). Evaluation and forensic psychiatric occupational therapy. British Journal of Occupational Therapy, 48, 137-140.

335.   Lloyd, C., & Guerra, F. (1988). A vocational rehabilitation programme in forensic psychology. British Journal of Occupational Therapy, 51, 123-126.

336.   Lombardo, L.X. (1985). Mental health work in prisons and jails: Inmate adjustment and indigenous correctional personnel. Criminal Justice and Behavior, 12, 17-27.

337.   Lomis, M.J., & Baker, L.L. (1985). Microtraining of forensic psychiatric patients for empathic counseling skills. Journal of Counseling Psychology, 32, 84-93.

338.   Losada-Paisey, G., & Paisey, T.J. (1988). Program evaluation of a comprehensive treatment package for mentally retarded offenders. Behavioral Residential Treatment, 3, 247-265.

339.   Maden, A., Swinton, M., & Gunn, J. (1994). Therapeutic community treatment: A survey of unmet need among sentenced prisoners. Therapeutic Communities International Journal for Therapeutic and Supportive Organizations, 15, 229-236.
        Surveyed the psychiatric disorders and treatment needs of sentenced prisoners in the United Kingdom and assessed the efficacy of therapeutic community treatment within prisons and found that the most common diagnoses were substance abuse (77%) and personality disorder (47%).   Results also suggested expanding therapeutic community treatment inside and outside of the prisons.

340.   Maier, G.J., Morrow, B.R., & Miller, R. (1989). Security safeguards in community rehabilitation of forensic patients. Hospital and Community Psychiatry, 40, 529-531.

341.   Mason, P. (1984). Services for the mentally abnormal offender: An overview. Issues in Criminological and Legal Psychology, 6, 12-16.
        Discusses how conflicting concerns between the public's desire for adequate protection from mentally ill offenders and the health service profession concern for adequate treatment of these offenders affect the development and implementation of policies regarding the handling and treatment of mentally ill offenders.

342.   McNamara, J.R., & Andrasik, F. (1982). Recidivism follow-up for residents released from a forensic psychiatry behavior change treatment program. Journal of Psychiatric Treatment and Evaluation, 4, 423-426.

343.   McNiff, M.A. (1973). Nursing in a psychiatric prison service. American Journal of Nursing, 73, 1586-1587.

344.   McShane, M.D. (1989). The bus stop revisited: Discipline and psychiatric patients in prison. Journal of Psychiatry and Law, 17, 413-433.

345.   Menditto, A.A., Baldwin, L.J., O'Neal, L.G., & Beck, N.C. (1991). Social learning procedures for increasing attention and improving basic skills in severely regressed institutionalized patients. Journal of Behavior Therapy and Experimental Psychiatry, 22, 265-269.

346.   Mollerstrom, W.W., Patchner, M.A., & Milner, J.S. (1992). Family violence in the Air Force: A look at offenders and the role of the Family Advocacy Program. Military Medicine, 157, 371-374.

347.   Morrison, E.F. (1991). Victimization in prison: implications for the mentally ill inmate and for health professionals. Archives of Psychiatric Nursing, 5, 17-24.
A qualitative study using interviews conducted with 13 subjects who were both inmates and staff members in a forensic halfway house found that the victimization experienced in prison poses particular problems for mentally ill inmates. The lack of social and economic resources, dependence, and need for attention common among mentally ill inmates make them particularly vulnerable. Implications of victimization of the mentally ill for health care professionals working in prisons is discussed.

348.   Morrissey, J.P., Swanson, J.W., Goldstrom, I., Rudolph, L., & Manderscheid, R.W. (1993). Overview of mental health services provided by state adult correctional facilities: United States, 1988. Mental Health Statistical Notes, May(207), 1-13.

349.   Musante, G., & Gallemore, J.L., Jr. (1973). Utilization of a staff development group in prison consultation. Community Mental Health Journal, 9, 224-232.

350.   National Institute of Mental Health. (1971). Civil commitment of special categories of offenders. DHEW Pub. No. (ADM)71-15. Washington, DC: U.S. Government Printing Office.

351.   National Institute of Mental Health. (1972). Directory of institutions for mentally disordered offenders. DHEW Pub. No. (HSM)72-9055. Washington, DC: U.S. Government Printing Office.

352.   Norton, K. (1992). Personality disordered individuals: The Henderson Hospital model of treatment. Criminal Behaviour and Mental Health, 2, 180-191.

353.   Pelissier, B.M. (1988). Mental health research in the Federal Bureau of Prisons: Current trends and future developments. Psychiatric Annals, 18, 702-705.

Discusses the involvement of mental health professionals in research in federal prisons and outlines the general function and importance of mental health research to the field of corrections and to mental health. Some of the topics covered are: organizational support for research, inmate population and mental health problems, the prediction of career criminal patterns, and issues surrounding treatment.

354. Peters, R.H. (1993). Substance abuse services in jails and prisons. Law and Psychology Review, 17, 85-116.
The author discusses the importance of jail-based substance abuse treatment programs in breaking the cycle of substance abuse and crime through comprehensive treatment planning. Factors deemed important to the success of such programs are links to community services, attention to acute health-related consequences of addiction, such as withdrawal symptoms, post-release transition planning, and coordinated systems of screening and referral.

355. Remington, B., & Remington, M. (1987). Behavior modification in probation work: A review. Criminal Justice and Behavior, 14, 156-174.

356. Rice, M.E., Harris, G.T., & Cormier, C.A. (1992). An evaluation of a maximum security therapeutic community for psychopaths and other mentally disordered offenders. Law and Human Behavior, 16, 399-412.
Studied the efficacy of a maximum security therapeutic community program in reducing recidivism among 176 mentally disordered offenders. Compared with "no program matched controls," treatment was associated with lower recidivism (especially violent recidivism) for nonpsychopaths and higher violent recidivism for psychopaths.

357. Robles, I.N. (1975). Meeting the mental health needs of the law offender. In D.J. Curren, et al., (Eds.), Proceedings of Puerto Rican conferences on human services. Washington, DC: National Coalition of Spanish-Speaking Mental Health Organizations.

358. Rold, W.J. (1992). Consideration of mental health factors in inmate discipline. Journal of Prison and Jail Health, 11, 41-49.

359. Ross, R.R., & Carlesso, M.L. (1991). The efficacy of drug rehabilitation programs for offenders. Delincuencia, 3, 35-94.
Reviews the literature on the efficacy of drug rehabilitation programs for offenders and discusses institutional programs, outcome research, mandatory urinalysis, court mandated treatment, matching clients and rehabilitation programs, methadone maintenance, criminal recidivism, and numerous treatment modalities.

360. Roth, L.H., & Ervin, F. (1971). Psychiatric care of federal prisoners. American Journal of Psychiatry, 128, 424-430.

361. Scannell, T.D. (1989). Community care and the difficult and offender patient. British Journal of Psychiatry, 154, 615-619.

362.   Schulte, J.L. (1985). Treatment of the mentally disordered offender. American Journal of Forensic Psychiatry, 6, 29-36.
       Discusses treatment for mentally ill offenders and presents guidelines for realistic assessment of time needed for rehabilitation, recruitment of qualified professionals, research and training, and studies of the prevalence of mental disorder in the prison populations.

363.   Schwitzgebel, R.K. (1979). Legal aspects of the enforced treatment of offenders. National Institute of Mental Health. DHEW Pub. No. (ADM)79-831. Washington, DC: U.S. Government Printing Office.

364.   Severson, M.M. (1992). Redefining the boundaries of mental health services: A holistic approach to inmate mental health. Federal Probation, 56, 57-63.

365.   Shah, S. (1990). The mentally disordered offenders: Some issues of policy and planning. In E.H. Cox-Feith & B.N. De Smit (Eds.), Innovations in mental health legislation and government policy: A European perspective. The Hague: The Netherlands Ministry of Justice.

366.   Shively, D., & Petrich, J. (1985). Correctional mental health. Psychiatric Clinics of North America, 8, 537-550.
       Describes a program for management of inmates with acute and chronic psychiatric illnesses in a maximum security facility. Program components include stabilization, diagnostic evaluation, and short-term treatment planning, assessment of risk of potential assaultiveness and self-destructiveness. Treatment goals are to teach the skills and knowledge theorized to help inmates cope with their psychiatric and behavioral problems as well as skills necessary for community survival and reintegration. Issues regarding the further development of similar programs are addressed including, punishment, due process, and the role of the psychiatrist.

367.   Sidley, N.T. (1974). The evaluation of prison treatment and preventive detention programs: Some problems faced by the Patuxent institution. Bulletin of the American Academy of Psychiatry and Law, 2, 73-95.

368.   Smith, J.A., Faubert, M. (1990). Programming and process in prisoner rehabilitation: A prison mental health center. Journal of Offender Counseling, Services and Rehabilitation, 15, 131-153.
       Describes a prison-based program that prepares mentally ill prison inmates for reentry into society. The process of client change is illustrated and the difficulties faced by the treatment team and the patients in correctional institutions are reviewed.

369.   Smith, L.D. (1989). Medication refusal and the rehospitalized mentally ill inmate. Hospital and Community Psychiatry, 40, 491-496.

370.   Steadman, H.J. (1977). A new look at recidivism among Patuxent inmates. Bulletin of the American Academy of Psychiatry and the Law, 5, 200-209.

371.   Steadman, H.J. (1985). Insanity defense research and treatment of insanity acquittees. Behavioral Sciences and the Law, 3, 37-48.

372.   Steadman, H.J., Holohan, E.J., Jr., & Dvoskin, J. (1991). Estimating mental health needs and service utilization among prison inmates. Bulletin of the American Academy of Psychiatry and Law, 19, 297-307
       Studied 3,684 inmates in the New York State prison system to determine the prevalence of psychiatric and functional disability and service utilization. It was estimated that 5% percent had a severe psychiatric disability, and 10% had significant psychiatric disability. The greater the disability, the more likely the inmate had received mental health services within the previous 30 days. However, just under half of the severely disabled group had no service contact in the prior 12 months. Differences in service utilization also differed by race and sex.

373.   Stein, L.I., & Diamond, R.J. (1985). The chronic mentally ill and the criminal justice system: When to call the police. Hospital and Community Psychiatry, 36, 271-274

374.   Steinfeld, G.J., & Mabil, J. (1974). Perceived curative factors in group therapy by residents of a therapeutic community. Criminal Justice and Behavior, 1, 278-288.

375.   Steinfeld, G.J., Rautio, E.A., Rice, A.H., & Egan, M.J. (1974). Group covert sensitization with narcotic addicts: Further comments. International Journal of the Addictions, 9, 447-464.

376.   Swanson, J.W., Morrissey, J.P., Goldstrom, I., Rudolph, L., & Manderscheid, R.W. (1993). Funding, expenditures, and staffing of mental health services in state adult correctional facilities: United States, 1988. Mental Health Statistical Note, Jul(208), 1-20.

377.   Tanay, E. (1973). Psychiatric morbidity and treatment of prison inmates. Journal of Forensic Sciences, 18, 53-59.

378.   Task Force on Psychiatric Services in Jails & Prisons. (1989). Position statement on psychiatric services in jails and prisons. American Journal of Psychiatry, 146, 1244. Outlines 6 fundamental principles for providing adequate mental health care and treatment to mentally ill persons in jails and prisons.

379.   Toch, H. (1982). The disturbed disruptive inmate: Where does the bus stop? Journal of Psychiatry and Law, 10, 327-349.

380.   Toch, H., Adams, K., & Grant, J.D. (1989). Coping: Maladaptation in prison. New Brunswick, NJ: Transaction.

381.   U.S. Government Accounting Office (1991). Mentally ill inmates: Better data would help determine protection and advocacy needs. GAO Pub. No. GGD-91-35. Washington, DC: Author.

382.   Von Holden, M.H. (1983). Providing quality mental health inpatient services to forensic clients: A five year experience. Psychiatric Quarterly, 55, 35-41.

The results of an evaluation of an on-site inpatient mental health program suggest that the program successfully integrated treatment and security concerns and that correctional staff accepted responsibility for providing supportive care to chronically mentally ill prisoners and actively supported efforts to reach this population.

383.   Von Holden, M.H. (1987). The Rochester Regional Forensic Unit: An innovative management approach to improving the continuum of care for forensic patients. Journal of Mental Health Administration, 14, 35-39.

384.   Washington, P.A. (1989). Mature mentally ill offenders in California jails. Special Issue: Older offenders: Current trends. Journal of Offender Counseling, Services and Rehabilitation, 13, 161-173.
Describes the mental health needs of 14 county jail prisoners over the age of 50. The men were mostly single, with a mean educational level of 10 years. Twenty-five percent had been arrested for drunk driving, and almost 90% were recidivists. Three quarters had DSM-III personality disorders, while 15% were schizophrenic and 15% were dysthymics. Over sixty percent were dependent on alcohol. Implications of findings for provision of mental health services is discussed.

385.   Webster, C.D., et al. (1985). Psychoeducational assessment programmes for forensic psychiatric patients. Canadian Psychology, 26, 50-53.

386.   Weller, M.P., & Weller, B.G. (1988). Crime and mental illness. Medicine, Science, and the Law, 28, 38-45.

387.   Wexler, D.B. (1973). Token and taboo: Behavior modification, token economics, and the law. California Law Review, 61, 81-109.

388.   Wideranders, M.R. (1992). Recidivism of disordered offenders who were conditionally vs. unconditionally released. Behavioral Sciences and the Law, 10, 141-148.
Compared arrests and state psychiatric hospitalizations of samples of conditionally and unconditionally released forensic patients. Conditionally released patients had a significantly lower post-release arrest rate than did the unconditionally released patients. However, when arrests and hospitalizations were combined to measure recidivism, the distribution of days-before-recidivism was comparable for the 2 groups. Further, revocation of conditional release within the first 240 days of community re-entry reduced the arrest rate for the conditional release group.

389.   Wiertsema, H.L., & Derks, F. (1994). Organizational aspects of residential forensic treatment. Therapeutic Communities International Journal for Therapeutic and Supportive Organizations, 15, 247-254.

390.   Williams, M. (1984). Reflections on data collected in the prison system. Issues in Criminological and Legal Psychology, 6, 28-35.

391.   Williams, T., Alves, E., & Shapland, J. (1984). The links in the system. Issues in Criminological and Legal Psychology, 6, 7-11.

392. Young, J.T., Bloom, J.D., Faulkner, L.R., Rogers, J.L., et al. (1987). Treatment refusal among forensic inpatients. <u>Bulletin of the American Academy of Psychiatry and the Law,</u> <u>15</u>, 5-13

5

Community-Based Programs and Services

393. Adams, K. (1983). Former mental patients in a prison and parole system: A study of socially disruptive behavior. Criminal Justice and Behavior, 10, 358-384.
Compared 287 former mental patients in a sample of federal prison inmates to 3,176 other inmates on measures of disciplinary infractions during incarceration and post-release adjustment. Mental patients had a higher rate of disciplinary infractions during incarceration than did other inmates and were more likely to fail in adjusting to community living after their release from prison. When possible confounds were accounted for, only the differences in prison infraction rates remained significant.

394. Arcaya, J. (1974). Probation and parole records considered as therapeutic tools. Criminal Justice and Behavior, 1, 150-161.

395. Ashley, M.C. (1922). Outcome of 1000 cases paroled from the Middletown State Homeopathic Hospital. State Hospital Quarterly, 8, 64-70.

396. Beran, N.J, & Hotz, A.M. (1984). A study of the civil commitment of mentally disordered criminals. Journal of Psychiatry and Law, 12, 257-262.
This study based on research conducted in 4 hospitals in Ohio covering the 2 years before and after the implementation of legislation authorizing the civil commitment of mentally disordered offenders from 1976 to 1980 (2 years before and 2 years after the legislation) showed no consistent evidence to support the notion that civil mental hospitals would be inundated with criminals. At only 2 hospitals was there any evidence that the legislation affected admissions. Further, it was found that mentally disordered offenders were already being admitted to civil hospitals in sizable numbers before the legislation was enacted.

397.   Bloom, J.D., & William, M.H. (1994). Management and treatment of insanity acquitees: A model for the 1990's. Washington, DC: American Psychiatric Press.

398.   Bloom, J.D., Rogers, J.L., & Manson, S.M. (1982). After Oregon's insanity defense: A comparison of conditional release and hospitalization. International Journal of Law and Psychiatry, 5, 391-402.

399.   Bloom, J.D., Rogers, J.L., Manson, S.M., et al. (1986). Lifetime police contacts of discharged Psychiatric Security Review Board clients. International Journal of Law and Psychiatry, 8, 189-202.

400.   Bloom, J.D., Williams, M.H., & Bigelow, D.A. (1991). Monitored conditional release of persons found not guilty by reason of insanity. American Journal of Psychiatry, 148, 444-448.
        This review highlights the community treatment programs for insanity defense acquitees based on treatment models for the chronically mentally ill. These community treatment programs appear cost-effective when compared with hospital-based programs.

401.   Bloom, J.D., Williams, M.H., Rogers, J.L., & Barbur, P. (1986). Evaluation and treatment of insanity acquittees in the community. Bulletin of the American Academy of Psychiatry and the Law, 14, 231-244.
        Describes an Oregon program for outpatient treatment of insanity acquittees.

402.   Bonovitz, J.C., & Bonovitz, J.S. (1981). Diversion of the mentally ill into the criminal justice system: the police intervention perspective. American Journal of Psychiatry, 138, 973-976.

403.   Bonovitz, J.C., & Guy, E.R. (1979). Impact of restrictive civil commitment procedures on a prison psychiatric service. American Journal of Psychiatry, 136, 1045-1048.
        A study of the effects of restrictive civil commitment procedures found that after implementation, mentally ill persons who might have previously been committed to psychiatric hospitalization, were more often arrested and incarcerated in order to remove them from the community.

404.   Borgman, R.D. (1975). Diversion of law violators to mental health facilities. Social Casework, 3, 418-426.

405.   Buchan, T. (1976). Some problems in the hospital management of criminal mental patients. South African Medical Journal, 50, 1252-1256.

406.   Buckley, R., & Bigelow, D.A. (1992). The Multi-Service Network: Reaching the unserved multi-problem individual. Community Mental Health Journal, 28, 43-50.
        Collaborations between the justice system and other human service agencies are rare. This study reports on a collaborative effort involving mental health, alcohol and drug treatment, corrections. and social and housing agencies that attempts to provide services to multi-problem individuals, those persons who have contact with multiple agencies and who have multiple problems including mental illness,

substance abuse, housing, and multiple police/law enforcement interactions. Two case studies are presented and some evidence of cost effectiveness from two evaluation studies is discussed.

407.   Carney, F.L. (1977). Outpatient treatment of the aggressive offender. American Journal of Psychotherapy, 31, 265-274.
Comparisons of inpatient and outpatient group treatment techniques for aggressive offenders do not significantly differ, focusing on awareness of feelings in order to facilitate behavioral control. Issues of personal control, trust, countertransference, and fear of patients by therapists, each of which impacts therapeutic dynamics, are also discussed.

408.   Cavanaugh, J.L., & Wasyliw, O.E. (1985). Treating the not guilty by reason of insanity outpatient: A two year study. Bulletin of the American Academy of Psychiatry and the Law, 13, 407-415.
Studied 44 NGRI acquittees receiving court-ordered outpatient treatment and found improvements in symptomatology, as measured by the SCL-90, the Global Assessment Scale, and the Schedule for Affective Disorders and Schizophrenia--Change Form, over two years. No arrests for violent or other crimes against persons occurred during the period of the study and only one case of recidivism and one conviction occurred.

409.   Cervantes, N.N., Kaulukukui, M., Poulson, J., & Kauffmen, H. (1987). Diverting the mentally ill from a county jail. American Journal of Public Health, 77, 367-368.

410.   Churgin, M. (1983). The transfer of inmates to mental health facilities. In, J. Monahan, & N. Steadman (Eds.), Mentally disordered offenders. New York: Plenum.

411.   Clarke, J.W. (1990). On being mad or merely angry: John W. Hinckley, Jr., and other dangerous people. Princeton, NJ: Princeton University Press.

412.   Cooke, D.J. (1991). Treatment as an alternative to prosecution: Offenders diverted for treatment. British Journal of Psychiatry, 158, 785-791.
Studied 150 offenders diverted from state prosecution in Scotland into psychological treatment prior to prosecution and found that selection of cases for diversion was generally appropriate and that cases were generally characterized by serious psychological problems but had failed to get appropriate services through the normal referral channels.

413.   Dank, N.R., & Kulishoff, M. (1983). An alternative to the incarceration of the mentally ill. Journal of Prison and Jail Health, 3, 95-100.
Arguing that no effective psychiatric intervention can occur in a prison or jail setting, the author describes a pre- and post-arrest psychiatric crisis intervention center as an alternative to incarceration of the mentally ill.

414.   Davis, S. (1994). Factors associated with diversion of mentally disordered offenders. Bulletin of the American Academy of Law and Psychiatry, 22, 389-397.

This study examined pre-trial diversion of mentally disordered offenders at the level of prosecutorial discretion. Diversion was most often associated with: (1) severity of offense, with offenders with lesser offenses more likely to be diverted from the justice system, (2) court characteristics, with non-urban courts more likely to divert mentally ill offenders, and (3) characteristics of the examining psychiatrist. The authors conclude that the level of discretion allotted to both court personnel (e.g., judges and prosecutors) and examining psychiatrists complicate the process of evaluating the efficacy of diversion programs and the reliability of diversion decisions.

415.   de St.Croix, S., Dry, R., & Webster, C.D. (1988). Patients on Warrants of the Lieutenant Governor in Alberta: A statistical summary with comments on treatment and release procedures. Canadian Journal of Psychiatry, 33, 14-20.

416.   Demone, H.W., & Sibelman, M. (1990). "Privatizing" the treatment of criminal offenders. Journal of Offender Counseling, Services, and Rehabilitation, 15, 7-26.

417.   Dix, G. (1983). Special disposition alternatives for abnormal offenders. In J. Monahan, & H. Steadman (Eds.), Mentally disordered offenders. New York: Plenum.

418.   Feder, L. (1991). A comparison of the community adjustment of mentally ill offenders with those from the general prison population: An 18 month followup. Law and Human Behavior, 15, 477-493.
Studied the post-imprisonment adjustment of mentally ill offenders and those in the general prison population over an 18 month period and found no differences in rearrest rates between the 2 groups or for types of offenses committed after release. As was the case with non-disturbed cases, rearrest among mentally ill offenders was associated with age and prior criminal record.

419.   Feder, L. (1991). A profile of mentally ill offenders and their adjustment in the community. Journal of Psychiatry and the Law, 19, 79-98.
Studied 147 mentally ill offenders released into the community for an 18 month period and found that most had at least one prior criminal justice or psychiatric contact, and had displayed a marginal existence prior to incarceration. Problems in community living and contacts with criminal justice or mental health agencies continued after release with 48% requiring at least one psychiatric commitment and 64% being rearrested. Recidivism was most associated with age and prior criminal record.

420.   Goldmeier, J., Sauer, R.H., & White, E.V. (1977). A halfway house for mentally ill offenders. American Journal of Psychiatry, 134, 45-49.
Discusses guiding principles for care and resocialization of high-risk recovering mentally ill offenders in a halfway house program. A 3-year evaluation showed lower than average recidivism rates, relatively low operating costs, and improved prediction of dangerousness.

421.   Goldmeier, J., White, E.V., Ulrich, C., & Klein, G.A. (1980). Community intervention with the mentally ill offender: A residential program. Bulletin of the American Academy of Law, 8, 72-82.

422.   Grounds, A. (1991). The transfer of sentenced prisoners to hospital 1960-1983: A study in one special hospital. British Journal of Criminology, 31, 54-71.

423.   Haddock, B.D. (1990). Substance abuse counseling in community corrections: A primer. Journal of Addictions and Offender Counseling, 11, 2-12.
Discusses substance abuse treatment modalities in community corrections. The most successful methods include social skills training, stress management, behavioral self-control training, and family therapy. Comprehensive outpatient services, including after-care services, hold promise for effective service delivery at an affordable price.

424.   Halleck, S.L. (1974). Rehabilitation of criminal offenders: A reassessment of the concept. Psychiatric Annals, 4, 61-85.
In light of the criticisms of the effectiveness of rehabilitation programs for criminal offenders, the author discusses 4 promising strategies for facilitating behavior change (manipulation of environmental contingencies, altering stressful environments, biological interventions, and provision of information). The author concludes that prisons teach nonproductive behaviors with little application for life outside of prison and advocates the use of family therapy in conjunction with structured post-release learning in group homes and halfway houses as an adjunct to rehabilitative interventions conducted in prisons.

425.   Hambridge, J.A. (1990). Use of an outpatient psychology service: The non-attenders. International Journal of Offender Therapy and Comparative Criminology, 34, 165-169.
In a study of first-time referrals to a regional forensic psychology service over a three year period, 25.6% of 270 new referrals did not attend any appointments or failed to complete the assessment process. Factors which differentiated non-attenders from attenders were being male, less than 30 years of age, and being referred for aggressive behavior.

426.   Hamm, M.B. (1988). Current perspectives on the prisoner self-help movement. Federal Probation, 52, 49-56.
Describes 4 types of prisoner self-help groups: (1) groups that deal with social stigma associated with criminal behavior, (2) those using a religious approach to rehabilitation which emphasize alcohol and drug abuse as causes of criminal behavior, (3) ethnic oriented groups, and (4) human potential groups. The author argues that prisoners should choose that group which best suits individual needs and is non-threatening to prison administrators, concluding that groups which serve the stigmatized or addicted are most likely to be perceived as non-threatening by prison administrators.

427.   Harmon, R.B. (1987). Mental health and corrections: Towards a working partnership. Journal of Forensic Sciences, 32, 233-241.

428.   Hochstedler, E. (1986). Criminal prosecution of the mentally disordered. Law and Society Review, 20, 279-292.
       Studied 379 criminal cases involving mentally disordered defendants and found that 85% were arrested for conduct normally considered a misdemeanor and that treatment for mental disorder was mandated by the court as often as was punishment.

429.   Hoffman, B.F. (1990). The criminalization of the mentally ill. Canadian Journal of Psychiatry, 35, 166-169.
       The author discusses 3 cases where psychiatric patients with psychotic illnesses were ordered to attend psychiatric treatment during the period preceding their trial. Although all three pleaded guilty to their charges, none was imprisoned. Charges were dismissed in one case, while the other 2 cases resulted in probation with continued psychiatric treatment.

430.   Howe, B.J., Howe, S.R., Ellison, T.K., & Rackley, M. (1976). The therapist and parole/probation officer as co-therapists with involuntary patients. Family Therapy, 3, 35-45.

431.   Inciardi, J.A., Martin, S.S., & Scarpitti, F.R. (1994). Appropriateness of assertive case management for drug-involved prison releases. Journal of Case Management, 3, 145-149.
       Studied the use of assertive case management with drug-involved parolees and found some modest effects on reducing relapse to drug use. It appears that assertive case management is of limited value for clients who are both unable to access services and quite assertive in their unwillingness to make use of these services.

432.   Ingram, G.L., & Swartzfager, A.K. (1973). Involving families and the community in rehabilitating offenders. Hospital and Community Psychiatry, 24, 616-618.

433.   Joseph, P.L., & Potter, M. (1993). Diversion from custody: I. Psychiatric assessment at the magistrates' court. British Journal of Psychiatry, 162, 325-330.

434.   Joseph, P.L., & Potter, M. (1993). Diversion from custody: II. Effect on hospital and prison resources. British Journal of Psychiatry, 162, 330-334.

435.   Justice, R.S. (1976). A regional and national network: Rehabilitation and the retarded offender. In P.L. Browning (Ed.), Rehabilitation and the retarded offender. Springfield, IL: Thomas.

436.   Komer, B., & Galbraith, D. (1992). Recidivism among individuals detained under a warrant of the Lieutenant-Governor living in the community. Canadian Journal of Psychiatry, 37, 694-698.

437.   Kunjukrishnan, R., & Bradford, J.M. (1985). Interface between the criminal justice system and the mental health system in Canada. Psychiatric Journal of the University of Ottawa, 10, 24-33.

438.   Laben, J.K., & Spencer, L.D. (1976). Decentralization of forensic services. Community Mental Health Journal, 12, 405-414.
Argues that decentralization of mental health services to mentally ill offenders in the community is essential to apply community mental health concepts. Factors supporting this argument include little evidence of the dangerousness of such persons, high costs of the isolated central facilities, and positive results where decentralization of services has been maintained.

439.   Lamb, H.R., & Goertzel, V. (1974). Ellsworth House: A community alternative to jail. American Journal of Psychiatry, 131, 64-68.

440.   Lamb, H.R., Weinberger, L.E., & Gross, B.H. (1988). Court-mandated outpatient treatment for insanity acquittees: Clinical philosophy and implementation. Hospital and Community Psychiatry, 39, 1080-1084.
Describes court-mandated outpatient treatment for insanity aquittees, in which insanity aquittees may be released into the community after serving part of their commitment in a forensic hospital. Elements of successful programs include emphasis on structure and supervision, the importance of neuroleptic drugs, a reality-based approach to therapy, a focus on problems of everyday living, and incorporation of principles of case management.

441.   Liss, R., & Frances, A. (1975). Court-mandated treatment: Dilemmas for hospital psychiatry. American Journal of Psychiatry, 132, 924-927.
Argues for creation of new kinds of institutions combining treatment modalities from hospital and correctional systems, citing the special treatment and management problems presented by mentally ill offenders, and the inadequacy of court-mandated treatment to patient, community, and mental hospital needs as the primary reasons for their suggestions.

442.   Mabli, J. (1985). Pre-release stress in prison inmates. Journal of Offender Counseling Services and Rehabilitation, 9, 43-56.
Examined pre-release stress in 37 female and 61 male inmates in a minimum security, coeducational federal corrections institution. Although anecdotal evidence supports the belief that inmates soon to be released are susceptible to stress-related behavior disorders, little research has been conducted to substantiate this belief. Results of this study suggest that pre-release stress existed in some inmates, and that females may be more susceptible to such stress than males.

443.   Maletzky, B.M. (1991). The use of medroxyprogesterone acetate to assist in the treatment of sexual offenders. Annals of Sex Research, 4, 117-129.
A study of 100 sex offenders in an outpatient treatment program who were receiving medroxyprogesterone acetat (MPA) found that MPA was a safe and effective short-term supplement to an ongoing treatment program using, cognitive-behavioral, group, and family therapy. Findings indicated that MPA did not indicate interfere with concurrent treatment approaches and had no irreversible side effects.

444.   Matthews, A. (1970). Observations on police policy and procedures for emergency detention of the mentally ill. Journal of Criminal Law, Criminology, and Police Science, 61, 283-295.

445.   Maynard, P.E., Hultquist, A. (1988). The Circumplex Model with adjudicated youths' families. Journal of Psychotherapy and the Family, 4, 249-266.

446.   McDonagh, E.W., Rudolph, C.J., & Cheraskin, E. (1983). The "health" of the parolee: Clinical considerations. International Journal of Biosocial Research, 5, 34-39.
       Studied the health of 27 male and 8 female parolees and found that, in general, the study sample was more unhealthy, both physically and mentally, than the average New York hospital patient.

447.   McGreevy, M.A., Steadman, H.J., Dvoskin, J.A., & Dollard, N. (1991). New York State's system of managing insanity acquittees in the community. Hospital and Community Psychiatry, 42, 512-517.

448.   Mendelson, E.F. (1993). Underlying patterns of practice in a regional forensic psychiatric service. Medicince, Science and the Law, 33, 55-62.
       A study of the variations in referral rates of diagnoses and the psychiatric histories of 306 mentally ill offenders referred to a forensic psychiatric practice found that the service was being used largely for second opinions on the mentally ill, but for cases of neurotic disorder or exacerbations of personality disorder it was more similar to a general psychiatric service.

449.   Menzies, R.J., & Webster, C.D. (1988). Fixing forensic patients: Psychiatric recommendations for treatment in pretrial settings. Behavioral Sciences and the Law, 6, 453-478.
       A study of 592 defendants referred to a clinical assessment agency found that 134 were considered in appropriate for outpatient care. Factors related to the decision to place in inpatient versus outpatient care were having a history of mental health rather than criminal justice contacts, to be arrested for nonviolent offenses, to exhibit psychotic behavior, to be found unfit for bail, incompetent to stand trial, or in need of further assessment and dangerous to self, and to experience higher rates of hospitalization.

450.   Miller, M.O., & Sales, B.D. (1986). Law and mental health professionals: Arizona. Washington, DC: American Psychological Association Press.

451.   Miller, R.D. (1992). Economic factors leading to diversion of the mentally disordered from the civil to the criminal commitment systems. International Journal of Law and Psychiatry, 15 1-12.

452.   Monahan, J. (1976). Introduction. In J. Monahan (Ed.), Community mental health and the criminal justice system. New York: Pergamon.

453.   Monahan, J. (Ed.) (1976). Community mental health and the criminal justice system. New York: Pergamon.

454.   Moser, A.L., & Levinson, T. (1990). The Program for Impaired Driving Offenders. Journal of Substance Abuse Treatment, 7, 195-197.

455. Pavelka, F.L. (1986). Psychosocial characteristics of parolees in forensic social work. Journal of Psychiatry and Law, 14, 217-223.
Parolees administered the MMPI were found to have personality characteristics of long-term pathological behavior recognizable in early adolescence. Recidivism correlated significantly with unemployment, substance use, and antisocial personality characteristics.

456. Pollock, H.M. (1938). Is the paroled patient a menace to the community? Psychiatric Quarterly, 12, 236-244.

457. Prandoni, J.R., et al. (1985). The use of an interagency team approach and mental health referral criteria to improve the effectiveness of pre-parole mental health evaluation. Journal of Offender Counseling, Services and Rehabilitation, 9, 5-18.

458. Pritchard, C., Cotton, A., Godson, D., Cox, M., et al. (1991-1992). Mental illness, drug and alcohol misuse and HIV risk Behaviour in 214 young adult (18-35 year) probation clients: Implications for policy, practice and training. Social Work and Social Sciences Review, 3, 227-242.
Studied 214 probation clients and found relationships between poverty, and illegal drug and alcohol misuse, which, in turn, was linked to HIV risk behavior. Further, a significant association between mental health and HIV risk behavior was found.

459. Reali, M., & Shapland, J. (1986). Breaking down barriers: The work of the Community Mental Health Service of Trieste in the prison and judicial settings. International Journal of Law and Psychiatry, 8, 395-412.

460. Robertson, G., Grounds, A., Dell, S., & James, K. (1994). A follow-up of remanded mentally ill offenders given court hospital orders. Medicine, Science and the Law, 34, 61-66.

461. Rogers, R., & Bagby, R.M. (1992). Diversion of mentally disordered offenders: A legitimate role for clinicians? Behavioral Sciences and the Law, 10, 407-418.

462. Schutte, N.S., Malouff, J.M., Lucore, P., & Shern, D. (1988). Incompetency and insanity: Feasibility of community evaluation and treatment. Community Mental Health Journal, 24, 143-150.
Surveyed 288 community mental health center and state hospital administrators and treatment staff members and found that, given enhanced community evaluation and treatment programs for forensic clients, (1) 41% of the sanity evaluations and 45% of the competency evaluations done at the hospital could be done in local communities, (2) 35-38% of the clients found incompetent could be treated in local communities, and (3) 39-50% of the clients found insane could be released to outpatient treatment 6 mo earlier than is current practice.

463. Scull, A. (1977). Decarceration, community treatment and the deviant: A radical view. Englewood Cliffs, NJ: Prentice-Hall.

464. Smith, A.B., Bassin, A. (1992). Kings County Court probation: A laboratory for offender rehabilitation. Journal of Addictions and Offender Counseling, 13, 11-22.

465.   Steadman, H.J. (1992). Boundary Spanners: A key component for effective interactions of the justice and mental health systems. Law and Human Behavior, 16, 75-87.
This review presents three case studies in which boundary spanners, positions that serve to link two or more social systems, were used in order to facilitate interactions between justice and mental health systems at the local level. Such positions allow the interchange of resources between systems and lead to more appropriate matching between mentally ill persons and mental health services within the justice system context through referral or diversion from the justice system at any of its levels. Problems faced by persons in boundary spanner positions, including burnout when faced with interfacing between systems with conflicting goals and purposes are discussed. The concept of boundary spanners is considered one of the few examples of system level interventions in the interactions of justice and mental health systems.

466.   Steadman, H.J., Barbera-Sharon, S.S., & Dennis, D.L. (1994). A national survey of jail diversion programs for mentally ill detainees. Hospital and Community Psychiatry, 45, 1109-1113.
In a mail survey of 1106 jails (return rate = 61.2%) with housing space for at least 50 inmates, it was estimated that only 52 jails (4.7%) had formal mental health diversion programs. Three quarters of the programs were located in mental health agencies, and two-thirds of program directors rated the programs as at least moderately successful.

467.   Steadman, H.J., Morris, S.M., & Dennis, D.L. (1995). Diversion of mentally ill persons from jails to community-based services: A profile of programs. American Journal of Public Health, 85, 1630-1635.
Studied the types and effectiveness of diversion programs for the mentally ill via three methods; a survey of all U.S. jails with a capacity of 50 or more detainees, a follow-up telephone survey of 115 selected respondents, and site visits at 18 jails. The most effective diversion programs were characterized by integrated services, regular meetings of key agency representatives, boundary spanners, strong leadership, early identification, and strong case management services. The most effective programs are well integrated with other community services such as community mental health centers, substance abuse and housing services.

468.   Stewart, S.D. (1994). Community-based drug treatment in the Federal Bureau of Prisons. Federal Probation, 58, 24-28.

469.   Swett, C. (1984). Use of the Michigan Alcohol Screening Test in a prison hospital. American Journal of Drug and Alcohol Abuse, 10, 563-569.

470.   Szasz, T.S. (1986). Insanity and irresponsibility: Psychiatric diversion in the criminal justice system. In H. Toch (Ed.), Psychology and criminal justice, 2nd ed. Prospect Heights, IL: Waveland Press.

471.   Teplin, L.A., & Pruett, N.S. (1992). Police as streetcorner psychiatrist: managing the mentally ill. International Journal of Law and Psychiatry, 15, 139-156.

472.   Toch, H., & Adams, K. (1987). The prison as dumping ground: Mainlining disturbed offenders. Journal of Psychiatry and Law, 15, 539-553.
Judges often consider prison for disturbed prisoners because they see prison as either a "secure hospital" or when the ability of the offender to cope in the community is questioned or the offender is disruptive or resistant to services. The authors suggest that these issues be addressed through diversion programs involving interagency arrangements, making imprisonment less likely.

473.   Trasler, G. (1972). Specialized hostels for homeless offenders 1. Types, numbers, and needs of the homeless offender. International Journal of Offender Therapy, 16, 224-249.

474.   Van Deusen, J., Yarbrough, J., & Cornelsen, D. (1985). Short-term system-therapy with adult probation clients and their families. Federal Probation, 49, 21-26.
Discusses the strategic use of individual and systems level therapy with probation and parole clients through an in-depth description of three cases and an evaluation of 46 cases showing improvements in drug use, employment status, and psychosocial functioning among probationers and parolees.

475.   Warren, M.Q. (1972). Correctional treatment in community settings. National Institute of Mental Health. DHEW Pub. No. (ADM)72-9129. Washington, DC: U.S. Government Printing Office.

476.   Wasyliw, O.E., Cavanaugh, J.L., & Grossman, L.S. (1988). Clinical considerations in the community treatment of mentally disordered offenders. International Journal of Law and Psychiatry, 11, 371-380.

477.   Webster, C.D., & Menzies, R.J. (1993). Supervision in the deinstitutionalized community. In S. Hodgins (Ed.), Mental disorder and crime. Newbury Park, CA: Sage.

478.   Wool, R. (1991). The present and future handling of the mentally disturbed offender (Part 1). Journal of the Royal Society of Health, 111, 203-205.

479.   Zverina, J. (1990). Results of compulsory treatment of 103 sexual delinquents. Cesko Slovenska Psychiatrie, 86, 249-259.
Conducted a three year study of 103 male sexual offenders in a compulsory outpatient treatment program that administered psychotherapy, sociotherapy, and psychopharmacotherapy.

6

Local Justice System
Issues

480. Abram, K.M. (1990). The problem of co-occurring disorders among jail detainees: Antisocial disorder, alcoholism, drug abuse, and depression. <u>Law and Human Behavior, 14</u>, 333-345.
This research investigated the extent of comorbidity among a sample of 688 male jail detainees in Chicago. Detainees were more likely to be diagnosed with at least 2 disorders than to be diagnosed with only a single disorder. Of the more than 40% who had a dual diagnosis, the most common pattern involved antisocial disorder as the primary diagnosis. Considering the poor prognosis of antisocial personality disorder, the author concludes that jail-based mental health treatment programs need to consider the possibility of differential treatment of antisocial inmates, including the possibility of long-term involuntary treatment, and use of "recovered" antisocial inmates on treatment teams in order to prevent manipulation of treatment staff by antisocial offenders.

481. Abram, K.M., & Teplin, L.A. (1991). Co-occurring disorders among mentally ill jail detainees: Implications for public policy. <u>American Psychologist, 46</u>, 1036-1045.
Studied 728 randomly selected male jail detainees and found evidence of co-occurring disorders (substance abuse, anti-social personality) among most severely mentally ill jail detainees. Suggestions for changes in public policy regarding health care delivery in correctional settings are discussed.

482. Abramson, M.F. (1972). The criminalization of mentally disordered behavior: A possible side-effect of a new mental health law. <u>Hospital and Community Psychiatry, 23</u>, 101-105.
In the original statement of the criminalization hypothesis, the author uses his personal experiences as a consulting psychiatrist in a local criminal justice system and the case of the Community Mental Health Services Law in California to

demonstrate the increased likelihood of diversion of mentally ill persons into the criminal justice system as a result of deinsitutionalization.

483.   Adams, J.J., Meloy, J.R., & Moritz, M.S. (1990). Neuropsychological deficits and violent behavior in incarcerated schizophrenics. Journal of Nervous and Mental Disease, 178, 253-256.
Based on scores on the Luria-Nebraska Battery, 12 of 37 schizophrenics in a county jail psychiatric unit were classified as neuropsychologically impaired. Compared to unimpaired schizophrenics, the impaired group had longer adult histories of violence and arrests for violent offenses, but were not rated by clinicians as more violent while they were hospitalized.

484.   American Medical Association. (1973). Medical care in U.S. jails. Chicago, IL: AMA.

485.   Arboleda-Florez, J., & Holley, H.L. (1988). Criminalization of the mentally ill: II. Initial detention. Canadian Journal of Psychiatry, 33, 87-95.
A longitudinal study of the movement of mental patients through the criminal justice system in Canada showed that police-identified mentally disordered offenders did not differ from police-identified "normals" on demographic, clinical or legal outcome variables.

486.   Arboleda-Florez, J.E., & Holley, H.L. (1987). General hospital forensic units: A new approach to forensic psychiatry. International Journal of Offender Therapy and Comparative Criminology, 31, 11-19.

487.   Arthur Bolton Associates. (1976). A study of the need for and availability of mental health services for mentally disordered jail inmates and juveniles in detention facilities. Sacramento, CA: California State Legislature.

488.   Ashford, J.B. (1989). Offense comparisons between mentally disordered and non-mentally disordered inmates. Canadian Journal of Criminology, 31, 35-48.
A case control study of mentally disordered and nonmentally disordered inmates in an urban jail found that when compared on current offense, history of violence, and criminal history, mentally disordered offenders were more likely to have a history of violence than were nonmentally disordered offenders. No differences in criminal history were found.

489.   Belcher, J.R. (1988). Are jails replacing the mental health system for the homeless mentally ill? Community Mental Health Journal, 24, 185-195.
Explores the process of how homeless mentally ill persons become involved with the criminal justice system. The unique demands of homelessness and chronic mental illness were specifically examined in this naturalistically based study. The author concludes that a combination of severe mental illness, a tendency to decompensate in a non-structured environment, and an inability or unwillingness to follow through with aftercare contributed to involvement with the criminal justice system. Changes in the mental health system that would prevent the criminalization of the homeless mentally ill are suggested.

490.   Bloom, J.D., Shore, J.H., & Arvidson, B. (1981). Local variations in arrests of psychiatric patients. Bulletin of the American Academy of Psychiatry and the Law, 9, 203-209.

491.   Bonovitz, J.C., & Bonovitz, J.S. (1981). Diversion of the mentally ill into the criminal justice system: the police intervention perspective. American Journal of Psychiatry, 138, 973-976.

492.   Bonovitz, J.C., & Guy, E.R. (1979). Impact of restrictive civil commitment procedures on a prison psychiatric service. American Journal of Psychiatry, 136, 1045-1048.
        A study of the effects of restrictive civil commitment procedures found that after implementation, mentally ill persons who might have previously been committed to psychiatric hospitalization, were more often arrested and incarcerated in order to remove them from the community.

493.   Bonta, J. (1983) Psychological services in jails. Canadian Psychology, 24, 135-139.

494.   Brodsky, S. (1982). Intervention models for mental health services in jails. In, C.S. Dunn & H.J. Steadman (Eds.), Mental health services in local jails. Washington, DC: National Institute of Mental Health.

495.   Carr, K., Hinkle, B., & Ingram, B. (1991). Establishing mental health and substance abuse services in jails. Journal of Prison and Jail Health, 10, 77-89.
        A mental health and substance abuse program in a Virginia county jail is described. Program components include evaluation of all inmates with previous psychiatric hospitalization, crisis intervention, individual and group psychotherapy, outside consultation and staff training. No empirical evidence of program efficacy is presented.

496.   Cimino, A.T. (1987). Management strategies for improving the delivery of mental health services in secure settings. Journal of Mental Health Administration, 14, 7-13.

497.   Coffler, D.B., & Hadley, R.G. (1973). The residential rehabilitation center as an alternative to jail for chronic drunkenness offenders. Quarterly Journal of Studies on Alcohol, 34, 543-548.

498.   Craig, T.J., McCoy, E.C., & Stober, W.C. (1988). Mental health programs in three county jails. Journal of Prison and Jail Health, 7, 15-26.
        Discusses seven years in the operation of mental health programs in three county jails. Jail staff, community mental and state hospital staff form teams the offer crisis services, support services (linkages with families, lawyers, probation departments, etc.), and coordination with medical services. Some of the benefits of the program are immediate contact with mentally ill upon arrival in jail, quick intervention with acute psychotic reactions, fewer transfers to other facilities, and facilitation of orderly jail management.

499.   Davis, S. (1992). Assessing the "criminalization" of the mentally ill in Canada. Canadian Journal of Psychiatry, 37, 532-538.

By comparing U.S. and Canadian studies of rates of mental disorder in jails and prisons, it was found that there were similar prevalence rates. However, data from other sources suggests that mentally ill offenders in Canada are more often diverted from the criminal justice system than are those in America. Taken together, the author argues for a "psychiatrization of the criminal" hypothesis, which states that mental hospitalization is an increasing occurrence for individuals with a criminal history.

500.   Diamond, R.J., Brooner, R.K., Lowe, D., & Savage, C. (1981). The use of minor tranquilizers with jail inmates. Hospital and Community Psychiatry, 32, 40-43.
Discusses issues surrounding the use of anxiety-reducing drugs which, although they may help jail inmates cope with environmental hardships, may also facilitate drug dependency. The use of medication-linked group therapy programs in jails may help overcome the distrust of minor tranquilizers on the part of mental health professionals and others working in jail settings.

501.   Draine, J., & Solomon, P. (1994). Jail recidivism and the intensity of case management services among homeless persons with mental illness. Journal of Psychiatry and the Law, 22, 245-261.
Recidivism in a sample of homeless mentally ill individuals released from jail who were assigned to intensive case management was found to be related to lower life satisfaction, fewer case management services provided in home, more face-to-face time spent with case managers, more time spent with other service providers (e.g., parole officers) over a six month period. The authors argue for spending more time on treatment rather than on monitoring mentally ill clients who are especially vulnerable to the stresses of poverty, addiction, homelessness, and arrest.

502.   Draine, J., Solomon, P., & Meyerson, A. (1994). Predictors of reincarceration among patients who received psychiatric services in jail. Hospital and Community Psychiatry, 45, 163-167.
This study identified several factors related to reincarceration within one year for 231 jail inmates who had received some form of mental health service while in jail. The most salient predictors of reincarceration were being young, a history of substance abuse, and previous incarceration. Further, those most likely to return to jail within the first year after release were those for whom there was less access to treatment resources available in the community.

503.   Dunn, C.S., & Steadman, H.J. (Eds.) (1982). Mental health services in local jails. National Institute of Mental Health. DHHS Pub. No. (ADM)82-1011. Washington, DC: U.S. Government Printing Office.

504.   DuRand, C.J., Butka, G.J., Federman, E.J., Haycox, J.A., & Smith, J. (1995). A quarter century of suicide in a major urban jail: Implications for community psychiatry. American Journal of Psychiatry, 152, 1077-1079.
A study of jail suicides over a twenty-five year period (1967-1992), was conducted at the Wayne County Jail in Michigan, where some of the earliest studies of jail suicide were undertaken. This history may explain the why so few suicides had taken place since the 1970's and why none had occurred in the previous five years. Of the 37 suicides studied, all were accomplished by hanging, including those of

women (N = 2). Suicides were more likely to occur at night in double occupancy cells (i.e., when cellmates were sleeping) and to occur within 31 days of admission. Finally, unlike findings from previous studies, persons charged with homicide manslaughter were 19 times more likely than those with other charges to successfully commit suicide.

505.   Durbin, J.R., Pasewark, R.A., & Albers, D. (1977). Criminality and mental illness: A study of arrest rates in a rural state. American Journal of Psychiatry, 134, 80-83.

506.   Feigenbaum, K.D. (1985). The criminalization of the mentally ill. American Psychologist, 40, 1063.

507.   Fishbein, D.H., & Reuland, M. (1994). Psychological correlates of frequency and type of drug use among jail inmates. Addictive Behaviors, 19, 583-598.
In an study of 76 male arrestees, information about childhood history, drug use and arrest histories, as well as, measures of mood, impulsivity and antisocial behavior were correlated with frequency of use of specific drugs and with drug preferences. Use of cocaine was most related to hostility and property crimes, while committing violent crimes was related to antisocial behavior. Further, antisocial behavior was correlated with an overall measure of frequency of drug use.

508.   Gibbs, J.L. (1987). Symptoms of psychopathology among jail prisoners: The effects of exposure to the jail environment. Criminal Justice and Behavior, 14, 288-310.
Studied the effects of incarceration upon psychological symptoms as measured by the SCL-90. Inmates completed the SCL-90 3 times (i.e., initial 72 hours of detention, after 2 days, and after 5 days). Results suggest that symptoms increased markedly over the first 2 days but stabilized after 5 days.

509.   Guy, E., Platt, J.J., Zwerling, I., & Bullock, S. (1985). Mental health status of prisoners in an urban jail. Criminal Justice and Behavior, 12, 29-53.

510.   Haley, M.W. (1980). Developing a program of mental health services in a rural county jail. Hospital and Community Psychiatry, 31, 631-632.

511.   Hammett, E., Lipper, S., & Mahorney, S.L. (1986). A reanalysis of arrest rates. American Journal of Psychiatry, 143, 675.

512.   Holley, H.L., & Arboleda-Florez, J. (1988). Criminalization of the mentally ill: I. Police perceptions. Canadian Journal of Psychiatry, 33 81-86.
A study of 611 offenders identified as mentally ill by police at arrest concluded that police perceptions concerning the presence of mental illness as opposed to substance abuse influenced the decision to recommend psychiatric examinations during subsequent phases of the justice process.

513.   Jemelka, R. (1990). The mentally ill in local jails: Issues in admission and booking. In H.J. Steadman (Ed.), Effectively addressing the mental health needs of jail detainees (pp. 35-63). Boulder, CO: National Institute of Corrections.

514.   Johnson, A.B. (1990). Out of bedlam: The truth about deinstitutionalization. New York: Basic Books.

515.   Johnson, J. (1983). "Minimum standards for mental health services": Comment. Journal of Prison and Jail Health, 3, 89-94.
        Based on a discussion of the mentally ill in local jails, the author suggests that attention needs to be given to the whole criminal justice system, not just corrections, in order to determine how the proposed mental health standards will actually function.

516.   Kal, E.F. (1977). Mental health in jail. American Journal of Psychiatry, 134, 463.

517.   Lamb, H.R., and Grant, R.W. (1982). The mentally ill in an urban county jail. Archives of General Psychiatry, 39, 17-22.
        Studied 102 inmates randomly selected from those referred for psychiatric evaluation and found that over 90% had prior arrest records and over half were arrested for felonies. Eighty percent exhibited signs of severe psychopathology and 75% met criteria for involuntary hospitalization. The authors suggest a need for more emphasis on ongoing involuntary treatment for this population.

518.   Lamb, H.R., Schock, R., Chen, P., Gross, B. (1984). Psychiatric needs in local jails. American Journal of Psychiatry, 141(6), 774-777.

519.   Landsberg, G. (1992). Developing comprehensive mental health services in local jails and police lockups. In P. Cooper and T.H. Lentner (Eds.), Innovations in community mental health. Sarsota, FL: Professional Resource Press/Professional Resource Exchange.

520.   Linde, P.R. (1993). How to avoid being manipulated by patients: notes from the county jail. Journal of the American Medical Association, 270, 1134-1135.

521.   Lombardo, L.X. (1985). Mental health work in prisons and jails: Inmate adjustment and indigenous correctional personnel. Criminal Justice and Behavior, 12, 17-27.

522.   Magura, S., Rosenblum, A., Lewis, C., & Joseph, H. (1993). The effectiveness of in-jail methadone maintenance. Journal of Drug Issues, 23, 75-99.
        Methadone maintenance programs conducted in local jails are a rarity. However, when participants in an in-jail methadone maintenance program (N = 308) were compared with a control group consisting of participants in a week-long in-jail detoxification program (N = 138) on post-release functioning, it was found that the program clients were significantly more likely than controls to apply for some form of drug treatment after release from jail and were more likely to still be in treatment after six months. Program participation was also linked with less drug use and criminal activity after six months. However, those most successful at follow-up were those who had been receiving methadone treatment at the time of their initial arrest.

523.   May, J.P., Ferguson, M.G., Ferguson, R., & Cronin, K. (1995). Prior nonfatal firearm injuries in detainees of a large urban jail. Journal of Health Care for the Poor and Underserved, 6, 162-176.

Surveyed 582 randomly selected detainees in the Cook County Department of corrections and found that 51% had been hospitalized previously for violence-related injuries, and that 26% had survived prior gunshot wounds. Factors related to previous firearm injury were witnessing a shooting at an early age, tattoos, previous sexually transmitted diseases, easy access to semiautomatic weapon, and prior incarceration.

524.   Meloy, J.R. (1985). Inpatient psychiatric treatment in a county jail. Journal of Psychiatry and Law, 13, 377-396.

525.   Meloy, J.R. (1986). Rapid classification of the functionally psychotic individual in custody. Criminal Justice and Behavior, 13, 185-195.

526.   Meyers, C.J. (1985). Arresting the patient instead of the illness: The jail as psychiatric service of last resort: A commentary on the criminalization of the mentally ill. Journal of Prison and Jail Health, 5, 20-28.
Argues that the legal revolution the led to increased protection of the civil rights of the mentally ill has had a paradoxical effect, in that many of the mentally ill who are no longer socially disruptive enough for involuntary admission into a psychiatric facility, nonetheless still night criteria for admission into jails. The result of this paradox is that local jails are becoming the repositories of the mentally ill.

527.   Michaels, D., Zoloth, S.R., Alcabes, P., & Braslow, C.A. (1992).Homelessness and indicators of mental illness among inmates in New York City's correctional system. Hospital and Community Psychiatry, 43(2), 150-155.
The prevalence of homelessness among detainees in the New York City correctional system was assessed is 3 samples of male inmates. One quarter to one third of each sample reported being homeless at some time in the 2 months prior to their arrest. Further, 20% were found to have been homeless the night before their arrest, and nearly twice as many of those who reported having been homeless in the past 3 years were positive to at least one mental health screening question than those who had not been homeless.

528.   Monahan, J, & McDonough, L. (1980). Delivering community mental health services to a county jail population: A research note. Bulletin of the American Academy of Psychiatry and the Law, 8, 28-32.

529.   Monahan, J., Caldeira, L., & Priedlander, A. (1979). Police and the mentally ill: A comparison of committed and arrested persons. International Journal of Law and Psychiatry, 2, 509-518.

530.   Morgan, C. (1982). Developing mental health services for local jails. Criminal Justice and Behavior, 8, 259-273.

531.   Morgan, C. (1982). Service delivery models: A summary of examples. In C. Dunn & H. Steadman (Eds.), Mental health services in local jails: Report of a special national workshop. Crime and delinquency issues: A monograph series (DHHS Pub. No. ADM 82-1181). Washington, DC: U.S. Government Printing Office.

532.   Morrissey, J.P., Steadman, H.J., & Kilburn, H.C. (1983). Organizational issues in the delivery of jail mental health services. Research in Community Mental Health, 3, 291-317.

533.   Morrissey, J.P., Steadman, H.J., Kilburn, H., & Lindsey, M.L. (1984). The effectiveness of jail mental health programs: An interorganizational assessment. Criminal Justice and Behavior, 11, 235-256.

534.   National Coalition for Jail Reform (1984). Removing the chronically mentally ill from jail. Case studies of collaboration between local criminal justice and mental health systems. Washington, DC: Author.

535.   National Coalition for Jail Reform (1989). Removing the chronically mentally ill from jail. Washington, DC: Author.

536.   National Coalition for Jail Reform (1990). Jail: The new mental institution. Washington, DC: Author.

537.   Nielsen, E.D. (1979). Community mental health services in the community jail. Community Mental Health, 15, 27-32.
       Describes the problems of the jail population and staff and suggests a policy of mental health intervention using the Mental Health Project in the Salt Lake County, Utah, Jail as an example.

538.   Ninzy, N.M. (1984). Mental health in an Ohio jail community. Ohio State Medical Journal, 80, 95-99.

539.   Ogloff, J.R., Tien, G., Roesch, R., & Eaves, D. (1991). A model for the provision of jail mental health services: An integrative, community-based approach. Journal of Mental Health Administration, 18, 209-222.
       Describes a program for providing mental health services to jails and pretrial facilities involving cooperation of several ministries in establishing the program, mental health screening of all inmates, careful tracking of mentally ill offenders with implementation of treatment plans by a nurse coordinator, coordination of community care following release by community social workers.

540.   Ogloff, J.R.P., & Otto, R.K. (1989). Mental health intervention in jails. In P.A. Keller, & S.R. Heyman (Eds.), Innovations in clinical practice: A sourcebook, Vol. 8. Sarasota, FL: Professional Resource Exchange.

541.   Oleski, M.S. (1977). The effect of indefinite pretrial incarceration on the anxiety level of an urban jail population. Journal of Clinical Psychology, 33, 1006-1008.
       A study of the anxiety levels of 60 males incarcerated in an urban jail over an 8 week period found that anxiety levels increased significantly from pre-test to post-test, leading the author to conclude that prolonged pretrial incarceration can increase the level of anxiety to that of psychological morbidity.

542.   Otto, R.K., & Ogloff, J.R.P. (1988). A manual for mental health professionals working with jails. Lincoln, NE: Nebraska Department of Public Institutions.

543.   Palermo, G.B., Smith, M.B., & Liska, F.J. (1991). Jails versus mental hospitals: The Milwaukee approach to a social dilemma. International Journal of Offender Therapy and Comparative Criminology, 35, 205-216.
In a replication of a national study which found a negative relationship between mental health admissions and jail census data, the authors found a positive relationship for Milwaukee county. The authors conclude that a cooperative mental health screening program at booking allows mentally ill offenders in the Milwaukee area to be promptly identified and referred to the Milwaukee County Mental Health Complex for psychiatric care.

544.   Palermo, G.B., Smith, M.B., & Liska, F.J. (1991). Jails versus mental hospitals: A social dilemma. International Journal of Offender Therapy and Comparative Criminology, 35, 97-106.
Analyses national jail census and psychiatric hospitalization data over several decades in order to determine the relationship between deinstitutionalization and criminalization of the mentally ill. Based on a negative correlation between jail census and psychiatric hospitalization data, the authors conclude that the mentally ill have assumed the status of criminal offenders, leading to jail overcrowding and limited psychiatric care.

545.   Peters, R.H. (1992). Referral and screening for substance abuse treatment in jails. Special Issue: Substance abuse services. Journal of Mental Health Administration, 19, 53-75.
The author discusses referral and screening programs for substance abusing jail inmates that have been implemented in several jails across the country. Elements of successful screening and referral services include comprehensive assessment, coordination with community resources, identification of dual diagnosed inmates, and attention to symptoms of withdrawal.

546.   Peters, R.H., & Kearns, W.D. (1992). Drug abuse history and treatment needs of jail inmates. American Journal of Drug and Alcohol Abuse, 18, 355-366.
In a study of 499 county jail inmates referred to substance abuse treatment, it was found that nearly all research participants were either primarily alcohol-dependent or cocaine-dependent. Among the alcohol-dependent inmates, the average length of time of regular alcohol involvement was over eight years, while for cocaine-dependent participants, the average length of regular involvement with cocaine was over four years. Nearly half of the participants reported heavy use of cocaine and alcohol in the 30 days prior to their arrest, while 70% had previous arrest records and had previous treatment for drugs or alcohol. The authors conclude that there is great need for compulsory treatment for substance abusers after their release, as well as, a great need for collaboration between jail treatment programs, the courts, and community-based treatment programs.

547.   Peters, R.H., & Schonfeld, L. (1993). Determinants of recent substance abuse among jail inmates referred for treatment. Journal of Drug Issues, 23, 101-117.
The majority (87%) of inmates in a city jail who were referred for drug treatment (N = 101) cited interpersonal reasons for their recent drug use, including coping with negative and positive emotional states. No differences in reasons for use were found for different types of drugs.

548.   Peters, R.H., Kearns, W.D., Murrin, M.R., & Dolente, A.S. (1992). Psychopathology and mental health needs among drug-involved inmates. Journal of Prison and Jail Health, 11, 3-25.
In a study of 535 jail inmates referred for substance abuse treatment in a county jail who were rated either high or low in psychopathology based on MMPI profiles, were compared on indices of drug use history, social and familial relationships, employment, and justice system involvement. Those in the high psychopathology group were more likely to report lifetime use of multiple drugs and to have used both alcohol and cocaine more frequently in the month preceding treatment than the low psychopathology group. Further, those in the high psychopathology group tended to have more employment and financial problems, more disturbances in social and familial relationships, poorer physical health, and more interactions with the justice system than those in the low psychopathology group.

549.   Peters, R.H., Kearns, W.D., Murring, M.R., & Dolente, A.S. (1993). Examining the effectiveness of in-jail substance abuse treatment. Journal of Offender Rehabilitation, 19, 1-39.
Compared 535 inmates admitted to a county jail substance abuse treatment program to 422 untreated inmate substance abusers. Program participants spent longer in the community before being rearrested, had fewer overall arrests, and served less time in jail than controls. Among program participants, improvements in coping with high-risk substance abuse situations, knowledge of relapse situations and potential, and overall knowledge of substance abuse recovery were found.

550.   Peters, R.H., May, R.L., & Kearns, W.D. (1992). Drug treatment in jails: Results of a nationwide survey. Journal of Criminal Justice, 20, 283-295.
This study reports findings of a survey of 1737 local and county jails in the U.S. Results indicate that only 28% of jails have any form of substance abuse treatment and only 7% offer comprehensive drug treatment for inmates. Considering the extent of substance abuse disorders among jail inmates, the authors conclude that the available treatment resources are woefully inadequate and that greater resource expenditures for jail-based substance abuse treatment services are warranted.

551.   Petrich, J. (1976). Introduction of a psychiatric acute care clinic into a metropolitan jail. Bulletin of the American Academy of Psychiatry and Law, 4, 37-44.

552.   Petrich, J. (1976). Psychiatric treatment in jail: An experiment in health care delivery. Hospital and Community Psychiatry, 27, 413-415.

553.   Petrich, J. (1976). Rate of psychiatric morbidity in a metropolitan county jail population, American Journal of Psychiatry, 133, 1439-1444.
In a sample of 122 jail inmates referred for psychiatric evaluation found that jail inmates were more likely to be diagnosed with schizophrenia and less likely to be diagnosed with alcoholism, anxiety neurosis, and anti-social personality that in studies of prison populations. The authors estimate the overall rate of psychiatric illness for the jail population to be 4.6%.

554.   Petrich, J. (1978). Metropolitan jail psychiatric clinic: A years experience. Journal of Clinical Psychiatry, 39, 191-195.

Two patterns of psychiatric syndromes and related intervention strategies were observed in a study of 524 jail inmates. The most common pattern was that of misdemeanants with psychotic illnesses requiring long-term antipsychotic medications and close contact with community treatment resources, while the second pattern involved suicidal ideation in patients with personality disorders who were treated with short-term anti-anxiety medications and environmental manipulations.

555.   Pogrebin, M.R. (1985). Symposium: The crisis in mental health care in our jails: Jail and the mentally disordered: The need for mental health services. Journal of Prison and Jail Health, 5, 13-19.
Based on a review of the literature, the author suggests that most jails are ill-equipped to provide necessary diagnostic and treatment services to the mentally ill, resulting in increased acute psychiatric distress. The author concludes by stating the need for increased mental health screening in jails and for more involvement of mental health professionals in addressing this growing problem.

556.   Pogrebin, M.R., & Regoli, R.M. (1985). Mentally disordered persons in jail. Journal of Community Psychology, 13, 409-412.
Discusses the increasing problem of the mentally ill in jails, suggesting that, despite the fact that many courts across the country have mandated mental health services in jails, jail administrators are often less equipped to treat disordered persons, requiring increased cooperation with mental health professionals.

557.   Reeder, D., & Meldman, L. (1991). Conceptualizing psychosocial nursing in the jail setting. Journal of Psychosocial Nursing and Mental Health Services, 29, 40-44.

558.   Rikard-Bell, C. (1985). Psychiatric treatment in gaol. Australian and New Zealand Journal of Psychiatry, 19, 448-449.
Concludes that the treatment of acutely ill psychotic patients in the Australian prison system is inadequate and recommends that formal evaluation and investigation take place to establish acceptable alternatives.

559.   Ringel, N.B., & Segal, A.C. (1986). A mental health center's influence in a county jail. Journal of Community Psychology, 14, 171-182.
Discusses the first twelve years in the operation of a community-based mental health service in a county jail, noting that the factors leading to success of the venture included strong leadership in each program component, acceptance of the value of those services by jail staff and administration, and the availability of community resources.

560.   Roesch, R., Ogloff, J.R.P., & Eaves, D. (1995). Mental health research in the criminal justice system: The need for common approaches and international perspectives. International Journal of Law and Psychiatry, 18, 1-14.
Provides an overview of research concerning mental disorders among prison inmates. Six specific topics are discussed: (1) the prevalence of mental disorders among prison inmates, (2) methods or models of detecting mental disorders in jails and prisons, (3) specific assessments that may be performed during jail incarceration, (4) intervention in jails and prisons, (5) diversion or transfer out of jails and prisons

to mental health facilities, and (6) gradual release programs and community management of offenders with mental disorders. Also discussed are some specific procedural aspects of working with the processing of people with mental disorders in the criminal justice system.

561.   Singer, R.G. (1983). Providing mental health services to jail inmates: Legal perspectives. In C.S. Dunn & H.J. Steadman (Eds.), Mental health services in local jails. Rockville, MD: National Institute of Mental Health.

562.   Snow, W.H., & Briar, K.H. (1990). The convergence of the mentally disordered and the jail population. Journal of Offender Counseling, Services and Rehabilitation, 15, 147-162.
Based both on reviews of the prevalence of substance abuse, mental disorder, and developmentally disabled in jails and upon data from a jail screening service, the authors argue that the presence of mentally impaired individuals in jails reflects the unintended consequences of deinsitutionalization and deterioration in adequate resources for community services.

563.   Solomon, P., & Draine, J. (1994). Jail recidivism in a forensic case management program. Health and Social Work, 20, 167-173.

564.   Solomon, P., & Draine, J. (1995). Issues in serving the forensic client. Social Work, 40, 25-33.

565.   Solomon, P., Draine, J., & Meyerson, A. (1994). Jail recidivism and receipt of community mental health services. Hospital and Community Psychiatry, 45, 793-797.
In a study of 105 homeless mentally ill forensic clients, it was found that 32% percent were reincarcerated within 6 months of release. Factors that contributed to reincarceration were receiving fewer services than participants reported they needed, especially help with independent living skills. The authors warn that case management services with homeless mentally ill forensic clients may resemble monitoring rather than treatment services, leading to increased recidivism rates.

566.   Solomon, P.L., Draine, J.N., Marchenko, M.O., & Myerson, A.T. (1992). Homelessness in a mentally ill urban jail population. Hospital and Community Psychiatry, 43, 169-171.
This study of 274 mentally ill jail inmates found that 31% were homeless at the time of their entry into the jail system and that those with the most severe psychiatric symptoms were at greater risk of homelessness

567.   Sosowsky, L. (1980). Explaining the increased arrest rate among mental patients: A cautionary note. American Journal of Psychiatry, 137, 1602-1605.

568.   Steadman, H.J. (Ed.) (1990). Effectively addressing the mental health needs of jail detainees (pp. 35-63). Boulder, CO: National Institute of Corrections.

569.   Steadman, H.J., and Ribner, S.A. (1980). Changing perceptions of the mental health needs of inmates in local jails. American Journal of Psychiatry, 137(9), 1115-1116.

570. Steadman, H.J., Cocozza, J.J., and Melick, M.E. (1978). Explaining the increased
      arrest rate among mental patients: the changing clientele of state hospitals. American
      Journal of Psychiatry, 135, 816-820.
      Compared 3 samples of psychiatric patients released from psychiatric centers over
      3 decades. Arrest rates were significantly higher only for the 2 most recent groups
      (1968 and 1975) than for the general population, while arrest rates for the earliest
      group (1946-1948) were not. Further, the number of patients with prior arrests had
      increased markedly over time.

571. Steadman, H.J., McCarty, D.W., & Morrissey, J.P. (1986). Developing jail mental
      health services: Practice and principles. National Institute of Mental Health. DHHS
      Pub. No. (ADM)82-1181. Washington, DC: U.S. Government Printing Office.

572. Steadman, H.J., McCarty, D.W., & Morrissey, J.P. (1989). The mentally ill in jail:
      Planning for essential services. New York: Guilford Press.

573. Swank, G.E., & Winer, D. (1976). Occurrence of psychiatric disorder in a county
      jail population. American Journal of Psychiatry, 133, 1331-1336.

574. Swank, G.E., & Winer, D. (1979). A psychiatric team provides services in a county
      jail. Hospital and Community Psychiatry, 29, 22-23.

575. Task Force on Psychiatric Services in Jails & Prisons. (1989). Position statement on
      psychiatric services in jails and prisons. American Journal of Psychiatry, 146, 1244.
      Outlines 6 fundamental principles for providing adequate mental health care and
      treatment to mentally ill persons in jails and prisons.

576. Teplin, L.A. (1990). Detecting disorder: The treatment of mental illness among jail
      detainees. Journal of Consulting and Clinical Psychology, 58, 233-236.
      Based on a random sample of 728 jail detainees who were diagnosed via the
      National Institute of Mental Health Diagnostic Interview Schedule, found that of
      those diagnosed with a major mental disorder (schizophrenia and major affective
      disorder), only 32% received treatment services within a week of their intake and
      diagnosis. Decisions to treat were more likely if there was an history of psychiatric
      hospitalization, if the diagnosis was schizophrenia rather than depression, and if the
      symptoms were documented by jail staff. The author suggests that these findings
      are discouraging since, even with a screening system, only about one-third received
      treatment, and because previous psychiatric hospitalization was such a strong
      predictor, rather than severity of illness.

577. Teplin, L.A. (1990). Policing the mentally ill: Styles, strategies, and implications. In
      H.J. Steadman (Ed.), Effectively addressing the mental health needs of jail detainees
      (pp. 35-63). Boulder, CO: National Institute of Corrections.

578. Teplin, L.A. (1990). The prevalence of severe mental disorder among male urban
      jail detainees: Comparison with the Epidemiological Catchment Area program.
      American Journal of Public Health, 80, 663-669.
      Using the NIMH Diagnostic Interview Schedule, the prevalence of severe mental
      disorder (e.g., Schizophrenia, Major Affective Disorders) among jail detainees in

Chicago was compared to that of the general population. Prevalence rates were 2 to 3 times higher for the jail sample (N = 728) than that of the general population after controlling for differences in age and race were controlled.

579. Teplin, L.A. (1994). Psychiatric and substance abuse disorders among male urban jail detainees. American Journal of Public Health, 84, 290-293.
The prevalence of mental disorders and substance abuse disorders in a random sample of 728 male jail detainees was assessed. It was found that two-thirds had experienced a mental disorder other than personality disorder during their lifetimes. Further, antisocial personality disorder was evident in about one-half of detainees. Nearly one-third were currently experiencing either a current mental disorder or a substance abuse disorder. Whites had significantly higher rates of depression, substance abuse disorders and antisocial personality disorders than blacks, while Hispanics had the highest rates of schizophrenia. Considering that mentally ill detainees were more likely to be charged with nonviolent misdemeanors, it is unfortunate that so few alternatives to incarceration are available and linkages between jails and community treatment are infrequent because diversion to community alternatives would seem more appropriate for these offenders.

580. Teplin, L.A., & Swartz, J. (1989). Screening for severe mental disorder in jails: The development of the Referral Decision Scale. Law and Human Behavior, 13, 1-18.

581. Teplin, L.A., Abram, K.M., & McClelland, G.M. (1994). Does psychiatric disorder predict violent crime among released jail detainees? A six-year longitudinal study. American Psychologist, 49, 335-342.
In a study of rearrests of jail detainees over a 6 year period, it was found that presence of neither major mental disorders and substance abuse disorders predicted probability of arrest for violent offenses in the six years following release. Although these findings suggest that the perception of mental patients as necessarily more violence-prone than non-mentally ill individuals is supported by these findings, the author notes that some studies have shown that mental patients may be more likely to be hospitalized rather than incarcerated during times of violent behavior.

582. Valdisseri, E.V., Carroll, K.R., & Hartl, A.J. (1986). A study of offenses committed by psychotic inmates in a county jail. Hospital and Community Psychiatry, 37, 163-166.

583. Virginia Department of Mental Health and Mental Retardation and the Virginia Department of Corrections (1984). The mentally ill in Virginia's jails: Final report of the Joint Task Force. Richmond, VA: Authors.

584. Walsh, J., & Bricout, J. (1996). Improving jail linkages of detainees with mental health agencies. Psychiatric Rehabilitation Journal, 20, 73-76.
Noting that deinstitutionalization has led to increases in arrests and imprisonment of persons with mental illnesses and that mental health treatment is not the mission or within the service capacity of most jails, a survey of 93 Virginia jails found that jail staff encouragement of family contact with the detainee is positively associated with the frequency of treatment linkages to mental health providers after discharge.

585. Washington, P.A. (1989). Mature mentally ill offenders in California jails. Special Issue: Older offenders: Current trends. Journal of Offender Counseling, Services and Rehabilitation, 13, 161-173.

586. Weinstein, H.C. (1989). Psychiatric services in jails and prisons: Who cares? American Journal of Psychiatry, 146, 1094-1095.

587. Weissman, J.C., Katsampes, P.L., & Giacinti, T.A. (1974). Opiate use and criminality among a jail population. Addictive Disorders, 1, 269-281.

588. Whitmer, G.E. (1980). From hospitals to jails: The fate of California's deinstitutionalized mentally ill. American Journal of Orthopsychiatry, 50, 65-75.

7

Individual Psychotherapy

589. Abrams, A.I., & Siegel, L.M. (1978). The Transcendental Meditation program and rehabilitation at Folsom State Prison: A cross validation study. Criminal Justice and Behavior, 5, 3-20.
      In two studies, significant decreases in anxiety, neuroticism, hostility, and insomnia were found for participants in a 14-week transcendental meditation program while no differences were found for controls.

590. Allen, D. (1979). TM at Folsom Prison: A critique of Abrams and Siegel. Criminal Justice and Behavior, 6, 9-12.

591. Ansbacher, H.L. (1990). Hypnosis for diagnostic purpose: Adlerian understanding: Comments on R. J. Corsini's "The case of Ken." Individual Psychology: Journal of Adlerian Theory, Research and Practice, 46, 516-521.

592. Balier, C. (1989). Psychiatry in a prison environment: Caretaking or treatment? Perspectives Psychiatriques, 28, 237-242.
      Argues that while limiting psychiatric interventions to symptom suppression may help maintain a satisfactory equilibrium of prison life, it denies the prisoner the ability to achieve autonomous psychological functioning. The prison environment may be a favorable setting for conducting dynamic therapy if the psychiatrist is able to identify the most important symptoms that make up the basic material for psychotherapeutic work.

593. Brosch, W. (1993). Sentenced to psychotherapy? Report of experiences from the Austrian central treatment institution for incompetent mentally abnormal criminals. Psychiatriques Praxis, 20, 176-180.

594.   Corsini, R.J. (1990). The case of Ken. Individual Psychology: Journal of Adlerian Theory, Research and Practice, 46, 508-515.

595.   Cox, M. (1982). "I took a life because I needed one": Psychotherapeutic possibilities with the schizophrenic individual. Psychotherapy and Psychosomatics, 37, 96-105.

596.   Cox, M. (1983). The contributions of dynamic psychotherapy to forensic psychiatry and vice versa. International Journal of Law and Psychiatry, 6, 89-99.

597.   Davison, F.M., Clare, I.C., Georgiades, S., Divall, J., & Holland, A.J. (1994). Treatment of a man with a mild learning disability who was sexually assaulted whilst in prison. Medicine, Science and the Law, 34, 346-353.

598.   Day, A., Maddicks, R., & McMahon, D. (1994). Brief psychotherapy in two-plus-one sessions with a young offender population. Behavioural and Cognitive Psychotherapy, 21, 357-369.

599.   Goldenberg, E.F. (1976). Psychotherapy and the offender. Corrective and Social Psychiatry and Journal of Behavior Technology, Methods and Therapy, 22, 12-13. Discusses the difficulty in conducting both individual and group psychotherapy in correctional institutions where security and restrictive environments are emphasized.

600.   Gomes, A.A. (1993). Psicoterapia institucional e psiquiatria de sector no meio prisional portugues. (Institutional psychotherapy and psychiatry in Portuguese prisons.) Analise Psicologica, 11, 61-73.

601.   Graham, S.A. (1980). Psychotherapists attitudes toward offender clients. Journal of Consulting and Clinical Psychology, 48, 796-797.

602.   Groh, T.R. (1976). A preliminary study of patient characteristics in a correctional setting. Corrective and Social Psychiatry and Journal of Behavior Technology, Methods and Therapy, 22, 21-23.
A study of 4 groups of offenders (e.g., individual psychotherapy, group psychotherapy, requesting therapy, and a general inmate population group) in a medium security prison found that inmates participating in both individual and group psychotherapy tended to be more intelligent, to be white, to have had previous experiences with psychotherapy and to be better educated. Offense characteristics, age, and income did not differ between the groups.

603.   Halleck, S. (1978). Psychotherapy in the penitentiary environment: Problems and perspectives. Quaderni Di Criminolicia Clinica, 20, 141-154.

604.   Meine, D. (1993). [Elements of power in so-called "evil": Psychoanalysis in prison]. Analytische Psychologie, 24, 39-54.

605.   Oberkirch, A. (1985). Psychotherapy of a murderer: Excerpts. American Journal of Psychotherapy, 39, 499-514.
Describes the case of a murderer judged not guilty by reason of insanity through dated excerpts from 26 month of process material. The patient was treated weekly

in a maximum security facility. The murderer is interpreted as an identification with the aggressor, the patient's mother. It is understood as a pathetic appeal for help.

606.   Panton, J.H. (1979). MMPI profiles associated with outcomes of intensive psychotherapeutic counseling with youthful first offender prison inmates. Research Communications in Psychology, Psychiatry and Behavior, 4, 383-395.
Results of pre- and post-test comparisons of MMPI profiles of 50 prisoners (aged 16 to 20) participating in an intensive psychotherapy program and a control group of similar prisoners not participating showed that pre-post-test changes in MMPI scales were found for only the experimental group. The experimental group showed significant pre- to post-test differences on 10 of the 15 scales analyzed, suggesting improvements in anxiety, depression, social alienation, and antisocial behavior.

607.   Peretti, P.G., Gorecki, M., & Cedeck, M. (1988). State prison clergy counselor role self-perceptions. Acta Psychiatrica Belgica, 88, 400-404.

608.   Rayburn, C.A. (1993). Prison. In R.J. Wicks, R.D. Parsons, & D. Capps (Eds.), Clinical handbook of pastoral counseling, Vol 1. New York: Paulist Press.

609.   Romig, C.A., & Gruenke, C. (1991). The use of metaphor to overcome inmate resistance to mental health counseling. Journal of Counseling and Development, 69, 414-418.

610.   Seager, M., & Jacobson, R. (1994). Two plus one: Confusions in conceptualization and methodology: A rejoinder to Day et al. Behavioural and Cognitive Psychotherapy, 22, 243-246.

611.   Sease, S.S. (1982). Grief associated with a prison experience: Counseling the client. Journal of Psychosocial Nursing and Mental Health Services, 20, 25-27.

612.   Smith, A.B., & Berlin, L. (1980). The place of psychotherapy in probation and parole: The patient as offender. Annals of the New York Academy of Science, 347, 157-166.

613.   Valliant, P.M., & Antonowicz, D.H. (1991). Cognitive behavior therapy and social skills training improves personality and cognition in incarcerated offenders. Psychological Reports, 68, 27-33.
Studied the use of cognitive behavioral therapy with maximum security inmates (34 general inmates and 19 sex offenders) over a 5 week period and found improvement in self-esteem and reduction in anxiety and aggressive traits in both groups.

614.   Zimmerman, R.R., Guest, R., & Geist, C. (1974). Improvement in self-concept during psychotherapy in a maximum security prison. Perceptual and Motor Skills, 39, 311-314.

8

Group, Marital, and Family Therapy

615. Batter, T.E. (1976). Group psychotherapy: A restructuring of the probation process. Corrective and Social Psychiatry and Journal of Behavior Technology, Methods, & Therapy, 22, 1-5.

616. Beidleman, W.B. (1981). Group assertive training in correctional settings: A review and methodological critique. Journal of Offender Counseling, Services and Rehabilitation, 6, 69-87.
      Reviews investigations of group assertiveness training in correctional settings, revealing an overall pattern of positive findings. However, methodological flaws, such as the lack of adequate control groups, restrict the conclusions which can be drawn from the research.

617. Ben-David, S. (1992). Influence, leadership, and social desirability in psychotherapeutic groups. Journal of Group Psychotherapy, Psychodrama and Sociometry, 45, 17-23.

618. Brown, D.R. (1992). A didactic group program for persons found unfit to stand trial. Hospital and Community Psychiatry, 43, 732-733.
      Describes an Illinois program designed to help persons with Axis I and Axis II disorders who have been found mentally incompetent to stand trial to attain fitness to stand trial, to provide clients with information about the criminal justice system, and to monitor progress in stabilizing the mental functioning of clients.

619. Caffaro, J.V. (1991). A room full of fathers. Journal of Family Psychotherapy, 2, 27-40.

620.   Camblin, L.M., Stone, W.N., & Merritt, L.C. (1990). An adaptive approach to group therapy for the chronic patient. Special Issue: Group work with the emotionally disabled. Social Work with Groups, 13, 53-65.
Discusses a model for group treatment of chronically mentally ill patients using a group of low SES clients with individuals with criminal records as an illustration. The group focuses on adaptive capacities of clients and encourages problem solving skills. Through development of successful problem skills, group members gained a sense of mastery and experienced increased self-esteem.

621.   Coyne, J.C., & Fabricatore, J.M. (1979). Group psychotherapy in a corrections facility: A case study of individual and institutional change. Professional Psychology, 10, 8-14.
Describes the shift from intrapsychic concerns to a focus on increased individual responsibility and prisoner-guard relations among members of a psychotherapy group in a community corrections center. The authors argue that changing the focus from intrapersonal to environmental change in the correctional environment is an appropriate and profitable transition for psychotherapy groups in correctional settings.

622.   Dan, D. (1992). The use of "alumni" in treatment for driving under the influence (DUI) clients. Alcoholism Treatment Quarterly, 9, 77-83.
Discusses a group treatment using former DUI offenders as group co-leaders. The presence of alumni provided role models for change and were instrumental in defusing authority issues in the group.

623.   Daniel, D.A. (1984). Effects of extensive group therapy on incarcerated young mens' attitudes toward themselves and prison staff. Journal of Offender Counseling, Services, and Rehabilitation, 8, 27-39.
A study comparing the effectiveness of extensive group therapy for drug abusers versus vocational training found no significant differences in attitudinal change between the groups. However, those offenders convicted of crimes against persons showed greater improvement in attitudes toward themselves and prison staff than did offenders convicted of property crimes.

624.   Forbes, M.R., Pratsinak, G.J., Fagan, T.J., & Ax, R.K. (1992). Effects of group prosocial skills training on anger control in prison inmates. Psychological Reports, 70, 66.
Describes a failed attempt to use prosocial skills training to facilitate anger management in 48 adult male prison inmates. The limited scope of the program, including eight group treatment sessions may have been too little to counteract years of experiential learning.

625.   Frager, S. (1978). Multiple family therapy: A literature review. Family Therapy, 5, 105-120.

626.   Freedman, B.J., & Rice, D.G. (1977). Marital therapy in prison: One partner "couple therapy." Psychiatry, 40, 175-183.

627.   Haskell, M.R. (1974). The contributions of J.L. Moreno to the treatment of the offender. Group Psychotherapy and Psychodrama, 27, 147-156.

628.   Hayman, P.M., & Weiss-Cassady, D.M. (1981). Structured learning therapy with mentally ill criminal offenders. Journal of Offender Counseling, Services and Rehabilitation, 6, 41-51.

629.   Hilkey, J.H., Wilhelm, C.L., & Horne, A.M. (1982). Comparative effectiveness of videotape pretraining versus no pretraining on selected process and outcome variables in group therapy. Psychological Reports, 50, 1151-1159.
        Randomly assigned 90 inmates of a medium security prison to either videotape group therapy pretraining or no pretraining conditions and found that those in the experimental group had clearer expectations of group therapy, demonstrated more desirable behaviors during group therapy, and made more progress in achieving individual goals according to ratings of both peers and therapists.

630.   Homant, R.J. (1976). Therapy effectiveness in a correctional institution. Offender Rehabilitation, 1, 101-113.
        This study of the effectiveness of group therapy found that, compared to controls, inmates in a maximum security state prison who participated in group therapy made significant gains in conduct, work behaviors, and institutional adjustment. These findings held for those who were rated either high or low in motivation, leading the author to conclude that group therapy should be more widely available in correctional settings.

631.   Homant, R.J. (1986). Ten years after: A follow-up of therapy effectiveness. Journal of Offender Counseling, Services, and Rehabilitation, 10, 51-57.
        A follow-up study of 92 prison inmates who began group therapy while incarcerated found that of the 86 inmates who had been released from prison, 39 showed successful adjustment to life in the community, while only 11 had been reincarcerated.

632.   Jones, E.J., & McColl, M.A. (1991). Development and evaluation of an interactional life skills group for offenders. Occupational Therapy Journal of Research, 11, 80-92.

633.   Kaufman, E. (1973). Group therapy techniques used by the ex-addict therapist. Group Process, 5, 3-19.

634.   Klabucar, L., & Pavlic, M. (1986). Group psychotherapy of schizophrenic murderers. Socijalna Psihijtrija, 14, 63-70.

635.   MacDevitt, J.W., & Sanislow, C. (1987). Curative factors in offenders' groups. Small Group Behavior, 18, 72-81.
        A study of curative factors involved in group therapy with 123 offenders in correctional settings ranging from probation to segregation units for prison inmates with severe behavioral problems found that catharsis was rated highest among offenders, while interpersonal learning was rated at varying levels depending on correctional setting. Existential awareness was also highly rated, while factors such as cohesiveness, family reenactment, and guidance were rated lower.

636.   Martin, J.V. (1989). Optimal timing for group therapy in the criminal justice system. Journal of Offender Counseling, Services, and Rehabilitation, 14, 149-158.

637.   Mathias, R.E., & Sindberg, R.M (1986). Time limited group therapy in minimum security. Journal of Offender Counseling, Services, and Rehabilitation, 11, 7-17. Evaluated a 10 session group therapy program designed to prepare individuals incarcerated in a minimum security prison for release. Results of comparisons of pre- and post-test MMPI and structured interview data suggested that the program reduced inmates distrust, suspicion and anxiety levels and increased feelings of self-worth and acceptance.

638.   Mattocks, A.L., & Jew, C.C. (1974). Comparison of self-actualization levels and adjustment scores of incarcerated male felons. Educational and Psychological Measurement, 34, 69-74. Compared scores on the Personal Orientation Inventory, a measure of self-actualization, and scores on the Q-Sort Adjustment Scale among a group of group psychotherapy participants in a correctional psychiatric facility. Those who were higher in self-actualization were found to be more well-adjusted than those who were low self-actualization.

639.   Milgram, D., & Rubin, J.S. (1992). Resisting resistance: Involuntary substance abuse group therapy. Social Work with Groups, 15, 95-110. Discusses a strategy for overcoming resistance in mandated group therapy with substance abusing federal offenders.

640.   Nolan, P. (1983). Insight therapy: Guided imagery and music in a forensic psychiatric setting. Music Therapy, 3, 43-51.

641.   Parloff, M.B., & Dies, R.R. (1977). Group psychotherapy outcome research 1966-1975. International Journal of Group Psychotherapy, 27, 281-319.

642.   Pueschel, J., & Moglia, R. (1977). The effects of the penal environment on familial relationships. Family Coordinator, 26, 373-375.

643.   Rappaport, R.G. (1971). Group psychotherapy in prison. International Journal of Group Psychotherapy, 21, 489-496,

644.   Rappaport, R.G. (1981). Group psychotherapy in prison: A proper role for the psychiatrist. Medical Trials Technical Quarterly, 27, 249-271.

645.   Resnick, R.J., Lira, F., & Wallace, J.H. (1977). On the effectiveness of group counseling: A look at the group leader in the correctional setting. Criminal Justice and Behavior, 4, 77-85. Compared the effectiveness of group counseling led by psychologists, social workers, and correctional counselors and found that groups led by psychologists had better adjustment in work settings. Similarly, group member motivation was higher in psychologist-led groups. Conclusions and recommendations for training are discussed.

646.   Rieger, W. (1973). A proposal for a trial of family therapy and conjugal visits in prison. American Journal of Orthopsychiatry, 43, 117-122.

647.   Robertson, J.M. (1990). Group counseling and the high risk offender. Federal Probation, 54, 48-51.

648.   Robinson, S., Vivian-Byrne, S., Driscoll, R., & Cordess, C. (1991). Family work with victims and offenders in a secure unit. Journal of Family Therapy, 13, 105-116.

649.   Rokach, A. (1987). Anger and aggression control training: Replacing attack with interaction. Psychotherapy, 24, 353-362.
        An evaluation of the effects of a time-limited group-treatment program designed to facilitate anger and aggression control among incarcerated males (N = 51) found that the brief program yielded significant decreases in susceptibility to anger and aggressive reactions while leading to increases in prosocial behaviors.

650.   Rummele, W. (1974). Report and considerations on group psychotherapy in a prison. Schweizer Archiv Fur Neurologie, Neurochirurgie und Psyciatrie, 115, 359-368.

651.   Savage, C., McCabe, O.L. (1973). Residential psychedelic (LSD) therapy for the narcotic addict: A controlled study. Archives of General Psychiatry, 28, 808-814.

652.   Schramski, T.G., Feldman, C.A., Harvey, D.R., & Holiman, M. (1984). A comparative evaluation of group treatments in an adult correctional facility. Journal for Group Psychotherapy, Psychodrama and Sociometry, 36, 133-147.
        Compared effects on psychiatric symptomology and perceived correctional institution and group social climate for 4 group therapy interventions (psychodrama, anger therapy, values clarification, and decision-making) as compared to no treatment controls among 66 male prisoners. Results suggest that overall, group treatment had significant benefits to inmates, although differential effects were found for group therapy type.

653.   Scott, E.M. (1993). History and treatment efforts for a prison special management unit: Prison group therapy with mentally and emotionally disturbed offenders. International Journal of Offender Therapy and Comparative Criminology, 37, 131-145.

654.   Stein, E., & Brown, J.D. (1991). Group therapy in a forensic setting. Canadian Journal of Psychiatry, 36, 718-722.
        Studied 30 violent offenders found not guilty by reason of insanity and found that these offenders had personality characteristics that precluded the development of therapeutic group dynamics. Among these characteristics were denial of responsibility, inability to form attachments, inability to form transference, inability to trust others, and egocentricity.

655.   Steinfeld, G.J., & Mabil, J. (1974). Perceived curative factors in group therapy by residents of a therapeutic community. Criminal Justice and Behavior, 1, 278-288.

656.   Steinfeld, G.J., Rautio, E.A., Rice, A.H., & Egan, M.J. (1974). Group covert sensitization with narcotic addicts: Further comments. International Journal of the Addictions, 9, 447-464.

657.   Towberman, D.B. (1993). Group vs. individual counseling: Treatment mode and the client's perception of the treatment environment. Journal of Group Psychotherapy, Psychodrama and Sociometry, 45, 163-174.
       Compared group and individual counseling effects on client perceptions of the treatment environment in a sample of 96 institutionalized adolescent female offenders and found that those in group counseling rated interpersonal relationships and the treatment program more positively than did those in individual counseling.

658.   Thaut, M.H. (1987). A new challenge for music therapy: The correctional setting. Music Therapy Perspectives, 4, 44-50.

659.   Wagoner, J.L., & Piazza, N.J. (1993). Group therapy for adult substance abusers on probation. Journal of Offender Rehabilitation, 19, 41-56.

660.   Waldram, J.B., & Wong, S. (1995). Group therapy of Aboriginal offenders in a Canadian forensic psychiatric facility. American Indian and Alaska Native Mental Health Research, 6, 34-56.

661.   Welldon, E.V. (1993). Forensic psychotherapy and group analysis. Group Analysis, 26, 487-502.

662.   Wolozin, D., & Dalton, E. (1990). Short-term group psychotherapy with the "family-absent father" in a maximum security psychiatric hospital. Annual Meeting of the Parenting Symposium (1986, Philadelphia, Pennsylvania). Social Work with Groups, 13, 103-111.

663.   Wunderlich, R.A., Lozes, J., & Lewis, J. (1974). Recidivism rates of group therapy participants and other adolescents processed by a juvenile court. Psychotherapy: Theory, Research and Practice, 11, 243-245.

664.   Zimpfer, D.G. (1984). Patterns and trends in group work. Journal for Specialists in Group Work, 9, 204-208.

665.   Zimpfer, D.G. (1992). Group work with adult offenders: An overview. Journal for Specialists in Group Work, 17, 54-61.
       Surveys the literature on group counseling in correctional settings and discusses the purpose of group counseling with offenders, therapeutic factors of groups, ethical issues in group counseling and the application of group therapy to differing offender populations.

9

Jail and Prison Suicide

666. Aks, S.E., Mansour, M., Hryhorczuk, D.O., Raba, J. (1993). Barium sulfide ingestions in an urban correctional facility population. Journal of Prison and Jail Health, 12, 3-122.
      Presents 5 cases studies of male jail inmates who ingested shaving products containing barium sulfide in attempts to commit suicide while in jail. One of the cases was successful. Noting that the suicide rate in jails is 3 times higher than that in the general population, the authors suggest that the use of such products should be restricted or safer products should be substituted for use by jail inmates.

667. Albrecht H., Chaplow, D., & Peters, J. (1992). Suicide in prison in Auckland. Lancet, 340(8823), 854.

668. Anonymous. (1991). Prison suicides. British Medical Journal, 302(6773), 410-411.

669. Ben-David, S., & Silfen, P. (1993). Rape death and resurrection: male reaction after disclosure of the secret of being a rape victim. Medicine and Law., 12, 181-189.
      In a study of the male rape victims, 23.8% of 235 prisoners that were interviewed disclosed past sexual abuse while incarcerated. Eleven suffered an acute reaction after disclosure. Over 3/4 of the prisoners who did not have an acute reaction after were sex offenders. Many male sexual abuse victims in prison have problems associated with gender identity and gender image after victimization. However, it seems that sex offenders come to terms with this fact by acting out or by proving their sexual virility in strange and cruel ways.

670. Bland, R.C., Newman, S.C., Dyck, R.J., & Orn, H. (1990). Prevalence of psychiatric disorders and suicide attempts in a prison population. Canadian Journal of Psychiatry, 35, 407-413.

671.   Bonner, R.L., & Rich, A.R. (1990). Psychosocial vulnerability, life stress, and suicide ideation in a jail population: A cross-validation study. Suicide and Life Threatening Behavior, 20, 213-224.
       Multiple regression analyses of responses of 146 male inmates of a county jail to a variety of measures of alienation, cognitive distortion. stress, mood, and suicidal ideation found that irrational beliefs, few reasons for living, jail stress and loneliness best accounted for the variance in suicidal ideation among jail inmates.

672.   Clark, D.C., & Horton-Deutsch, S.L. (1992). Assessment in absentia: The value of the psychological autopsy method for studying antecedents of suicide and predicting future suicides. In R.W. Maris, A.L. Berman, J.T. Maltsberger, & R.I. Yufit (Eds.), Assessment and prediction of suicide. New York: Guilford.

673.   Copeland, A.R. (1989). Fatal suicidal hangings among prisoners in jail. Medicine, Science and the Law, 29, 341-345.

674.   Cox, J., McCarty, D., Landsberg, G., & Paravati, M.P. (1990). Local jails and police lockups. In M.J. Rothedam-Boros, J. Bradely, & N. Obolensky (Eds.), Evaluating and treating suicidal teens in community settings. Tulsa, OK: National Resource Center for Youth Services.

675.   Cox, J.F., & Landsberg, G. (1989). Future directions. Special Issue: Jail suicide: A comprehensive approach to a continuing national problem. Psychiatric Quarterly, 60, 185-188.
       Implementation of the elements that experts deem essential to identifying and managing suicidal and mentally ill inmates is crucial to the success of any jail suicide prevention program.

676.   Cox, J.F., McCarty, D.W., Landsberg, G., & Paravati, M.P. (1988) A model for crisis intervention services within local jails. Special Issue: Forensic administration. International Journal of Law and Psychiatry, 11, 391-407.

677.   Danto, B.L. (1971). Suicide at the Wayne County jail, 1967 -1970. Police Law Quarterly. January, 34-41.

678.   Danto, B.L. (1981). Crisis behind bars: The suicidal inmate. Warren, MI: The Dale Corporation.

679.   Danto, B.L., Taff, M.L., & Mirchandani, H.G. (1985). Cases of self-destructive behavior involving multiple methods during a single episode. American Journal of Forensic Psychiatry, 6, 38-45.

680.   Duclos, C.W., LeBeau, W., & Gasil, L. (1994). American Indian adolescent suicide behavior in detention environments: Cause for continued basic and applied research. American Indian and Alaska Native Mental Health Research, 4, 189-221.

681.   DuRand, C.J., Butka, G.J., Federman, E.J., Haycox, J.A., & Smith, J. (1995). A quarter century of suicide in a major urban jail: Implications for community psychiatry. American Journal of Psychiatry, 152, 1077-1079.

A study of jail suicides over a twenty-five year period (1967-1992) was conducted at the Wayne County Jail in Michigan, where some of the earliest studies of jail suicide were undertaken. This history may explain the why so few suicides had taken place since the 1970's and why none had occurred in the previous five years. Of the 37 suicides studied, all were accomplished by hanging, including those of women (N = 2). Suicides were more likely to occur at night in double occupancy cells (i.e., when cellmates were sleeping) and to occur within 31 days of admission. Finally, unlike findings from previous studies, persons charged with homicide manslaughter were 19 times more likely than those with other charges to successfully commit suicide.

682.   Esparza, R.E. (1973). Attempted and committed suicide in county jails. In B.L. Danto (Ed.). Jail house blues. Orchard Lake, MI: Epic.

683.   Felthous, A.R. (1994). Preventing jailhouse suicides. Bulletin of the American Academy of Psychiatry and Law, 22, 477-488.
This paper reviews the literature on suicide in jail and prison noting the various discrepancies in risk factors noted in these studies. These discrepancies may be due to situational/ geographical differences in correctional systems and hence, present a problem for those wishing to develop broad-based suicide prevention programs for jails and prisons. The author presents a detailed description of a number of procedures which appear to be the most efficacious in preventing jailhouse suicides including screening within the first 24 hours, crisis intervention, psychological support, close monitoring, development of clear and consistent precautionary procedures, and treatment or transfer to psychiatric hospitals when possible.

684.   Foxman, J. (1990). A practical guide to emergency and protective crisis intervention with the violent and self-destructive person. Springfield, IL: Charles C. Thomas.

685.   Franklin, R.K. (1988). Deliberate self-harm: Self-injurious behavior within a correctional mental health population. Criminal Justice and Behavior, 15, 210-218.
Studied variables that distinguished suicidal inmates from those engaging in deliberate self-harm in a prison treatment program. Half of the self-harm inmates indicated that manipulation was their primary goal, while diagnoses of borderline personality disorder was over-represented among those engaging in deliberate self-injurious behaviors. Deliberate self-harm was associated with a greater history of self-injurious behavior than was suicidal behavior.

686.   French, L.A. (1985-86). Forensic suicides and attempted suicides. Omega: Journal of Death and Dying, 16, 335-345.

687.   Guarner, J., & Hanzlick, R. (1987). Suicide by hanging: A review of 56 cases. American Journal of Forensic Medicine and Pathology, 8, 23-26.

688.   Haycock, J. (1989). Manipulation and suicide attempts in jails and prisons. Psychiatric Quarterly, 60, 85-98.

689.   Haycock, J. (1989). Race and suicide in jails and prisons. Journal of the National Medical Association, 81, 405-411.

690.   Haycock, J. (1991). Capital crimes: Suicides in jail. Death Studies, 15, 417-433.
In a review of the literature on in-jail suicides, the author considers alternative explanations of the increased risk for suicide among jail inmates, concluding that their are generally two opposing views: (1) the "importation hypothesis," which suggests that the high rate of jail suicide is explained by the types of individuals who find themselves in jail, and (2) the "deprivation hypothesis," which attributes the high rate of jail suicides to the stresses associated with jails. Although the empirical knowledge base on jail suicides is severely limited, and support for either hypothesis is problematic, some risk factors for suicide in the general population are over-represented in the jail population, including being male, undergoing family disruption at the time of arrest, and being from a lower socioeconomic category.

691.   Haycock, J. (1991). Crimes and misdemeanors: A review of recent research on suicides in prison. Omega Journal of Death and Dying, 23, 81-94.
Although others have reported that the suicide rate in jail is 5 to 8 times greater than that of the general population, and 2 to 3 times greater than that of inmates in prison, the author argues that for some subgroups of prison inmates, the risk of completed suicide are even greater than that of jail inmates. These subgroups include the "graying" of the prison populations and the increasing prevalence of AIDS in prisons.

692.   Hayes, L.M. (1992). Can jail suicide be prevented? Crisis, 13, 60-62.

693.   Hayes, L.M. (1992). Jail suicide--an overview of yesterday. Crisis, 13, 11-13.

694.   Hayes, L.M. (1993). Jail suicide--prevention through written protocol (Part 1). Crisis, 14, 11-13.

695.   Hayes, L.M. (1993). Jail suicide--prevention through written protocol (Part 2). Crisis, 14, 57-58, 60.

696.   Hayes, L.M. (1994). Jail suicide in Mississippi. Crisis, 15, 105-107.

697.   Hayes, L.M. (1994). Jail suicide: Overcoming obstacles to prevention. Crisis, 15, 59-61.

698.   Hayes, L.M. (1994). Prison suicide: An overview and guide to prevention (Part 1). Crisis, 15, 155-8.

699.   Hayes, L.M. (1995). Prison suicide: An overview and guide to prevention (Part 2). Crisis, 16, 9-12.

700.   Hayes, L.M. (1995). Prison suicide: An overview and guide to prevention (Part 3). Crisis, 16, 63-65.

701.   Hayes, L.M., & Rowan, J.R. (1988). National study of jail suicides: Seven years later. Alexandria, VA: National Center on Institutions and Alternatives.

702.   Herranz-Bellido, J., Martin-Escudero, R., Garrido-Martinez, A., & Nunez-Machaco, J.L. (1990). Analysis of suicidal behaviour in a psychiatric penitentiary. Analisis y Modificacion de Conducta, 16, 471-487.

703.   Hess, A.K. (1987). The self-imposed death sentence. Psychology Today, 21, 50-53. Suggests six steps necessary to prevent jail suicide including: (1) city/county acceptance of responsibility for inmate welfare, (2) appropriate budgeting, (3) mental health training for jail personnel, (4) development of suicide screening devices, (5) involvement of behavioral scientists in the design of jails, and (6) innovative approaches to deal with the suicidal inmate directly.

704.   Hillbrand, M. (1993). Self-injurious behavior in correctional and noncorrectional psychiatric patients: Prevalence and correlates. Journal of Offender Rehabilitation, 19, 95-102.

705.   Ivanoff, A. (1989). Identifying psychological correlates of suicidal behavior in jail and detention facilities. Psychiatric Quarterly, 60, 73-84.

706.   Ivanoff, A., & Jang, S.J. (1991). The role of hopelessness and social desirability in predicting suicidal behavior: a study of prison inmates. Journal of Consulting and Clinical Psychology, 59, 394-399.

707.   Ivanoff, A., Smyth, N.J., Grochowski, S., Jang, S.J., & Klein, K.E. (1992). Problem solving and suicidality among prison inmates: another look at state versus trait. Journal of Consulting and Clinical Psychology, 60, 970-973.

708.   Johnson, R. (1978). Youth in crisis: Dimensions of self-destructive conduct among adolescent prisoners. Adolescence, 13, 461-82.

709.   Karp, J.G., Whitman, L., & Convit, A. (1991). Intentional ingestion of foreign objects by male prison inmates. Hospital and Community Psychiatry, 42, 533-535.

710.   Kerkhof, A.J., & Bernasco, W. (1990). Suicidal behavior in jails and prisons in the Netherlands: Incidence, characteristics, and prevention. Suicide and Life Threatening Behavior, 20, 125-137.

711.   Landsberg, G. (1994). Issues in the prevention and detection of suicide potential in correctional facilities. In R. Rosner (Ed.), Principles and practice of forensic psychiatry. New York: Chapman & Hall.

712.   Lester, D. (1987). Suicide and homicide in USA prisons. Psychological Reports, 61, 126.

713.   Lester, D. (1990). Overcrowding in prisons and rates of suicide and homicide. Perceptual and Motor Skills, 71, 274.

714.   Lester, D. (1992). State regulations for suicide prevention in jails and the jail suicide rate. Psychological Reports, 71(3 Pt 2), 1170.

715.   Lester, D., & Danto, B.L. (1993). Suicide behind bars: Prediction and prevention. Philadelphia, PA: Charles Press.

716.   Library Information Specialists, Inc. (1983). Corrections information series: Suicide in jails. (Contract DI-7) Boulder, CO: National Institute on Corrections.

717.   Marcus, P., & Alcabes, P. (1993). Characteristics of suicides by inmates in an urban jail. Hospital and Community Psychiatry, 44, 256-261.
In a study of jail suicides in New York city over a 9 year period, it was shown that suicides were most likely to be committed during the first 30 days of incarceration, with the highest rate being for those incarcerated within 3 days of a court appearance. The vast majority of suicides were by hanging (90%) and were committed by persons housed alone. Further, about half had either a diagnosis of major psychiatric disorder or a history of psychiatric hospitalization. The authors argue for early identification of inmates with psychiatric histories, treatment for those identified as being high in suicide potential, avoiding housing inmates alone, and increased training for jail staff.

718.   New York University Symposium. (1974). Report on the NYU symposium: Suicide in prison. Journal of Psychiatry and Law, 2, 73-92.

719.   Rakis, J. (1984). Suicide prevention measures in urban detention facilities throughout the United States. Journal of Prison and Jail Health, 4, 91-95.

720.   Rakis, J., & Monroe, R. (1989). Monitoring and managing the suicidal prisoner. Psychiatric Quarterly, 60, 151-160.

721.   Rieger, W. (1971). Suicide attempts in a Federal prison. Archives of General Psychiatry, 24, 532-535.

722.   Rood, L.R., & Faison, K. (1988). Identifying suicidal risk in prisoners. In Mental health basics for correctional officers. Lincoln, NE: Nebraska Department of Public Institutions.

723.   Salive, M.E. (1990). Series of jail suicides in Dade County, Florida. Medicine, Science and the Law, 30, 273.

724.   Skegg, K., & Cox, B. (1991). Impact of psychiatric services on prison suicide. Lancet, 338(8780), 1436-1438.

725.   Sloane, B.C. (1973). Suicide attempts in the District of Columbia prison system. Omega: Journal of Death and Dying, 4, 37-50.

726.   Sovronsky, H.R., & Shapiro, I. (1989). The New York State Model Suicide Prevention Training Program for local corrections officers. Psychiatric Quarterly, 60, 139-149.
Describes the four components of a training program for correctional officers that enables these officers to better identify and manage suicidal and mentally ill inmates.

The program includes a training manual, and interactive videotape, and officer handbook, and pre- and post-evaluations leading to certification.

727.   Spellman, A., & Heyne, B. (1989). Suicide? Accident? Predictable? Avoidable? The psychological autopsy in jail suicides. Psychiatric Quarterly, 60, 173-183.

728.   Stone, W.E. (1984). Means of the cause of death in Texas jail suicides. Americas Jails, 4, 50-53.

729.   Thorburn, K.M. (1984). Self-mutilation and self-induced illness in prison. Journal of Prison and Jail Health, 4, 40-51.

730.   Topp, D.O. (1979). Suicide in prison. British Journal of Psychiatry, 134, 24-27. Findings of a study of 186 prison suicides suggest that suicide is 3 times more likely in a prison population than the general population, that the most salient predictor of prison suicide are sentences of more than 18 months, and that suicide is most likely to be committed in the first few weeks of incarceration.

731.   Winfree, L.T. (1988). Rethinking American jail death rates. Policy Studies Review, 7, 641-659.

732.   Winkler, G.E. (1992). Assessing and responding to suicidal jail inmates. Community Mental Health Journal, 28, 317-326.
Based on a literature review and personal experience, the author discusses suicidal risk among jail inmates. Intoxication, isolation, and the initial 24 hours of incarceration are considered to be among the most significant risk factors.

733.   Wooldredge, J.D., & Winfree, L.T. (1992). An aggregate-level study of inmate suicides and deaths due to natural causes in U.S. jails. Journal of Research in Crime and Delinquency, 29, 466-479.
In a study of possible influences on number of inmate suicides in 204 U.S. jails, using both crosssectional and longitudinal data, it was found that suicides had become less prevalent over time in larger, urban facilities where inmate suicide potential was routinely assessed. Suicides were also less prevalent in jails with the highest staff-to-inmate ratios.

10

Violence and Aggression

734.   Adams, J.J., Meloy, J.R., & Moritz, M.S. (1990). Neuropsychological deficits and
        violent behavior in incarcerated schizophrenics. Journal of Nervous and Mental
        Disease, 178, 253-256.
        Based on scores on the Luria-Nebraska Battery, 12 of 37 schizophrenics in a county
        jail psychiatric unit were classified as neuropsychologically impaired. Compared to
        unimpaired schizophrenics, the impaired group had longer adult histories of violence
        and arrests for violent offenses, but were not rated by clinicians as more violent
        while they were hospitalized.

735.   Adams, K.A. (1974). The child who murders. Criminal Justice and Behavior, 1, 51-
        61.

736.   American Psychiatric Association. (1974). Clinical aspects of the violent individual.
        Task Force Report #8. Washington, DC: Author.

737.   Andrew, J.M. (1974). Violent crime indices among community-retained delinquents.
        Criminal Justice and Behavior, 1, 123-130.

738.   Ashford, J.B. (1989). Offense comparisons between mentally disordered and
        non-mentally disordered inmates. Canadian Journal of Criminology, 31, 35-48.
        A case control study of mentally disordered and nonmentally disordered inmates in
        an urban jail found that when compared on current offense, history of violence, and
        criminal history, mentally disordered offenders were more likely to have a history
        of violence than were nonmentally disordered offenders. No differences in criminal
        history were found.

739. Barnard, G.W., Robbins, L., Newman, G., & Carrera, F. (1984). A study of violence within a forensic treatment facility. Bulletin of the American Academy of Psychiatry and the Law, 12, 339-348.
Investigated the incidence of four types of aggressive acts (passive aggression, verbal abuse, threats of violence, and acts of violence) at a maximum security treatment facility for mentally disordered offenders over a four month period. All of the 188 incidents recorded were committed by about 25% of the 255 patients. Findings show that environmental factors were more important in explaining institutional violence than were more traditional predictors such as race or diagnosis.

740. Belfrage, H., Lidberg, L., & Oreland, L. (1992). Platelet monoamine oxidase activity in mentally disordered violent offenders. Acta Psychiatrica Scandinavica, 85, 218-221.
Found that there was lower monoamine oxidase (MAO) activity in violent offenders (n=37) than in non-violent offenders (n=22) and that the difference increased when history of psychosis was controlled. Among those participants who were mentally disordered, there was no difference in MAO activity for violent and non-violent offenders.

741. Beran, N.J., & Hotz, A.M. (1984). The behavior of mentally disordered criminals in civil mental hospitals. Hospital and Community Psychiatry, 35, 585-589.
Compared 393 civil admission patients and 404 forensic patients in 4 Ohio state civil mental hospitals on demographic, diagnostic and behavioral variables. Few differences were found. However, forensic patients were higher on some indices of dangerousness, were more likely to leave without discharge, and to be described as manipulative by staff. Civil patients were more often involved in violence and property damage and reported more frequent placement in restraints and seclusion. The authors conclude that differences in the mental disorders of forensic and civil patients have been exaggerated and that the need for different treatment modalities is unwarranted.

742. Bergman, B., & Brismar, B. (1994). Characteristics of imprisoned wife-beaters. Forensic Science International, 65, 157-167.

743. Blankstein, H. (1988). Organizational approaches to improving institutional estimations of dangerousness in forensic psychiatric hospitals: A Dutch perspective. Special Issue: Forensic administration. International Journal of Law and Psychiatry, 11, 341-345.
Discusses organizational characteristics of a treatment setting that are important to effective treatment and to more accurate predictions of dangerous behavior. These characteristics include adequate information flow about patient behavior and treatment progress, division of responsibility for treatment and policy decisions, confidentiality, and the need to build social networks for patients once they return to the community.

744. Bourget, D., & Labelle, A. (1992). Homicide, infanticide, and filicide. Psychiatric Clinics of North America, 15, 661-673.

Discusses homicidal behavior in relation to developmental, environmental, and clinical factors. Homicide is best viewed as a multifaceted phenomenon in which multiple causes hinder unitary prevention strategies.

745. Brown, C.R. (1978). The use of benzodiazepines in prison populations. Journal of Clinical Psychiatry, 39, 219-222.
Findings of a study of the use of benzodiazepines in anxiety control in a prison populations found that the benefits derived in terms of patient control were outweighed by frequent appearance of paradoxical rage reactions and increases in hostility and aggressive behaviors. However, findings indicate that Serax was superior to Valium in terms of antianxiety qualities and side effects of rage and aggression.

746. Campion, J.F., Cravens, J.M., & Covan, Fred (1988). A study of filicidal men. American Journal of Psychiatry, 145, 1141-1144.
A study of 12 filicidal men found that most suffered from severe mental impairments due to psychosis, neurological disorders, substance abuse, or mental retardation. Most of the filicidal acts committed resulted from isolated explosive behavior.

747. Chamberlain, T.J. (1986). The dynamics of parricide. American Journal of Forensic Psychiatry, 7, 11-23.

748. Clannon, T.L., & Jew, C. (1985). Predictions from assessments of violent offenders under stress: A fifteen year experience. Criminal Justice and Behavior, 12, 485-499.

749. Clarke, J.W. (1990). On being mad or merely angry: John W. Hinckley, Jr., and other dangerous people. Princeton, NJ: Princeton University Press.

750. Cocozza, J., & Steadman, H.J. (1974). Some refinements in the measurement and prediction of dangerous behavior. American Journal of Psychiatry, 131, 1012-1020. KW ASSESSING

751. Cocozza, J., Melick, M., & Steadman, H.J. (1978). Trends in violent crime among ex-mental patients. Criminology, 16, 317-334.

752. Cohen, M., Groth, A., & Seigel, R. (1978). The clinical prediction of dangerousness. Crime and Delinquency, 1, 28-39. KW

753. Colaizzi, J. (1989). Homicidal insanity, 1800-1985. Tuscaloosa, AL: The University of Alabama Press.

754. Copello, A.G., & Tata, P.R. (1990). Violent behaviour and interpretative bias: An experimental study of the resolution of ambiguity in violent offenders. British Journal of Psychology, 29, 417-428.
Studies differences in interpretation of sentences that ambiguous for violent or neutral meaning across three groups, violent offenders, non-violent offenders, and non-offenders. Results indicate that both offender groups interpreted ambiguous violent sentences as more threatening than did the non-offender group. This tendency to infer violent threat was found to correlate with hostility.

755. Craven, J.M, et al. (1985). A study of 10 men charged with patricide. <u>American Journal of Psychiatry</u>, <u>142</u>, 1089-1092.

756. Dabbs, J.M., Jr., Jurkovic, G.J., & Frady, R.L. (1991). Salivary testosterone and cortisol among late adolescent male offenders. <u>Journal of Abnormal Child Psychology</u>, <u>19</u>, 469-78.
A study relating levels of salivary testosterone and cortisol concentration to personality, criminal violence, prison behavior and parole board decisions among 113 adolescent offenders found that offenders high in testosterone committed more violent crimes, were judged more harshly by the parole board, and violated prison rules more often than those low in testosterone. No main effects for cortisol emerged. However, as expected, a significant interaction between testosterone and cortisol was found, in which cortisol moderated the correlation between testosterone and violence of crime. Measures of personality and behavior showed little relationship to hormones.

757. Daniel, C. (1992). Anger control bibliotherapy with a convicted murderer under life sentence: A clinical report. <u>Journal of Offender Rehabilitation</u>, <u>18</u>, 91-100.

758. Elliot, F. (1978). Neurological factors in violent behavior (the dyscontrol syndrome). In R. Sadoff (Ed.), <u>Violence and responsibility</u>. New York: Spectrum.

759. Farley, G., Sikorski, C., & Benedek, E.P. (1975). Dissociation and violence. <u>Psychiatric Opinion</u>, <u>12</u>, 36-42

760. Feldman, M., Mallouh, K., & Lewis, D.O. (1986). Filicidal abuse in the histories of 15 condemned murderers. <u>Bulletin of the American Academy of Psychiatry and the Law</u>, <u>14</u>, 345-352.
Explored in depth the characteristics the families of origin of 15 murderers on death row through interviews with relatives, psychiatric evaluations, and official records and found evidence of extraordinary physical and/or sexual abuse by parents of the inmates in 13 cases, and murderous behaviors of parents in 8 cases. The mechanisms by which parental violence is linked to violent behaviors are discussed.

761. Feldman, T.B., Johnson, P.W., & Bell, R.A. (1990). Cofactors in the commission of violent crimes: A self-psychology examination. <u>American Journal of Psychotherapy</u>, <u>44</u>, 172-179.
Argues that many violent crimes are precipitated or elicited by interpersonal situations which interact with perpetrator personality factors, often narcissistic or borderline pathology, to produce violent outcomes. Through the use of 2 case examples, the authors use a self-psychology framework to explain the violence process.

762. Fendrich, M., Mackesy-Amiti, M.E., Goldstein, P., Spunt, B., & Brownstein, H. (1995). Substance involvement among juvenile murderers: Comparisons with older offenders based on interviews with prison inmates. <u>International Journal of the Addictions</u>, <u>30</u>, 1363-1382.
Evaluated substance involvement among incarcerated juvenile offenders convicted of murder or manslaughter. Patterns of substance use among juvenile offenders were

compared with patterns found in older offenders. In both age groups, nearly 1/3 of homicide perpetrators reported that they were affected by alcohol prior to the offense. In every age group, alcohol was the substance showing the highest rate of "regular" lifetime use and the highest rate of ingestion in the week preceding the homicide.

763.   Fisher, R. (1976). Factors influencing the prediction of dangerousness: Authoritarianism, dogmatism, and data quality. Unpublished doctoral dissertation, Department of Psychology, University of Alabama.

764.   Gordon, R. (1977). A critique of the evaluation of Patuxent Institution, with particular attention to the issues of dangerousness and recidivism. Bulletin of the American Academy of Psychiatry and the Law, 5, 210-255.

765.   Gottlieb, P., & Gabrielsen, G. (1990). The future of homicide offenders: Results from a homicide project in Copenhagen. International Journal of Law and Psychiatry, 13, 191-205.

766.   Gottschalk, L.A., Rebello, T., Buchsbaum, M.S., Tucker, H.G., & Hodges, E.L. (1991). Abnormalities in hair trace elements as indicators of aberrant behavior. Comprehensive Psychiatry, 32, 229-237.
       It has been suggested that impulsive and violent behavior may stem from brain dysfunction or damage secondary to head injury, disease, or toxic chemical substances. This study examined the relationship between potentially toxic metals and aberrant behavior, especially violent activity, through the nonintrusive technique of hair analysis for trace elements. Results suggested that significantly higher levels of manganese were found in violent versus non-violent offenders.

767.   Greene, A.F., Coles, C.J., Johnson, E.H. (1994). Psychopathology and anger in interpersonal violence offenders. Journal of Clinical Psychology, 50, 906-912.
       A study of 40 men ordered referred for anger-management psychotherapy found 4 clusters of interpersonal violence offenders based on scores form the MMPI and the State-Trait Anger Expression Inventory. The most pathological cluster type reported the highest level of total anger experience, while the histrionic cluster type reported the lowest anger expression. Results provide some support for a positive relationship between psychopathology and anger, as well as for the distinction between overcontrolled and undercontrolled anger in subtypes of interpersonal violence offenders.

768.   Grunberg, F., Klinger, B.I., and Grumet, B.R. (1977). Homicide and the deinstitutionalization of the mentally ill. American Journal of Psychiatry, 134, 685-687.

769.   Hambridge, J.A. (1990). The grief process in those admitted to Regional Secure Units following homicide. Journal of Forensic Sciences, 35, 1149-1154.

770.   Hamparian, D., Schuster, R., Dinitz, S., & Conrad, J. (1978). The violent few: A study of dangerous juvenile offenders. Lexington, MA: Lexington Books.

771.   Hart, S.D., Kropp, P.R., Roesch, R., Ogloff, J.R.P., et al. (1994). Wife assault in community-resident offenders. Canadian Journal of Criminology, 36, 435-446.
Findings of a study of prevalence of wife assault in a random sample of 256 offenders on bail, probation, or parole, showed that 21.5% of male offenders in the region had a documented current or lifetime history of wife assault. In comparison to other offenders, those in the assaultive group were more likely to be older, involved in a current relationship, member of an ethnic minority, and on probation.

772.   Hillbrand, M., Foster, H.G., & Hirt, M. (1988). Variables associated with violence in a forensic population. Journal of Interpersonal Violence, 3, 371-380.
Eighty-five male forensic hospital patients were classified as violent or nonviolent and were administered a self-report questionnaire assessing personality traits. Results indicate that a characterological type of dysphoria was found to have the strongest association with violence, followed by the absence of temporal lobe damage and a passive style of response to threat.

773.   Hodgins, S., & Cote, G. (1993). The criminality of mentally disordered offenders. Criminal Justice and Behavior, 20, 115-129.

774.   Holcomb, W.R., & Adams, N. (1982). Racial influences on intelligence and personality measures of people who commit murder. Journal of Clinical Psychology, 38, 793-796.
137 persons (91 whites and 46 blacks) who were charged with first degree murder and admitted to a state forensic unit were administered the MMPI, the Peabody Picture Vocabulary Test and the Revised Beta Examination. Results show that blacks scored significantly lower than whites on both verbal and nonverbal intelligence and on the Social Introversion Scale of the MMPI. However, they scored higher on the Hypomania scale. Overall, the intelligence measures discriminated better between black and white offenders than did the personality measures. Implications for future research are discussed.

775.   Howells, K. (1982). Aggression: Clinical approaches to treatment. Issues in Criminological and Legal Psychology, 2, 26-33.

776.   Hunter, M., & Carmel, H. (1992). The cost of staff injuries from inpatient violence. Hospital and Community Psychiatry, 43, 586-588.
In a study of the cost figures of 134 employee injuries resulting from inpatient violence at a state forensic hospital it was found that injuries resulting from battery were more costly than containment-related injuries, that injuries to female employees, especially from battery, were more costly than injuries to males, and that a major proportion of workers' compensation costs went to a small number of employees who litigated their cases and did not return to work.

777.   Hurley, W. (1972). Psychiatry and the dangerous offender. Medical Journal of Australia, 1, 283-284.

778.   Justice, B., Justice, R., & Kraft, J. (1974). Early warning signs of violence: Is a triad enough? American Journal of Psychiatry, 131, 457-459.

779.   Klabucar, L., & Pavlic, M. (1986). Group psychotherapy of schizophrenic murderers. Socijalna Psihijjtrija, 14, 63-70.

780.   Kozol, H. (1975). The diagnosis of dangerousness. In S. Pasternack (Ed.), Violence and victims. New York: Spectrum.

781.   Kozol, H., Boucher, R., & Garofolo, R. (1972). The diagnosis and treatment of dangerousness. Crime and Delinquency, 18, 371-392.

782.   Kozol, H., Boucher, R., & Garofolo, R. (1973). Dangerousness: A reply to Monahan. Crime and Delinquency, 19, 554-555.

783.   Kuhlman, T. (1988). Gallows humor for a scaffold setting: Managing aggressive patients on a maximum-security forensic unit. Hospital and Community Psychiatry, 39, 1085-1090.

784.   Lavergne, M.P., & Lavergne, T. (1990). A father, murderer of his two daughters. Information Psychiatrique, 66, 669-676.

785.   Levine, D. (1977). The concept of dangerousness: Criticism and compromise. In B. Sales (Ed.), Psychology in the legal process. New York: Spectrum.

786.   Lira, F.T., Fagan, T.J., & White, M.J. (1979). Violent behavior and differential WAIS characteristics among black prison inmates. Psychological Reports, 45, 356-358.

787.   Lurigio, A.J., & Lewis, D.A. (1987). The criminal mental patient: A descriptive analysis and suggestions for future research. Criminal Justice and Behavior, 14, 268-287.

788.   Maier, G.J. (1976). Therapy in prisons. In J.R. Lion & D.J. Madden (Eds.), Rage, hate, assault and other forms of violence (pp. 113-133). New York: Spectrum.

789.   Mandelzys, N., Lane, E.B., & Marceau, R. (1981). The relationship of violence to alpha levels in a biofeedback training paradigm, Journal of Clinical Psychology, 37, 202-209.

790.   Mark, V.H., & Ervin, F.R. (1970). Violence and the brain. New York: Harper & Row.

791.   Martell, D.A. (1991). Homeless mentally disordered offenders and violent crimes: Preliminary research findings. Law and Human Behavior, 15, 333-347.
       Studied the rate of homelessness in a population of 150 maximum security forensic patients and found that forensic patients were 25 times more likely to be homeless than non-incarcerated mentally ill persons and 50 times more likely to be homeless than the general population. Results suggest that homelessness increases the risk of forensic hospitalization among the mentally ill and is highly related to indictments for violent crimes.

792.   Martell, D.A., & Dietz, P.E. (1992). Mentally disordered offenders who push or attempt to push victims onto subway tracks in New York City. Archives of General Psychiatry, 49, 472-475.

793.   McDougall, C., & Boddis, S. (1991). Discrimination between anger and aggression: Implications for treatment. Issues in Criminological and Legal Psychology, 2(17), 101-106.

794.   McGuire, J. (1976). Prediction of dangerous behavior in a federal correctional institution. Unpublished doctoral dissertation, Department of Psychology, Florida State University.

795.   Megargee, E. (1973). Recent research on overcontrolled and undercontrolled personality patterns among violent offenders. Sociological Symposium, 9, 37-50.

796.   Megargee, E.I. (1976). The prediction of dangerous behavior. Criminal Justice and Behavior, 3, 3-21.

797.   Megargee, E.I. (1986). A psychometric study of incarcerated presidential threateners. Criminal Justice and Behavior, 13, 243-260.
Compared MMPI scores of 45 presidential threateners and 48 nonthreateners evaluated at mental health facilities for federal prisoners and found that threateners' MMPI profiles and were more elevated and that classifications into Megargee's (1979) MMPI-based typology of offenders were significantly more deviant than in previously tested samples. Threateners tended to be more anti-social and prone to violence than had been previously suggested.

798.   Menuck, M. (1983). Clinical aspects of dangerous behavior. Journal of Psychiatry and Law, 11, 277-304.

799.   Menzies, R.J., Webster, C.D., & Sepejak, D.S. (1987). "At the mercy of the mad": Examining the relationship between violence and mental illness. Advances in Forensic Psychology and Psychiatry, 2, 63-100.
Investigated the relationship between mental illness and violence in persons referred to a forensic clinic from the criminal courts for pretrial assessment. Results indicate little evidence of heightened frequency of violence among mentally disordered forensic patients.

800.   Meyer, C.K. (1982). An analysis of factors related to robbery-associated assaults on police officers: II. Journal of Police Science and Administration, 10, 127-150.
Presents data on the officer and assailant characteristics in robbery-related assaults on police officers. Victimized officers tended to be younger, with lower rank and experience. Assailants tended to be male, non-white, and to have previous criminal records. Assailants were also predominately from lower socioeconomic groups and tended to be unemployed. Contrary to findings from studies of general police assaults, few of the assailants in robbery-related assaults showed signs of mental derangement or were under the influence of drugs or alcohol.

801.	Miller, R.D., & Maier, G.J. (1992). Factors affecting the decision to prosecute mental patients for criminal behavior. Hospital and Community Psychiatry, 38, 50-55.
	Discusses, through the use of 4 case examples, the factors affecting decisions by hospital staff to prosecute patients for assaultive or criminal behavior. The changes in the profile of the public mental hospital patient and the implications of these changes on therapeutic relationships and the therapist's responsibility for to protect the public from patient's behavior are discussed along with the need to educate mental health and legal professionals with regard to the prosecution of psychiatric patients.

802.	Monahan, J. (1973). Dangerous offenders: A critique of Kozol, et al. Crime and Delinquency, 19, 418-420.

803.	Monahan, J. (1976). The prevention of violence. In J. Monahan (Ed.), Community mental health and the criminal justice system. New York: Pergamon Press.

804.	Monahan, J. (1977). Strategies for empirical analysis of the prediction of violence in civil commitment. Law and Human Behavior, 1, 363-371.

805.	Monahan, J. (1978). Prediction research and the emergency commitment of dangerous mentally ill persons: A reconsideration. American Journal of Psychiatry, 135, 198-201.

806.	Monahan, J. (1978). The prediction of violent criminal behavior: A methodological critique and prospectus. In A. Blumstein, J. Cohen, & D Nagin (Eds.), Deterrence and incapacitation: Estimating the effects of criminal sanctions on crime rates. Washington, DC: National Academy of Sciences.

807.	Monahan, J. (1981). The clinical prediction of violent behavior. Rockville, MD: National Institute of Mental Health.

808.	Monahan, J. (1992). Mental disorder and violent behavior: Perceptions and evidence. American Psychologist, 47, 511-521.
	Noting the widespread public and professional perception that mentally ill persons are more violent than the non-mentally ill, and the numerous studies that purport to show a negative relation between mental illness and violence, the author presents evidence from a number of sources to support the notion that there is a positive, albeit moderate, relationship between mental illness and violence.

809.	Monahan, J., & Cummings, L. (1975). The prediction of dangerousness as a function of its perceived consequences. Journal of Criminal Justice, 2, 239-242.

810.	Monahan, J., & Geis, G. (1976). Controlling "dangerous" people. Annals of the American Academy of Political and Social Science, 423, 142-151.

811.	Monahan, J., & Hood, G. (1978). Ascriptions of dangerousness: The eye (and age, sex, education, location, and politics) of the beholder. In R. Simon (Ed.), Research in law and sociology. Greenwich, CT: Johnson.

812.   Mullen, J.M., Dudley, H.K., Craig, E.M. (1978). Dangerousness and the mentally ill offender: Results of a pilot survey. Hospital and Community Psychiatry, 29, 424-425.

813.   Murdoch, D., Pihl, R.D., & Ross, D. (1990). Alcohol and crimes of violence: Present issues. International Journal of the Addictions, 25, 1065-1081.
        Reviewed correlational studies between alcohol and violent crime and found that alcohol is associated with violent crime at a greater than chance level than is nonviolent crime, with heavy drinking a verbal arguments usually preceding the violent act. The research also indicates that victims are equally as likely as offenders to initiate the altercation, but the perpetrator is more likely to be intoxicated. Concomitant psychopathology exacerbates the connection between alcohol and violent crime. However, due to the nature of most studies, establishment of causal links between alcohol and violent crime is prohibited.

814.   Myers, W.C., & Mutch, P.J. (1992). Language disorders in disruptive behavior disordered homicidal youth. Journal of Forensic Sciences, 37, 919-922.

815.   National Council on Crime and Delinquency, Board of Directors. (1973). The non-dangerous offender should not be imprisoned: A policy statement. Crime and Delinquency, 19, 449-456.

816.   Norton, S.C. (1988). Predictor variables of violent behavior. American Journal of Forensic Psychology, 6, 53-66.
        Studied case histories of 93 violent and 109 nonviolent adult male prisoners committed to a psychiatric hospital and found that certain characteristics distinguished violent from nonviolent offenders. Twenty-one variables were associated violent group with available weapon and specific victim being the most salient. Seven variables were associated with membership in the nonviolent group, with history of minor charges being the most salient

817.   Palmer, S., & Humphrey, J.A. (1980). Offender-victim relationships in criminal homicide followed by offender's suicide, North Carolina, 1972-1977. Suicide and Life Threatening Behavior, 10, 106-118.

818.   Perkins, D. (1983). Assessment and treatment of dangerous sexual offenders. In J. Hinton (Ed.), Dangerousness: Problems of assessment and prediction. London: Allen & Unwin.

819.   Pfohl, S. (1977). The psychiatric assessment of dangerousness: Practical problems and political implications. In J. Conrad, & S. Dinitz (Eds.), In fear of each other. Lexington, MA: Lexington Books.

820.   Pihl, R.O., & Ervin, F. (1990). Lead and cadmium levels in violent criminals. Psychological Reports, 66, 839-844.

821.   Prins, H. (1990). Some observations on the supervision of dangerous offender patients. British Journal of Psychiatry, 156, 157-162.

822.   Prins, H. (1990). The supervision of potentially dangerous offender-patients in England and Wales. International Journal of Offender Therapy and Comparative Criminology, 34, 213-221.

823.   Quinsey, V.L., & Ambtman, R. (1979). Variables affecting psychiatrists' and teachers' assessments of the dangerousness of mentally ill offenders. Journal of Consulting and Clinical Psychology, 47, 353-362

824.   Rabiner, C.J. (1992). Releasing NGRI offenders: The Larsen case. Psychiatric Annals, 22, 574-578.

825.   Raine, A. (1993). Features of borderline personality and violence. Journal of Clinical Psychology, 49, 277-281.
        A study of borderline and schizotypal personality in 3 groups of male prisoners: murderers, violent offenders, and nonviolent offenders, found that murderers had higher borderline personality scores than did nonviolent offenders. No group differences were observed for schizotypal personality. Borderline traits associated with extreme violence consisted of unstable, intense relationships and affective instability.

826.   Rappeport, J.R. (1973). A response to "Implications from the Baxtrom experience." Bulletin of the American Academy of Psychiatry and the Law, 1, 197-198.

827.   Rector, M. (1973). Who are the dangerous? Bulletin of the American Academy of Psychiatry and the Law, 1, 186-188.

828.   Rennie, Y. (1978). The search for criminal man: A conceptual history of the dangerous offender. Lexington, MA: Lexington Books.

829.   Rice, M.E., & Harris, G.T. (1991). Firesetters admitted to a maximum security psychiatric institution: Offenders and offenses. Journal of Interpersonal Violence, 6, 461-475.
        Compared 243 male arsonists in a maximum security psychiatric facility with 100 non-arsonists admitted to the same institution and found that the arsonist group was more likely to be less socially isolated and less likely to be socially competent. Further, few mentally disordered firesetters were characterized by either pyromania, as determined by DSM-III-R criteria, or sexual motivation for firesetting.

830.   Rizzo, N.D. (1982). Murder in Boston: Killers and their victims. International Journal of Offender Therapy and Comparative Criminology, 26, 36-42.
        Based on court data of 243 accused murderers (14-67 yrs old), the authors report that: (1) 90% of all alleged murders were committed by males (average age = 26 yrs); (2) Most cases involved acquaintances, friends or relatives; (3) Controlled drugs (heroin, cocaine, hashish, PCP, marijuana) were the principle substances in illicit transactions complicated by murder; (4) Few cases of murder were committed for sexual thrills; and (5) The smallest proportion of murders were committed by the mentally ill.

831. Roth, L.H. (1978). Clinical and legal considerations in the therapy of violence-prone patients. In J. Masserman (Ed.), Current psychiatric therapies. New York: Grune & Stratton.

832. Rubin, B. (1972). Prediction of dangerousness in mentally ill criminals. Archives of General Psychiatry, 72, 397-407.

833. Scarnati, R., Madry, M.A., Wise, A., Moore, H.D., et al. (1991). Religious beliefs and practices among most-dangerous psychiatric inmates. Forensic Reports, 4, 1-16.

834. Scarnati, R.A. (1986). Most-violent psychiatric inmates and neuroleptics. Journal of Psychiatry and Law, 14, 447-468.
The benefits of neuroleptics in the control of violent episodes were studied with a sample of 47 violent adult psychiatric inmates. Subjects were more likely to develop a therapeutic alliance after benefits of the therapy became apparent. The authors also note some success with using carbamazepine in combination with lithium carbonate in reducing violence in a bipolar patient.

835. Scarnati, R.A. (1992). Prison psychiatrist's role in a residential treatment unit of dangerous psychiatric inmates. Forensic Reports, 5, 367-384.

836. Scott, P. (1977). Assessing dangerousness in criminals. British Journal of Psychiatry, 131, 127-142.

837. Serin, R.C. (1991). Psychopathology and violence in criminals. Journal of Interpersonal Violence, 6, 423-431.
Studied the relationship between criminal psychopathology and violent behavior and found that psychopaths scored higher than non-psychopaths on measures of impulsiveness and aggression and were more likely to act violently, to have committed more crimes involving weapons, threats, and instrumental aggression, and to have been abused as children. Violent psychopaths felt more anger and attributed greater hostile intent to others than violent non-psychopaths when presented with hypothetical frustrating situations.

838. Shaffer, C.E., Jr., Waters, W.F., & Adams, S.G., Jr. (1994). Dangerousness: Assessing the risk of violent behavior. Journal of Consulting and Clinical Psychology, 62, 1064-1068.
Studied a hospital sample (N = 100) to determine which factors discriminated dangerous from non-dangerous patients. Discriminant analysis yielded a discriminant function containing 5 variables, which correctly classified 85% of the sample. Analysis of a prison sample (N = 100) yielded a discriminant model with 6 variables, correctly classified 72% of the sample. A discriminant analysis of the combined sample (N = 200) yielded a discriminant function containing 8 variables, which correctly classified 75% of the sample. The authors conclude that population-specific models were the most valid.

839. Shah, S.A. (1975). Dangerousness and civil commitment of the mentally ill: Some public policy considerations. American Journal of Psychiatry, 132, 505-505.

840.   Shah, S.A. (1977). Dangerousness: Some definitional, conceptual and public policy issues. In B. Sales (Ed.), Perspectives in law and psychology. New York: Plenum.

841.   Shah, S.A. (1978). Dangerousness and mental illness. Some conceptual, prediction and policy dilemmas. In C. Frederick (Ed.), Dangerous behavior: A problem in law and mental health. DHEW Pub. No. (ADM) 78-563. Rockville, MD: NIMH.

842.   Shah, S.A. (1978). Dangerousness: A paradigm for exploring some issues in law and psychology. American Psychologist, 33, 224-238.

843.   Shah, S.A. (1981). Dangerousness: Conceptual, prediction, and public policy issues. In J.R. Hays, T.K. Roberts, & K.S. Solway (Eds.), Violence and the violent individual. New York, NY: SP Medical & Scientific Books.

844.   Sigal, M., Altmark, D., & Gelkopf, M. (1001). Munchausen syndrome by adult proxy revisited. Israel Journal for Psychiatry and Related Sciences, 28, 33-36.

845.   Silberman, C.E. (1978). Criminal violence, criminal justice. New York: Random House.

846.   Siomopoulos, V. (1979). Drug involvement in crimes committed by mentally ill offenders. Psychological Reports, 45, 875-879.

847.   Sosowsky, L. (1978). Crime and violence among mental patients reconsidered in view of the new legal relationship between the state and the mentally ill. American Journal of Psychiatry, 135, 33-42.

848.   Steadman, H.J. (1981). Critically reassessing the accuracy of public predictions of the dangerousness of the mentally ill. Journal of Health and Social Behavior, 22, 310-316.

849.   Sterling, S., Edelmann, R.J. (1988). Reactions to anger and anxiety provoking events: Psychopathic and nonpsychopathic groups compared. Journal of Clinical Psychology, 44, 96-100.
        A study of the cognitive appraisals and anticipated reactions of self and others made by a group of psychopathic offenders (N = 17) and a group of nonpsychopathic, non-offenders after being presented with scenarios depicting anxiety-provoking and anger provoking situations found that psychopathic offenders tended to rate the anxiety provoking situations as more anxiety and threat inducing than did controls. Further, the psychopathic subjects saw both types of scenario as more anger inducing than did controls. The implications of findings for cognitive-oriented interventions dealing with anger management are discussed.

850.   Stermac, L.E. (1986). Anger control treatment for forensic patients. Journal of Interpersonal Violence, 1, 446-457.
        Evaluated the efficacy of a brief cognitive-behavioral anger control intervention in combination with stress inoculation treatment with 40 forensic patients, half of whom received the cognitive-behavioral intervention and half of whom received a control psychoeducational treatment (random assignment), and found greater

improvements in anger, impulsivity, and coping between pre- and pot-intervention testing for the cognitive-behavioral group than the psychoeducational group.

851. Stokman, C.L. (1984). Dangerousness and violence in hospitalized mentally ill offenders. Psychiatric Quarterly, 56, 138-143.
Presents an interactive framework involving both organismic and environmental variables in both determining the likelihood, type, and severity of violent episodes and in the clinical judgement process. Suggestions for improving the predictive validity of assessments of dangerousness are presented.

852. Tardiff, K. (1992). Mentally abnormal offenders: Evaluation and management of violence. Psychiatric Clinics of North America, 15, 553-567.

853. Tennent, T.G. (1975). The dangerous offender. British Journal of Psychiatry, Spec #9, 308-315.

854. Tingle, D., Barnard, G.W., Robbins, L., Newman, G., et al. (1986). Childhood and adolescent characteristics of pedophiles and rapists. International Journal of Law and Psychiatry, 9, 103-116.
Studied 64 consecutive voluntary admissions to a program for mentally disordered sex offenders and found that developmental differences between pedophiles and rapists were evident even in early youth. Rapists were more likely to come from disruptive families and to have histories of violence while pedophiles were more likely to have close attachments to their mothers.

855. Tobey, L.H., & Bruhn, A.R. (1992). Early memories and the criminally dangerous. Journal of Personality Assessment, 59, 137-152.
Using the Early Memory Aggressiveness Potential Score System (EMAPSS), 73% of criminally dangerous (N = 30) and nondangerous (N = 30) forensic patients were correctly classified with 15 of 16 (94%) classified as dangerous actually being dangerous.

856. Toch, H. (1977). Police, prisons, and the problem of violence. National Institute of Mental Health. DHEW Pub. No. (ADM)76-364. Washington, DC: U.S. Government Printing Office.

857. Toch, H. (1981). Psychological treatment of imprisoned offenders. In S. Hays, T. Roberts, A Freedman, and B. Sadok (Eds.), Violence and the violent individual. New York: Medical and Scientific Books.

858. Toch, H., & Adams, K. (1989). The disturbed violent offender. New Haven, CT: Yale University Press.

859. Van Dine, S., Dinitz, S., & Conrad, J. (1978). The incapacitation of the dangerous offender: A statistical experiment. In J. Conrad & S. Dinitz (Eds.), In fear of each other. Lexington, MA: Lexington Books.

860. Volavka, J., Mertell, D., & Convit, A. (1992). Psychobiology of the violent offender. Journal of Forensic Science, 37, 237-251.

The authors suggest that, along with psychosocial antecedents of violent crime, such as childhood victimization, alcohol and drug abuse, and head injuries, neuropsychological findings suggest that temporal and frontal lobe dysfunctions, especially in the dominant hemisphere, are also associated with violent offending, while other studies indicate a relationship between central serotonergic functions are associated with impulsive homicide and arson. The authors conclude that these findings support an interdisciplinary approach to violent offending, using neurochemical, neuropsychological, and psychosocial approaches together in future research with violent offenders.

861. Walker, N. (1991). Dangerous mistakes. British Journal of Psychiatry, 158, 752-757.

862. Webster, C.D. (1990). Prediction of dangerousness polemic. Canadian Journal of Criminology, 32, 191-196.

863. Wenk, E., Robison, J., & Smith, G. (1972). Can violence be predicted? Crime and Delinquency, 18, 393-402.

864. Wexler, D.B. (1976). Criminal commitments and dangerous mental patients: Legal issues of confinement, treatment, and release. National Institute of Mental Health. DHEW Pub. No. (ADM)72-9129. Washington, DC: U.S. Government Printing Office.

865. Whiteford, H.A., & Westmore, B. (1991). Biopsychosocial psychiatry and the criminal justice system: A case report. Australian and New Zealand Journal of Psychiatry, 25, 211-214.

866. Wilcox, D.E. (1987). Characteristics of seventy-one convicted murderers. American Journal of Forensic Psychiatry, 7, 48-52.

867. Williams, W., & Miller, K. (1977). The role of personal characteristics in perceptions of dangerousness. Criminal Justice and Behavior, 4, 421.

868. Yelsma, P., & Yelsma, J. (1977). Self-esteem of prisoners committing directly versus indirectly destructive crimes. Perceptual and Motor Skills, 44, 375-380.

869. Zitrin, A., Hardesty, A.S., & Burdock, E.I. (1976). Crime and violence among mental patients. American Journal of Psychiatry, 133, 142-149.

870. Zona, M.A., Sharma, K.K., & Lane, J. (1993). A comparative study of erotomanic and obsessional subjects in a forensic sample. Journal of Forensic Sciences, 38, 894-903.
In a study of 74 case files of the Threat Management Unit of the Los Angeles Police Department, three distinct clusters of obsessional offenders were differentiated: (1) erotomanics, (2) love obsessionals, and (3) general obsessional. The general obsessional category contained offenders who harassed persons they had once had either a casual or intimate relationship with, while erotomanics harassed strangers. The love obsessionals were similar to the erotomanics, except that other delusions

about the victim also accompanied the erotomanic delusion. The three groups differed on several variables other than relationships with victims, with the erotomanic group having longer histories of psychiatric disturbance and more severe symptoms than the other groups.

11

Sex Offenders

871.   Abel, G.G., Barlow, D., Blanchard, E., & Guild, D. (1977). The components of rapists' sexual arousal. Archives of General Psychiatry, 34, 895-903.

872.   Abel, G.G., Blanchard, E.B., Becker, J.V., & Djenderedijian, A. (1978). Differentiating sexual aggressiveness with penile measures. Criminal Justice and Behavior, 5, 315-332.
        Argues that penile transducers have great potential for assisting therapists in assessing the treatment needs and treatment responses of rapists, child molesters and other sexually aggressive patients.

873.   Abel, G.G., Mittelman, M.S., & Becker, J.V. (1985). Sexual offenders: Results of assessment and recommendations for treatment. In M.H. Ben-Aron, S.J. Hucker, & C.D. Webster (Eds.), Clinical criminology: The assessment and treatment of criminal behavior. Toronto: M&M graphics.

874.   Abel, G.G., Osborn, C.A., Anthony, D., & Gardos, P. (1992). Current treatments of paraphiliacs. Annual Review of Sex Research, 3, 255-290.
        Reviews current approaches to treatment of paraphiliacs and other male sex offenders with a primary focus on cognitive-behavioral interventions. The cognitive-behavioral treatments discussed include behavior therapy, social skills training, modification of distorted cognitions, and relapse prevention. Other modes of treatment, including pharmacological, psychodynamic and family systems approaches are also discussed.

875.   Adler, C. (1984). The convicted rapist: A sexual or violent offender? Criminal Justice and Behavior, 11, 157-177.

Compared convicted rapists to other sexual offenders, property offenders and violent offenders in a sample of 722 inmates in state correctional institutions. Although rapists tended to be African American more often than did property or violent offenders, rapists were considerable more similar to violent and property offenders than to other sex offenders leading the author to conclude that rapists are more appropriately understood as aggressive rather than sexually disturbed.

876.   Anechiarico, B. (1990). Understanding and treating sex offenders from a self-psychological perspective: The missing piece. Clinical Social Work Journal, 18, 281-292.
Contrasts the classical psychoanalytic drive theory of sex and aggression with the self-psychological theory of Kohut. The self-psychological formulation suggests that voyeurism and exhibitionism are the disintegration products of the fragmenting self. Case studies of the treatment of male sex offenders are used to illustrate the application of the self-psychological model in individual and group psychoanalytic psychotherapy.

877.   Aubrey, M., & Dougher, M.J. (1990). Ethical issues in outpatient group therapy with sex offenders. Journal for Specialists in Group Work, 15, 75-82.

878.   Barker, J.G., & Howell, R.J. (1992). The plethysmograph: a review of recent literature. Bulletin of the American Academy of Psychiatry and the Law, 20, 13-25.
Based on a review of the literature, the authors conclude that although the penile plethysmograph is the best objective measure of male sexual arousal and can be useful in the assessment and treatment of sex offenders, there are limitations involved with its use as a predictive test. These limitations include lack of standards for administration and interpretation, lack standardized norms, and susceptibility to controlling results. Despite these limitations, the plethysmograph is often used as the single most important source of predictive data in court rooms, boards of pardons, and in inmate classification systems. The method is probably most effective in predictive situations when it is used in conjunction with multiple data sources.

879.   Baxter, D.J., et al. (1984). Deviant sexual behavior: Differentiating sex offenders by criminal and personal history, psychometric measures, and sexual response. Criminal Justice and Behavior, 11, 477-501.

880.   Becker, J.V., et al. (1978). Evaluating social skills of sexual aggressives. Criminal Justice and Behavior, 5, 357-368.

881.   Ben-David, S., & Silfen, P. (1993). Rape death and resurrection: Male reaction after disclosure of the secret of being a rape victim. Medical Law, 12, 181-189.
In a study of the male rape victims, 23.8% of 235 prisoners that were interviewed disclosed past sexual abuse while incarcerated. Eleven suffered an acute reaction after disclosure. Over 3/4 of the prisoners who did not have an acute reaction after were sex offenders. Many male sexual abuse victims in prison have problems associated with gender identity and gender image after victimization. However, it seems that sex offenders come to terms with this fact by acting out or by proving their sexual virility in strange and cruel ways.

882. Berlin, F.S. (1988). Issues in the exploration of biological factors contributing to the etiology of the "sex offender." Annals of the New York Academy of Science, 528, 183-192.

883. Berner, W., Berger, P., Guitierrez, K., Jordan, B., et al. (1992). The role of personality disorders in the treatment of sex offenders. Journal of Offender Rehabilitation, 18, 25-37.
Twenty-three of 30 consecutively admitted male sex offenders at a prison treatment facility were diagnosed with personality disorder. The distribution of diagnoses did not differ significantly from a sample of patients in a general outpatient clinic with the exception of a relatively high rate of sadistic personality disorder among offenders. A case example is presented and the meaning of this diagnosis and promising therapeutic strategies are discussed.

884. Berner, W., Brownstone, G., & Sluga, W. (1983). The Cypro-teronacetat treatment of sexual offenders. Neuroscience and Biobehavioral Reviews, 7, 331-443.

885. Borduin, C.M., Henggeler, S.W., Blaske, D.M., & Stein, R.J. (1990). Multisystemic treatment of adolescent sexual offenders. International Journal of Offender Therapy and Comparative Criminology, 34, 105-113.
Sixteen male adolescent sexual offenders in outpatient treatment were randomly assigned to either multisystemic or individual therapy conditions. Recidivism data were collected on each participant at a three-year follow-up. Between-groups comparisons showed that significantly fewer adolescents in the multisystemic therapy condition had been rearrested for sexual crimes and that the frequency of sexual rearrests was significantly lower in the multisystemic condition than in the individual therapy condition. The authors conclude that the efficacy of multisystemic therapy was due to its emphasis on changing behavior and interpersonal relations within the offender's natural environment, including family, peer and school environments.

886. Bowden, P. (1991). Treatment: Use, abuse and consent. Criminal Behaviour and Mental Health, 1, 130-136.
Reviews different treatments for sex abuse offenders including drug therapies such as cyproterone acetate and medroxyprogesterone acetate, hormonal ablation, and castration. It is recommended that drugs be used in combination with other intensive therapies such as sex therapy, sex education, family therapy, cognitive therapy, and covert sensitization. However, there is a substantial amount of evidence testifying to the failure of psychotherapy and behavioral methods to treat serious or dangerous sexual deviants.

887. Bradford, J.M., & McLean, D. (1984). Sexual offenders and testosterone: A clinical study. Canadian Journal of Psychiatry, 29, 335-343.
A study of 50 male sex offenders convicted for crimes ranging from exhibitionism to rape found no support for the relationship between plasma testosterone levels and sexual violence. However findings did substantiate the relationship between alcoholism and violence and found that low levels of plasma testosterone were related to diagnoses of dysthymia.

888. Bradford, J.M., & McLean, D. (1984). Sexual offenders, violence and testosterone: A clinical study. Canadian Journal of Psychiatry, 29, 335-343.

889. Brodsky, S.L., & Hobart, S.C. (1978). Blame models and assailant research. Criminal Justice and Behavior, 5, 379-388.

890. Caffaro, J.V. (1991). A room full of fathers. Journal of Family Psychotherapy, 2, 27-40.

891. Card, R.D., Farrall, W. (1990). Detecting faked penile responses to erotic stimuli: A comparison of stimulus conditions and response measures. Annals of Sex Research, 3, 381-396.

892. Carnes, P.J. (1988). Sexually addicted families: Clinical use of the circumplex model. Journal of Psychotherapy and the Family, 4, 113-140.

893. Cole, W. (1992). Incest perpetrators: Their assessment and treatment. Psychiatric Clinics of North America, 15, 689-701.
Outlines the characteristics of incest offenders, including sexual preferences, reported psychopathologies, and psychosocial features. Dynamics present within incest families that relate to the offender are reviewed. Incest families have been reported to be dysfunctional, with power imbalances; control struggles; indirect, unclear communication; and inappropriate coalitions among family members. Offender-oriented treatment and the multimodal, family-oriented systems approach to treatment are examined.

894. Coleman, E., Cesnik, J., Moore, A.M., & Dwyer, S.M. (1992). An exploratory study of the role of psychotropic medications in the treatment of sex offenders. Journal of Offender Rehabilitation, 18, 75-88.

895. Cook, D.A., Fox, C.A., Weaver, C.M., & Rooth, F.G. (1991). The Berkeley Group: Ten years' experience of a group for non-violent sex offenders. British Journal of Psychiatry, 158, 238-243.
Studied the effectiveness of group treatment of nonviolent sex offenders and found that many offenders demonstrate a high degree of commitment to the group while attendance levels run consistently at 70%. Of 63 men who came to the group during the 10-year study period, 33 completed their stay at the group, 11 left the group prematurely, and 11 never engaged satisfactorily. The remaining 8 were still attending the group. Of the 55 participants whose contact with the group had ended, 36 had not been convicted of further sex offenses after attending the group.

896. Cook, R.F., Fosen, R.H., & Pacht, A. (1971). Pornography and the sex offender: Patterns of previous exposure and arousal effects of pornographic stimuli. Journal of Applied Psychology, 55, 503-511.

897. Cordoba, O.A., & Chapel, J.L. (1983). Medroxyprogesterone acetate antiandrogen treatment of hypersexuality in a pedophiliac sex offender. American Journal of Psychiatry, 140, 1036-1039.

898. Cowburn, M. (1991). Treatment in prison: "What happens to the nonces?" Criminal Behaviour and Mental Health, 1, 145-151.

899. Craissati, J., & Hodes, P. (1992). Mentally ill sex offenders: The experience of a regional secure unit. British Journal of Psychiatry, 161, 846-849.
Studied 11 psychotic male sex offenders who formed an important small group in a regional secure unit's patients. Ten of the 11 participants had a diagnosis of schizophrenia. There was a complex relationship between their mental illness and offending. Two cases are discussed.

900. Cullen, K., & Travin, S. (1990). Assessment and treatment of Spanish-speaking sex offenders: Special considerations. Psychiatric Quarterly, 61, 223-236.

901. Dix, G. (1975). Determining the continuing dangerousness of psychologically abnormal sex offenders. Journal of Psychiatry and the Law, 3, 327-344.

902. Dwyer, S.M. (1988). Exhibitionism/voyeurism. Journal of Social Work and Human Sexuality, 7, 101-112.
Data from interviews with sex offenders over a 10 year period for the basis for this discussion of psychological, social, and familial characteristics of sexual offenders, as well as, useful treatment modalities.

903. Dwyer, S.M., Bockting, W.O., Robinson, B., & Miner, M.H. (1994). Sex offender case study: The truth? Journal of Forensic Sciences, 39, 241-245.

904. Dwyer, S.M., Rosser, B.S. (1992). Treatment outcome research cross-referencing a six-month to ten-year follow-up study on sex offenders. Annals of Sex Research, 5, 87-97.
Results of a four year study of seventy sex offenders indicated overall improvement and increased ability to maintain a life-style free from offending behavior. Self-report data corresponded with results on the Tennessee Self Concept Scale, the BEM Sex Role Inventory and the Derogatis Sexual Functioning Inventory. Four years after treatment, participants reported total confidence for not re-offending.

905. Earls, C.M. (1988). Aberrant sexual arousal in sexual offenders. Annals of the New York Academy of Science, 528, 41-48.

906. Earls, C.M., & Proulx, J. (1986). The differentiation of Francophone rapists and nonrapists using penile circumferential measures. Criminal Justice and Behavior, 13, 419-429.

907. Eisenman, R. (1993). Denigration of a victim in group psychotherapy by violent vs seductive sex offenders. Psychological Reports, 72, 413-414.

908. Emory, L.E., Cole, C.M., & Meyer, W.J. (1992). The Texas experience with DepoProvera: 1980-1990. Journal of Offender Rehabilitation 18, 125-139.
Compared 40 male sex offenders who were treated with DepoProvera to 21 male sex offenders who had the same clinical and legal problems of sexual offenses but who refused pharmacological treatment. Both groups received group therapy,

individual therapy, and sometimes family therapy. Results suggest that DP may allow carefully selected men to participate in an outpatient treatment.

909. Fedora, O., Reddon, J.R., Morrison, J.W., Fedora, S.K., Pascoe, H., & Yeudall, L.T. (1992). Archives of Sexual Behavior, 21, 1-15.

910. Freeman-Longo, R.E., & Wall, R.V. (1986). Changing a lifetime of sexual crime. Psychology Today, 20, 58-64.
Describes a program for chronic sex offenders which involves group psychotherapy, social skills training, covert sensitization, aversive conditioning, minimum arousal conditioning, and drug treatment. Evaluation results show that less than 10% of those completing all phases of the program have committed further sex offenses.

911. Freund, K., & Watson, R.J. (1992). The proportions of heterosexual and homosexual pedophiles among sex offenders against children: An exploratory study. Journal of Sex and Marital Therapy, 18, 34-43.

912. Freund, K., Watson, R., Dickey, R. (1990). Does sexual abuse in childhood cause pedophilia: An exploratory study. Archives of Sexual Behavior, 19, 557-568.

913. Ganzarain, R. (1992). Narcissistic and borderline personality disorders in cases of incest. Group Analysis, 25, 491-494.

914. Ganzarain, R., & Buchele, B.J. (1990). Incest perpetrators in group therapy: A psychodynamic perspective. Bulletin of the Menninger Clinic, 54, 295-310.
Reports data on 20 incest perpetrators in a psychoanalytically oriented psychotherapy group, focusing on the psychodynamics of such offenders. Available treatments are outlined, including medication and behavior modification through aversive conditioning and major obstacles to treatment are discussed.

915. Graber, B., Hartmann, K., Coffman, J.A., Huey, C.J., & Golden, C.J. (1982). Brain damage among mentally disordered sex offenders. Journal of Forensic Science, 27, 125-134.
Studied the incidence of structural brain dysfunction in a group of mentally disordered sex offenders and found that half of those tested showed brain dysfunction assessed by multiple measures.

916. Groth, A.N., & Burgess, A.W. (1977). Rape: A sexual deviation. American Journal of Orthopsychiatry, 47, 400-406.

917. Groth, N. (1979). Men who rape: The psychology of the offender. New York: Plenum.

918. Groth, N. (1982). Treatment of the sexual offender in a correctional institution. Sommers, CT: Sex Offender Program.

919. Grubin, D., & Prentky, R. (1993). Sexual psychopathy laws. Criminal Behaviour and Mental Health, 3, 381-392.

920.   Grubin, D., & Thornton, D. (1994). A national program for the assessment and treatment of sex offenders in the English prison system. Criminal Justice and Behavior, 21, 55-71.

921.   Hall, G.C. (1989). Sexual arousal and arousability in a sexual offender population. Journal of Abnormal Psychology, 98, 145-149.

922.   Hall, G.C., Graham, J.R., & Shepherd, J.R. (1991). Three methods of developing MMPI taxonomies of sexual offenders. Journal of Personality Assessment, 56, 2-13.

923.   Hall, J.N. (1992). Correctional services for inmates with mental retardation: Challenge or catastrophe? In R.W. Conley, R. Luckasson, & G.H. Bouthilet (Eds.), The criminal justice system and mental retardation: Defendants and victims. Baltimore, MD: Paul H. Brooks.

924.   Hanson, R.K., Steffy, R.A., & Gauthier, R. (1993). Long-term recidivism of child molesters. Journal of Consulting and Clinical Psychology, 61, 646-652.
       A study of 197 child molesters found that 42% of the total sample were reconvicted for sexual crimes, violent crimes, or both, with only 10% of the sample reconvicted after 10 or more years after release. Factors associated with increased recidivism were, never being married and previous sexual offenses with offenders who selected only boys having the highest recidivism rate while incest perpetrators had the lowest. Neither scores on the Eysenck Personality Inventory or the Minnesota Multiphasic Personality Inventory were significantly associated with recidivism.

925.   Hedlund, E. (1987). Two years' counseling and psychotherapy of male sexual offenders. Nordisk Sexologi, 5, 116-123
       Discusses the use of brief or long-term counseling, and group therapy with 25 male sexual offenders as part of a pilot treatment program within the Swedish criminal system. Six common reactive characteristics and 6 therapeutic goals of treatment are described. The usefulness of this psychodynamic model with rapists, child molesters, and exhibitionists is emphasized.

926.   Herrera-Hernandez, E., Marvan, L., Saavedra, M., & Contreras, C.M. (1993). [Anxiety and depression levels in rape offenders]. Acta Psiquiatrica and Psicologica de America Latino, 39, 53-57.

927.   Hillbrand, M., Foster, H., Jr., & Hirt, M. (1990). Rapists and child molesters: Psychometric comparisons. Archives of Sexual Behavior, 19, 65-71.
       Compared three groups of offenders (child molesters, child rapists, and adult rapists) on factorial derived psychological and social history indicators and found few differences between child molesters and child rapists. Adult rapists, however, were characterized by higher levels of dysphoria, subjective distress, and inhibition than the other two groups. The authors conclude that the prognosis for adult rapists is more favorable than that for the other two groups.

928.   Hodges, J., Lanyado, M., Andreou, C. (1994). Sexuality and violence: Preliminary clinical hypotheses from psychotherapeutic assessments in a research programme on young sexual offenders. Journal of Child Psychotherapy, 20, 283-308.

929. Holmes, R.M. (1991). Sex crimes. Newbury Park, CA: Sage.

930. Houston, J., & Adshead, G. (1993). The use of repertory grids to assess change: Application to a sex offenders group. Issues in Criminological and Legal Psychology, 19, 43-51.

931. Huckle, P.L., & Jones, G.H. (1993). Mentally ill sex offenders. British Journal of Psychiatry, 162, 568.

932. Ingersoll, S.L., & Patton, S.D. (1990). Treating perpetrators of sexual abuse. Lexington, MA: Lexington Books.

933. Johnston, P., Hudson, S.M., & Marshall, W.L. (1992). The effects of masturbatory reconditioning with nonfamilial child molesters. Behavior Research and Therapy, 30, 559-561.

934. Kilmann, P.R., et al. (1982). The treatment of sexual paraphilias: A review of outcome research. Journal of Sex Research, 18, 193-252.

935. Knight, R.A., & Prentky, R.A. (1987). The developmental antecedents and adult adaptations of rapist subtypes. Criminal Justice and Behavior, 14, 403-426.

936. Konecni, V., Mulcahy, E., & Ebbeson, E. (1980). Prison or mental hospital: Factors affecting the processing of persons suspected of being "mentally disordered sex offenders." In P. Lipsitt, & B. Sales (Eds.), New directions in psychological research. New York: Van Nostrand Reinhold.

937. LaCalle, J.J. (1987). Incest: Offender treatment and family therapy. American Journal of Forensic Psychology, 5, 43-46.

938. Lang, R.A., Lloyd, C.A., & Fiqia, N.A. (1985). Goal attainment scaling with hospitalized sexual offenders. Journal of Nervous and Mental Disease, 173, 527-537.

939. Langevin, R., Wright, P., & Handy, L. (1988). What treatment do sex offenders want? Annals of Sex Research, 1, 363-385.
   Studied 87 male sex offenders being assessed pretrial, presentence, or posttrial regarding desire for treatment and the perceived nature of problems and found that 51% of participants did not want any form of treatment at the time of assessment. Of participants who wanted treatment, 40% perceived changing their sexually anomalous behavior as a therapy goal. Preferred therapies were individual psychotherapy, social skills training, and group therapy. Evidence of disparity between therapists' application of treatment and offenders' perceptions of their needs implies that improving congruence between therapist and patient goals may enhance treatment compliance and therapy success for sex offenders.

940. Launay, G. (1994). The phallometric assessment of sex offenders: Some professional and research issues. Criminal Behaviour and Mental Health, 4, 48-70.

Research suggests that penile plethysmography, in spite of many as yet unresolved methodological problems, is reliable and valid. Plethysmography is useful in challenging sex offenders' denial, in assessing treatment needs, and in evaluation of treatment. This technique cannot be relied on alone to establish guilt or predict future deviant sexual behavior. Areas where future research is needed are discussed.

941. Lawrence, S. (1984). Manual for the Lawrence psychological forensic examination. San Bernardino, CA: Associates in Forensic Psychology.

942. Laws, D.R. (Ed.) (1989). Relapse prevention with sex offenders. New York: Guilford.

943. Laws, D.R., & Holmen, M.L. (1978). Sexual response faking by pedophiles. Criminal Justice and Behavior, 5, 343-356.

944. Laws, D.R., & Marshal, W.L. (1990). A conditioning theory of the etiology and maintenance of deviant sexual preference and behavior. In W.L. Marshall, D.R. Laws, & H.E. Barbaree (Eds.). Handbook of sexual assault: Issues theories, and treatment of the offender. New York: Plenum.

945. Lundervold, D.A., & Young, L.G. (1992). Treatment acceptability ratings for sexual offenders: effect of diagnosis and offense. Research in Developmental Disabilities, 13, 229-237.

946. Maletzky, B.M. (1991). The use of medroxyprogesterone acetate to assist in the treatment of sexual offenders. Annals of Sex Research, 4, 117-129.

947. Marks, I., Gelder, M., & Bancroft, J. (1970). Sexual deviants two years after electric aversion. British Journal of Psychiatry, 117, 173-185.

948. Marques, J.K. (1988). The Sex Offender Treatment and Evaluation Project: California's new outcome study. Annals of the New York Academy of Science, 528, 235-243.
      Describes a state mandated relapse prevention model treatment program for sex offenders in California prisons. The objectives, treatment model, and research design of the program are discussed.

949. Marques, J.K., Day, D.M., Nelson, C., & West, M.A. (1993). Findings and recommendations from California's experimental treatment program. In G.C. Hadayam Hall, R. Hirschman, J.R. Graham, & M.S. Zaragoza (Eds.), Sexual aggression: Issues in etiology, assessment, and treatment. Washington, DC: Taylor & Francis.

950. Marshall, W.L. (1993). A revised approach to the treatment of men who sexually assault adult females. In G.C. Hadayam Hall, R. Hirschman, J.R. Graham, & M.S. Zaragoza (Eds.), Sexual aggression: Issues in etiology, assessment, and treatment. Washington, DC: Taylor & Francis.

951.   Marshall, W.L. (1994). Treatment effects on denial and minimization in incarcerated sex offenders. Behaviour Research and Therapy, 32, 559-564.
Studied 81 incarcerated sex offenders and found an overall positive effect on reducing denial and minimization. Also, different types of offenders (rapists, incest offenders, and nonfamilial child molesters) benefitted equally from the treatment.

952.   Marshall, W.L., & Barbaree, H.E. (1978). The reduction of deviant arousal: Satiation treatment for sexual aggressors. Criminal Justice and Behavior, 5, 294-303.

953.   Marshall, W.L., Eccles, A., & Barbaree, H.E. (1993). A three-tiered approach to the rehabilitation of incarcerated sex offenders. Behavioral Sciences and the Law, 11, 441-455.
Discusses an intervention with convicted sex offenders that includes incarceration and treatment of high risk offenders in maximum and medium security facilities, while lower risk offenders are exposed to a less extensive treatment program in a minimum security facility, followed by possible release to the community where offenders are reassessed, treated, and begin supervised relapse prevention. Evidence suggests that this approach is both effective in reducing recidivism, and cost-effective in reducing the expense to the community in dealing with reoffenders.

954.   Medella, J.T., Travin, S., & Cullen, K. (1989). Legal and ethical issues in treating sex offenders. Bulletin of the American Academy of Psychiatry and the Law, 17, 223-232.

955.   Mendelson, E.F. (1989). Sex offenders: Anyone to help? Sexual and Marital Therapy, 4, 7-10.
Discusses various ideas about treatment for sexual offenders and describes a group therapy program that focuses on (1) adverse consequences that such offenders could face; (2) adverse effects on victims; (3) behaviors and fantasies that led to sexual offenses; and (4) strategies and psychological techniques for resisting temptation (including use of fantasization and pornography).

956.   Menghini, P., & Ernst, K. (1991). Anti-androgenic treatment judged by 19 offenders. Nervenarzt, 62, 303-307.

957.   Monahan, J., & Davis, S. (1983). Mentally disordered sex offenders. In J. Monahan & H. Steadman (Eds.), Mentally disordered offenders. New York: Plenum.

958.   Murrin, M.R., & Laws, D.R. (1990). The influence of pornography on sexual crimes. In W.L. Marshall, D.R. Laws, & H.E. Barbaree (Eds.). Handbook of sexual assault: Issues, theories, and treatment of the offender. New York: Plenum.

959.   Neidigh, L., & Krop, H. (1992). Cognitive distortions among child sexual offenders. Journal of Sex Education and Therapy, 18, 208-215.
Examines specific cognitive distortions and rationalizations used by outpatient child sexual offenders with regard to their maladaptive behavior. Participants were 101 adult males undergoing outpatient group psychotherapy as sexual offenders. Participants completed an open-ended questionnaire, generating 357 statements

concerning their behavior, which were sorted into a list of 38 cognitive distortions and rationalizations. Applications of this list for clinical work and as a base for future research are discussed.

960. O'Connell, M.A. (1986). Reuniting incest offenders with their families. Journal of Interpersonal Violence, 1, 374-386.

961. O'Connor, A. (1987). Female sex offenders. British Journal of Psychiatry, 150, 615-620.
Studied 81 women convicted of sex offenses and found that those convicted of indecency (n= 19) were characterized by poor social skills and a high incidence of mental illness, mental retardation, and alcoholism. Those convicted of more serious offenses were found to have victimized children more often than adults. Of those who victimized children, nearly 50% had a history of psychiatric disorder.

962. O'Donohue, W.T., Letourneau, E. (1993). A brief group treatment for the modification of denial in child sexual abusers: Outcome and follow-up. Child Abuse and Neglect, 17, 299-304.
Investigated whether brief structured group treatment could produce a reduction of denial of sexual offenses in males convicted of child sexual abuse. The group treatment contained elements of victim empathy, cognitive restructuring, sex education, assertiveness and social skills, education about sex offender therapy, and a discussion of the possible consequences of continued denial. 17 adult child sexual offenders in denial were run in 2 groups. Despite an average length of denial of nearly 2 yrs, by post-treatment the majority of offenders had come out of denial. Moreover, follow-up denial data indicated continued admission, and above-average compliance with subsequent sex offender therapy. Although the lack of an experimental design precludes causal inference, these results are suggestive of an effective method for modifying denial in child sex offenders.

963. Pacht, A.R., & Cowden, J.E. (1974). An exploratory study of five hundred sex offenders. Criminal Justice and Behavior, 1, 13-20.
Compared sex offenders defined as sexually deviant and in need for psychiatric treatment to those who were not found in need of treatment and found that the sexual deviant sex offenders demonstrated long term histories of personality disturbance and substantial problems in many areas of interpersonal functioning, while other offenders tended to be more aggressive towards their victims.

964. Perkins, D. (1986). Sex offending: A psychological approach. Issues in Criminological and Legal Psychology, 9, 56-66.

965. Pithers, W.D. (1994). Process evaluation of a group therapy component designed to enhance sex offenders' empathy for sexual abuse survivors. Behaviour Research and Therapy, 32, 565-570.

966. Pollock, N.L. (1988). Sexual assault of older women. Annals of Sex Research, 1, 523-532.
A study comparing the clinical histories of 5 males who had sexually assaulted women 60 years old or older with those of 6 males who had sexually assaulted

younger women found that assaults of older women tended to be more violent and to be more motivated by anger, need for power and sadistic intent, while males who assaulted older women were found to be characterized by more severe, often psychotic, psycho-pathological problems than those who assaulted younger women.

967.   Quinsey, V.L., & Laws, D.R. (1990). Validity of physiological measures of pedophilic sexual arousal in a sexual offender population: A critique of Hall, Proctor, and Nelson. Journal of Consulting and Clinical Psychology, 58, 886-891.

968.   Rada, R.T. (1978). Legal aspects in treating rapists. Criminal Justice and Behavior, 5, 369-378.

969.   Rada, R.T. (1980). Plasma androgens and the sex offender. Bulletin of the American Academy of Psychiatry and the Law, 8, 456-464.

970.   Rada, R.T., Kellener, R., Laws, D.R., & Winslow, W.W. (1978). Drinking, alcoholism, and the mentally disordered sex offender. Bulletin of the American Academy of Psychiatry and the Law, 6, 296-300.

971.   Romero, J.J., & Williams, L.M. (1983). Group psychotherapy and intensive probation supervision with sex offenders: A comparative study. Federal Probation, 47, 36-42.
A 10-year follow-up study of 231 sex offenders who received either intensive probation supervision with group psychotherapy or without group psychotherapy found no significant differences in rearrest rates (for sex offenses) between the two groups.

972.   Roys, D.T. (1995). Exit examinations for sexual offenders. Sexual Abuse Journal of Research and Treatment, 7, 85-106.

973.   Ryan, G., Lane, S., Davis, J., & Issac, C. (1987). Juvenile sex offenders: Development and correction. Child Abuse and Neglect, 11, 385-395.
Uses three case studies to discuss the developmental nature of sexually abusive behaviors in juvenile males and discusses treatment issues that reduce the risk of further offending and decrease the incidence of sexual victimization.

974.   Sagatun, I.J. (1982). Attributional effects of therapy with incestuous families. Journal of Marital and Family Therapy, 8, 99-104.
Studied a group of 57 male incest offenders and 35 spouses who participated in a self-help program (Parents United) for incestuous families. Survey results suggest that the program was successful in increasing feelings of personal responsibility and reducing recidivism, but did not affect whether families remained intact or dissolved.

975.   Scheela, R.A. (1992). The remodeling process: A grounded theory study of perceptions of treatment among adult male incest offenders. Journal of Offender Rehabilitation, 18, 167-189.

976.   Schwartz, B.K. Effective treatment techniques for sex offenders. Psychiatric Annals, 22, 315-319.

Critiques the "nothing works" attitude in the treatment of sex offenders, noting that what works depends on where the treatment is taking place, who is providing the treatment, and what types of issues a particular offender has to deal with. A popular model currently operating in a number of states combines group therapy, behavioral techniques designed to recondition sexual arousal, relapse prevention, and cognitive-behavioral approaches for use in the treatment of sexual deviance.

977.   Scott, W. (1994). Group therapy for male sex offenders: Strategic interventions. Journal of Family Psychotherapy, 5, 1-20.

978.   Serber, M., & Wolpe, J. (1971). Treatment of the sex offender: Behavior therapy techniques. International Psychiatry Clinics, 8, 53-68.

979.   Silver, S.N. (1976). Outpatient treatment for sexual offenders. Social Work, 21, 134-140.

980.   Small, M.A. (1992). The legal context of mentally disordered sex offender (MDSO) treatment programs. Criminal Justice and Behavior, 19, 127-142.
Summarizes constitutional challenges of MDSO statutes, and discusses the relationship between legislation and treatment for a number of current state programs. It is critical that conclusions about treatment efficacy and offender recidivism should account for the legal context in which treatment programs operate.

981.   Spodak, M.K., Falck, Z.A., & Rappeport, J.R. (1978). The hormonal treatment of paraphilias with Depo-provera. Criminal Justice and Behavior, 5, 304-314.
Discusses the use of the female hormone medroxyprogesterone acetate (Depo-provera) and cyproterone as a reversible form of chemical castration. The action of these hormones is to decrease the functioning of the male hormone, testosterone, and hence decrease overall sexual drive to allow the sex offender to gain control over his aggressive sexual urges. Case studies are presented to show that, when coupled with psychotherapy, these drugs may be an important adjunct to treatment of paraphilias.

982.   Stermac, L.E., & Hall, K. (1989). Escalation in sexual offending: Fact or fiction? Annals of Sex Research, 2, 153-162.

983.   Stermac, L.E., & Hucker, S. (1988). Combining cognitive-behavioral therapy and pharmacotherapy in the treatment of pedophilic incest offenders. Behavioral Sciences and the Law, 6, 257-266.

984.   Sturup, G. (1972). Castration: The total treatment. In H. Resnick & M.E. Wolfgang (Eds.), Sexual behavior. Boston, MA: Little, Brown.

985.   Swanson, C.K., & Garwick, G.B. (1990). Treatment for low-functioning sex offenders: Group therapy and interagency coordination. Mental Retardation, 28, 155-161.
Outlines the procedures and results of an outpatient therapy group for low-functioning sex offenders (IQ 55-85). The group treatment philosophy focuses

on teaching the client right from wrong in sexual aggression, realistically appraising the client's intellectual strengths and weaknesses to lower the chances of future offenses, training the client in sexuality topics and in positive social and sexual skills, and encouraging the client to take personal responsibility for sex offenses. Rates of goal attainment and recidivism are presented.

986. Tingle, D., Barnard, G.W., Robbins, L., Newman, G. (1986). Childhood and adolescent characteristics of pedophiles and rapists. International Journal of Law and Psychiatry, 9, 103-116.
Studied 64 consecutive voluntary admissions to a program for mentally disordered sex offenders and found that developmental differences between pedophiles and rapists were evident even in early youth. Rapists were more likely to come from disruptive families and to have histories of violence while pedophiles were more likely to have close attachments to their mothers.

987. Valliant, P.M., Furac, C.J., & Antonowicz, D.H. (1994). Attitudes toward sex offenders by female undergraduate university students enrolled in a psychology program. Social Behavior and Personality, 22, 105-110.

988. Van Lankveld, J. (1991). Treating perpetrators of sexual violence: Contact and relational aspects. Tijdschrift voor Psychotherapie, 17, 172-183.
Discusses the methodology of establishing a therapeutic relationship with sex offenders. The problems associated with treating sex offenders are discussed. It is maintained that the therapist must recognize his or her own prejudices and avoid behavior that could hinder therapy. A case study is described.

989. Walker, P., & Meyer, W. (1981). Medroxyprogesterone acetate treatment for paraphiliac sex offenders. In S. Hays, T. Roberts, & K. Solway (Eds.), Violence and the violent individual. New York: SP Medical and Scientific Books.

990. Watson, R.J., & Stermac, L.E. (1994). Cognitive group counseling for sexual offenders. International Journal of Offender Therapy and Comparative Criminology, 38, 259-270.
Studied two groups of sex offenders; those treated in a psychiatric hospital and those treated in a correctional facility. Significant positive treatment effects were observed in both groups indicating that cognitive group counseling can be effective in helping child sexual abusers to reevaluate and remodel their cognitions about their victims and offenses.

991. Wiederholt, I.C. (1992). The psychodynamics of sex offenses and implications for treatment. Journal of Offender Rehabilitation, 18, 19-24.

992. Wormith, J.S., Bradford, J.M., Pawlak, A., Borzecki, M., & Zohar, A. (1988). The assessment of deviant sexual arousal as a function of intelligence, instructional set and alcohol ingestion. Canadian Journal of Psychiatry, 33, 808.

993. Zverina, J. (1989). Attempt to define the goals in the therapy of sex offenders. Ceskoslovenska Psychiatrie, 85, 316-322.

Discusses a comprehensive therapy of sexual deviations that includes social, psychotherapeutic, and biological approaches. The main goals of this therapy are: (1) education about normal and deviant sexuality; (2) modification of attitudes toward the client's own and other people's sexuality; and (3) acquainting the client with the results of the complex diagnostic and therapeutic process. Other individualized treatments include developing understanding of the sexual deviation and working out an individual life style, and inhibition of sexuality by short-term (pharmacological) or long-term (castration) biological treatment. The modalities of treatment are selected in accordance with the client's status and acute life situations.

12

Adolescent Offenders

994. Allen, J.F., Urco, N., & Burger, G. (1982). Structure of personality needs in a young, deviant, male population. Professional Psychology, 13, 744-751.
      Group profiles and personality trait factor structures on Form B of the PRF are compared for 122 male prisoners and a normative sample of 1,000 male college students. The expected mean level differences in the group profiles were found. Further, interesting variations appeared in the factor structure of the 2 groups, suggesting that the PRF measures some group-specific personality dimensions in inmates. Implications of prisoner PRF factors are discussed.

995. Andrew, J.M. (1977). Delinquency: Intellectual imbalance? Criminal Justice and Behavior, 4, 99-104.

996. Andrew, J.M. (1982). Memory and violent crime among delinquents. Criminal Justice and Behavior, 9, 364-371.

997. Anonymous. (1970). Psychiatric services and the young offender. Lancet, 1(636), 30.

998. Apter, A., Ratzoni, G., Iancu, I., Weizman, R., & Tyano, S. (1993). The Ganser syndrome in two adolescent brothers. Journal of the American Academy of Child and Adolescent Psychiatry, 32, 582-584.
      Considers the case of two adolescent brothers diagnosed with Ganser syndrome after incarceration who later developed signs and symptoms of affective disorder. Diagnosis and management of such cases are discussed.

999. Archer, R.P. (1989). Use of the MMPI with adolescents in forensic settings. Forensic Reports, 2, 65-87.

1000. Atkinson, B.J., & McKenzie, P.N. (1987). Family therapy with adolescent offenders: A collaborative treatment strategy. American Journal of Family Therapy, 15, 316-325.

1001. Beal, D., & Duckro, P. (1977). Family counseling as an alternative to legal action for the juvenile status offender. Journal of Marriage and Family Counseling, 3, 77-81.

1002. Borduin, C.M., Henggeler, S.W., Blaske, D.M., & Stein, R.J. (1990). Multisystemic treatment of adolescent sexual offenders. International Journal of Offender Therapy and Comparative Criminology, 34, 105-113.
Sixteen male adolescent sexual offenders in outpatient treatment were randomly assigned to either multisystemic or individual therapy conditions. Recidivism data were collected on all participants at a 3-year follow-up. Between-groups comparisons showed that significantly fewer adolescents in the multisystemic therapy condition had been rearrested for sexual crimes and that the frequency of sexual rearrests was significantly lower in the multisystemic condition than in the individual therapy condition. The authors conclude that the efficacy of multisystemic therapy was due to its emphasis on changing behavior and interpersonal relations within the offender's natural environment, including family, peer and school environments.

1003. Borduin, C.M., Mann, B.J., Cone, L.T., Henggeler, S.W., et al. (1995). Multisystemic treatment of serious juvenile offenders: Long-term prevention of criminality and violence. Journal of Consulting and Clinical Psychology, 63, 569-578.
Results of s study comparing multisystemic and individual therapy with 176 serious juvenile offenders found that multisystemic therapy was more effective than individual therapy in improving family correlates of antisocial behavior and in ameliorating adjustment problems in individual family members. Results from a 4-year follow-up of rearrest data showed that multisystemic therapy was more effective than individual therapy in preventing future criminal behavior, including violent offenses.

1004. Bradford, J., & Dimock, J. (1986). A comparative study of adolescents and adults who willfully set fires. Psychiatric Journal of the University of Ottawa, 11, 228-234.
A comparison of 57 adult and 45 juvenile arsonists found that mental retardation was diagnosable in about 10% of cases in both groups. Conduct disorders were common among juveniles, while alcoholism, personality disorders, and schizophrenia were common among adults. About 40% of adolescents came from single parent homes and adult psychopathology and physical abuse were common in the homes of juvenile adolescents.

1005. Brannon, J.M., & Troyer, R. (1991). Peer group counseling: A normalized residential alternative to the specialized treatment of adolescent sex offenders. International Journal of Offender Therapy and Comparative Criminology, 35, 225-234.

1006. Burdsal, C., Force, R.C., & Klingsporn, M.J. (1989). Treatment effectiveness in young male offenders. Residential Treatment for Children and Youth, 7, 75-88. Studied the effectiveness of three types of treatment; low-intensive, high-intensive, and no inpatient (stay at home); in a residential treatment program for male juvenile offenders with follow-ups at 2 and/or 5 years after treatment. Findings indicated that high-intensive treatment was more effective (based on interview data and scores on a socialized coping scale) than low-intensive treatment. The stay-at-home group, however, had the highest scores on the coping measure.

1007. Burgess, A.M., Hartman, C.R., & McCormack, A. (1987). Abused to abuser: Antecedents to socially deviant behaviors. American Journal of Psychiatry, 144, 1431-1436.
A comparison of 34 adolescents and young adults (aged 14-21 years) who had been sexually abused as children with a group of 34 non-abused controls showed positive associations between childhood sexual abuse and later drug abuse, juvenile delinquency, and criminal behaviors.

1008. Camp, B.H., & Thyer, B.A. (1993). Treatment of adolescent sex offenders: A review of empirical research. Journal of Applied Social Sciences, 17, 191-206.
Reviewed the literature on psychosocial treatment of juvenile offenders and found that recidivism rates were the most often used outcome measures, although some studies used data from other sources. Further, the use of matched samples or control groups was rare, as were attempts to determine which treatment components contributed to successful outcomes.

1009. Connor, D.G. (1984). Multifamily educational groups in juvenile court settings with drug/alcohol offenders. Journal for Specialists in Group Work, 9, 21-25.
Describes an innovative court service for adolescent offenders who have committed minor drug or alcohol offenses. The program consists of 7 group meetings for adolescents and their parents or guardians. Topics of the sessions include effective communication, family roles, and effective problem-solving strategies.

1010. Corder, B.F., Cornwall, T., & Whiteside, R. (1984). Techniques for increasing effectiveness of co-therapy functioning in adolescent psychotherapy groups. International Journal of Group Psychotherapy, 34, 643-654.

1011. Daniel, C. & Dodd, C. (1989). Preventing alcohol-related crimes among incarcerated juvenile offenders via covert sensitization. Delincuencia, 1, 331-348. Studied the effects of covert sensitization coupled with alcohol education and counseling in two adolescent offenders over a three month period with followup assessments at nine and twenty-four month intervals after treatment.

1012. Day, A., Maddicks, R., & McMahon, D. (1993). Brief psychotherapy in two-plus-one sessions with a young offender population. Behavioural and Cognitive Psychotherapy, 21, 357-369.

1013. Dougherty, A.M., & Horne, A.M. (1977). The helpfulness of three counseling models as perceived by institutionalized adolescent males. Criminal Justice and Behavior, 4, 273-284.

1014. Eisenman, R. (1993). Characteristics of adolescent felons in a prison treatment program. Adolescence, 28, 695-699.
Based on data collected in psychotherapy and official records concerning 43 adolescent offenders in a prison treatment program, the most common characteristics of the sample included having anti-social or anti-authority values, lack of marketable skills, history of emotional, physical, or sexual abuse, were members of a minority group, and reported gang membership.

1015. Ellis, M.J. (1977). Custody, treatment and the abnormal young male offender. Practitioner, 218, 818-822.

1016. Faltico, G.J. (1975). An after-school without failure: A new therapy model for juvenile offenders. Corrective and Social Psychiatry and Journal of Behavior Technology, Methods, & Therapy, 21, 17-20.

1017. Fehrenbach, P.A., Smith, W., Monastersky, C., & Deisher, R.W. (1986). Adolescent sexual offenders: Offender and offense characteristics. American Journal of Orthopsychiatry, 56, 225-223.
Results of a survey of 307 adolescent sex offenders showed that over 60% had sexually victimized a child under the age of 12 and 33% victimized a family member. Only about 10% of cases involved rape of a peer-aged female.

1018. Fendrich, M., Mackesy-Amiti, M.E., Goldstein, P., Spunt B., & Brownstein, H. (1995). Substance involvement among juvenile murderers: Comparisons with older offenders based on interviews with prison inmates. International Journal of the Addictions, 30, 1363-1382.
Evaluated substance involvement among incarcerated juvenile offenders convicted of murder or manslaughter. Patterns of substance use among juvenile offenders were compared with patterns found in older offenders. In both age groups, nearly 1/3 of homicide perpetrators reported that they were affected by alcohol prior to the offense. In every age group, alcohol was the substance showing the highest rate of "regular" lifetime use and the highest rate of ingestion in the week preceding the homicide.

1019. Flaherty, M.G. (1983). The national incidence of juvenile suicide in adult jails and juvenile detention centers. Suicide and Life Threatening Behavior, 13, 85-94.

1020. Gabel, S., & Frances, R.J. (1991). Establishing links between residential placements for youths and prisons for adults. Hospital and Community Psychiatry, 42, 1203-1204.

1021. Genoves, V.G., & Redondo, S. (1993). The institutionalization of young offenders. Criminal Behaviour and Mental Health, 3, 336-348.
Argues that imprisonment can be a positive force in the rehabilitation of juvenile offenders and presents evidence that community alternatives do not necessarily yield better results for individual youths or for the community. When based on sound developmental and environmental models, institutionally based programs often yield similar results.

1022. Gold, M., Mattlin, J., & Osgood, D.W. (1989). Background characteristics and responses to treatment of two types of institutionalized delinquent boys. Criminal Justice and Behavior, 16, 5-33.

1023. Goncalves, R.A. (1992). Research in delinquency and prisons in Portugal: Role and contributions of psychology. Jornal de Psicologia, 10, 3-12.

1024. Gordon, D.A., Arbuthnot, J., Gustafson, K.E. (1988). Home-based behavioral systems family therapy with disadvantaged juvenile delinquents. American Journal of Family Therapy, 16, 243-255.
This study of recidivism in two groups of juvenile offenders found that juvenile offenders who were placed in time-limited, in-home family therapy were less likely than a similar comparison group of juvenile offenders who were referred to probation only to be recidivists (11% vs. 67%) over a 30 month follow-up.

1025. Haapala, D.A., & Kinney, J.M. (1988). Avoiding out-of-home placement of high-risk status offenders through the use of intensive home-based family preservation services. Criminal Justice and Behavior, 15, 334-348.

1026. Hains, A.A., Herrman, L.P., Baker, K.L., & Graber, S. (1986). The development of a psycho-educational group program for adolescent sex offenders. Journal of Offender Counseling, Services, and Rehabilitation, 11, 63-76.
Evaluated a 7-week psychotherapy group designed to improve incarcerated adolescents sex offenders' sexual knowledge, problem-solving skills, and moral assessment abilities. Compared to controls, those in the therapy group showed significant increases in sexual knowledge, attitudes, and problem-solving skills. However, participation in the group had no significant effect on moral reasoning.

1027. Halpern, A.L. (1978). Anticipated misuse of psychiatry under the New York Juvenile Offender Law. Bulletin of the American Academy of Psychiatry and the Law, 6, 382-387.

1028. Hamparian, D., Schuster, R., Dinitz, S., & Conrad, J. (1978). The violent few: A study of dangerous juvenile offenders. Lexington, MA: Lexington Books.

1029. Henggeler, S.W., Borduin, C.M., & Melton, G.B., Mann, B.J., et al. (1991). Effects of multisystemic therapy on drug use and abuse in serious juvenile offenders: A progress report from two outcome studies. Family Dynamics of Addiction Quarterly, 1, 40-51.
Compared the efffectiveness of multisystemic therapy to that of individual counseling in treating the substance use and abuse of 200 serious antisocial juvenile offenders and found that at an average 4 year follow-up, the multisystemic therapy group had a significantly lower rate of substance-related arrests than controls. Similar findings emerged from a second study of 47 juveniles.

1030. Henggeler, S.W., et al. (1986). Multisystemic treatment of juvenile offenders: Effects on adolescent behavior and family interaction. Developmental Psychology, 22, 132-141.

A comparison of the pre- and post-treatment functioning of a group of 57 adolescent offenders receiving family ecological treatment with a group of 23 adolescents receiving an alternative treatment, and a group of 44 non-offender controls found that the adolescents in the family ecological treatment group showed decreases in conduct problems, anxiety, withdrawal, immaturity, and number of contacts with delinquent peers. No significant changes were observed for the alternative treatment group suggesting that multisystemic therapy shows great promise for addressing the behavioral problems of adolescents in trouble with the law.

1031. Henggeler, S.W., Melton, G.B., & Smith, L.A. (1992). Family preservation using multisystemic therapy: An effective alternative to incarcerating serious juvenile offenders. Journal of Consulting and Clinical Psychology, 60, 953-961.

1032. Johnson, T.F. (1978). A contextual approach to treatment of juvenile offenders. Offender Rehabilitation, 3, 171-179.

1033. Kramp, P., Israelson, L., Mortensen, K., & Aarkrog, T. (1987). Serious juvenile offenders: Demographic variables, diagnostic problems, and therapeutic possibilities. International Journal of Law and Psychiatry, 10, 63-73.

1034. Laben, J.K., Dodd, D., & Sneed, L. (1991). King's theory of goal attainment applied in group therapy for inpatient juvenile sexual offenders, maximum security state offenders, and community parolees, using visual aids. Issues in Mental Health Nursing, 12, 51-64.

1035. Leeman, L.W., Gibbs, J.C., & Fuller, D. (1993). Evaluation of a multi-component group treatment program for juvenile delinquents. Aggressive Behavior, 19, 281-292.
Randomly assigned 57 male juvenile offenders incarcerated at a medium-security correctional facility, to either a multi-component group treatment program or to one of 2 control groups. Significant improvements in institutional behavior and significantly lower recidivism rates were found for the group treatment group relative to the two controls.

1036. Lewis, D.O. (1976). Diagnostic evaluation of the juvenile offender: Toward a clarification of often overlooked psychopathology. Child Psychiatry and Human Development, 6, 198-213.

1037. Lewis, D.O., Balla, D.A., & Shanok, S.S. (1979). Some evidence of race bias in the diagnosis and treatment of the juvenile offender. American Journal of Orthopsychiatry, 49, 53-61.
In a comparison of African American and white juvenile offenders, it was found that African American juvenile offenders and their families were less likely than their white counterparts to receive adequate psychiatric and medical services.

1038. Locke, T.P., Johnson, G.M., Kirigin-Ramp, K., Atwater, J.D., et al. (1986). An evaluation of a juvenile education program in a state penitentiary. Evaluation Review, 10, 281-298.

1039. Margolin, L. (1983). A treatment model for the adolescent sex offender. Journal of Offender Counseling, Services and Rehabilitation, 8, 1-12.

1040. Maynard, P.E., Hultquist, A. (1988). The Circumplex Model with adjudicated youths' families. Journal of Psychotherapy and the Family, 4, 249-266.

1041. McNeil, J.K, & Hart, D.S. (1986). The effect of self-government on the aggressive behavior of institutionalized delinquent adolescents. Criminal Justice and Behavior, 13, 430-445.

1042. Megargee, E.I. (1974). Applied psychological research in a correctional setting. Criminal Justice and Behavior, 1, 43-50.

1043. Michaels, K.W., & Green, R.H. (1979). A child welfare agency project: Therapy for families of status offenders. Child Welfare, 58, 216-220.

1044. Mio, J.S., Nanjundappa, G., Verieur, D.E., and de Rios, M.D. (1986). Drug abuse and the adolescent sex offender: A preliminary analysis. Journal of Psychoactive Drugs, 18, 65-72.

1045. Mulvey, E.P., & Repucci, N.D. (1984). Perceptions of appropriate services for juvenile offenders. Criminal Justice and Behavior, 11, 401-422.
        A survey of 168 juvenile justice gatekeepers, including juvenile court, social service agency, and community mental health center personnel found that personnel in each of the three juvenile justice settings found that alternative services without a therapeutic intent were disfavored, while services involving individual or family therapy were rated highest. Further, each of the agencies viewed the type of service that they provided to be superior to those provided in other settings.

1046. Novy, D.M., Gaa, J.P., Frankiewicz, R.G., Liberman, D., & Amerikaner, M. (1992). The association between patterns of family functioning and ego development of the juvenile offender. Adolescence, 27, 25-35.

1047. O'Connell, B.A. (1975). The assessment of the adolescent offender. Irish Medical Journal, 68, 459-465.

1048. Pearson, M.A. (1994). Therapy with felony-convicted male juvenile offenders. Special Issue: Innovations in psychiatric nursing theory, practice, and research. Issues in Mental Health Nursing, 15, 49-57.

1049. Phillips, S.L., & Fields, J. (1975). An experiment in activity groups for juvenile offenders. Corrective and Social Psychiatry and Journal of Behavior Technology, Methods, & Therapy, 21, 4-6.

1050. Polischuk, D., Collins, D. (1991). Sharks, mice and bears: A group-counseling experience with adolescents. Journal of Child and Youth Care, 6, 41-47.

1051. Porter, S. (1990). Adolescent sex offenders: A study of the relationship between self-concept and sexual behavior in adolescent males. American Journal of Forensic Psychology, 8, 61-73.

1052. Saunders, E., Awad, G.A., & White, G. (1986). Male adolescent offenders: The offender and the offense. Canadian Journal of Psychiatry, 31, 542-549.
Divided a group of male adolescent sex offenders into three groups: (1) courtship disorders, (2) sexual assault, and (3) pedophiles. Those in group 1 were more likely to come from less disorganized homes, were better adjusted in school and community, and were viewed as less disturbed than those in the other groups. Group 2 offenders came from homes with high levels of parent-child separations, had committed more violent offenses and were more likely to classified in the Borderline Range of Intelligence. Group 3 offenders had witnessed more parental violence, had more siblings who were truant and were described as not enjoying cuddling when infants.

1053. Scavo, R., & Buchanan, B.D. (1989). Group therapy for male adolescent sex offenders: A model for residential treatment. Residential Treatment for Children and Youth, 7, 59-74.
Describes a mandatory 13-week group treatment model for male adolescent sex offenders in a residential treatment program that encourages self-disclosure in a supportive confrontational environment which is geared towards eliciting honest responses from group members. The focus of the group is on (1) development of group cohesiveness, (2) awareness of denial and projection, (3) development of empathy for the victim, (4) the dual-status offender, (5) homophobia, (6) interpersonal skills, and (7) sex education.

1054. Scherer, D.G., Brondino, M.J., Henggeler, S.W., Melton, G.B., et al. (1994). Multisystemic Family Preservation Therapy: Preliminary findings from a study of rural and minority serious adolescent offenders. Journal of Emotional and Behavioral Disorders, 2, 198-206.
Analyses assessed the impact of multisystemic therapy on family functioning and the problem behavior of the delinquent adolescent in 55 White and Black rural families with a chronically delinquent son. Compared to a control group, the multisystemic group showed significant improvements in problem behavior and mother's psychological distress.

1055. Smets, A.C., & Cebula, C.M. (1987). A group treatment program for adolescent sex offenders: Five steps toward resolution. Child Abuse and Neglect, 11, 247-254.

1056. Stouthamer-Loeber, M., & Loeber, R. (1988). Parents as intervention agents for children with conduct problems and juvenile offenders. Child and Youth Services, 11, 127-148.

1057. Thomas, J.N. (1982). Juvenile sex offender: Physician and parent communication. Pediatric Annals, 11, 807-812.

1058. Watson, S.M., Henggeler, S.W., Borduin, C.M. (1985). Interrelations among multidimensional family therapy outcome measures. Family Therapy, 12, 185-196.

1059. White, S.L. (1976). Providing family-centered consultation to a juvenile court in Massachusetts. Hospital and Community Psychiatry, 27, 692-693.

1060. Wunderlich, R.A., Lozes, J., & Lewis, J. (1974). Recidivism rates of group therapy participants and other adolescents processed by a juvenile court. Psychotherapy: Theory, Research and Practice, 11, 243-245.

1061. Zimpfer, D.G. (1992). Group work with juvenile delinquents. Journal for Specialists in Group Work, 17, 116-126.

13

Female Mentally Ill Offenders

1062. Baridon, P.C., & Rosner, K. (1981). Characteristics of women forensic patients in a federal hospital. Hospital and Community Psychiatry, 32, 50-53.
A study of 2 cohorts of 72 women forensic patients found that over the ten-year period separating the groups, admissions of women convicted of non-violent and victimless crimes had decreased from 12 to 50%, while admissions for violent offenders had increased by 17%. Typical female forensic patients were black, unmarried, in their mid thirties, undereducated and likely to be diagnosed as schizophrenic.

1063. Birecree, E.A., Bloom, J.D., Leverette, M.D., & Williams, M. (1994). Diagnostic efforts regarding women in Oregon's prison system: A preliminary report. International Journal of Offender Therapy and Comparative Criminology, 38, 217-230.
Studied 91 women in Oregon's prison system via psychometric testing and clinical interviews to assess their need for mental health services. The incidence of mental disorders was high in this population with a high rate of dual diagnosis. Substance abuse/dependence (91%) and affective disorders (42%) were the most prevalent disorders. Psychotic disorders were not often identified. Results suggest that there are 2 overlapping diagnostic groups in need of treatment while in prison, those with affective and/or substance abuse problems.

1064. Blount, W.R., Danner, T.A., Vega, M., & Silverman, I.J. (1991). The influence of substance use among adult female inmates. Journal of Drug Issues, 21, 449-467.
The extent of substance abuse among over a thousand adult women prisoners was found to be inversely related to age at first arrest as an adult, age at incarceration, and employment at time of arrest. The extent of substance use was directly related to number and percent of prior offenses and incarcerations, being from a broken

home, and parental criminality. Although nonusers were more likely to be convicted of homicide, casual/recreational users were the most violent.

1065. Bourget, D., & Bradford, J.M. (1989). Female arsonists: A clinical study. <u>Bulletin of the American Academy of Psychiatry and the Law</u>, <u>17</u>, 293-300.
A study of 17 female arsonists found that most were single or separated but were not of any specific age group. Further, these women seemed to be characterized by poor impulse control. Demographic and clinical differences between female and male arsonists are also discussed.

1066. Brodsky, A.M. (1974). Planning for the female offender: Directions for the future. <u>Criminal Justice and Behavior</u>, <u>1</u>, 392-400.

1067. Brooks, P.W., & Mitchell, G. (1975). A fifteen-year review of female admissions to Carstairs State Hospital. <u>British Journal of Psychiatry</u>, <u>127</u>, 448-455.
Contrasts two groups of female admissions to a state hospital: (1) persistently violent patients and (2) patients referred from prison. The prison group are more likely to have committed a single violent act, usually involving a family member, and are more likely to suffer from schizophrenia. Those in the transfer group were more likely to be characterized by persistent violent interactions and to suffer from personality disorders and to have poorer prognoses than the prison group.

1068. Brownstone, D.Y., & Swaminath, R.S. (1989). Violent behaviour and psychiatric diagnosis in female offenders. <u>Canadian Journal of Psychiatry</u>, <u>34</u>, 190-194.
A study of 91 female offenders found that an early age of onset of criminal behavior was associated with personality disorder, while women over 30 yrs of age were often diagnosed as having a psychotic disorder. There was no association between age at first crime and age at index admission with the type of crime committed.

1069. Cooper, A.J., Swaminath, S., Baxter, D., & Poulin, C. (1990). A female sex offender with multiple paraphilias: A psychologic, physiologic (laboratory sexual arousal) and endocrine case study. <u>Canadian Journal of Psychiatry</u>, <u>35</u>, 334-337.

1070. D'Orban, P.T. (1979). Women who kill their children. <u>British Journal of Psychiatry</u>, <u>134</u>, 560-571.
A study of 89 women charged with killing or attempting to kill their children found six subtypes: (1) battering mothers, (2) mentally ill mothers, (3) neonaticides, (4) retaliating mothers, (5) mothers killing unwanted children, and (6) mercy killers. Social and clinical features that distinguish the groups are discussed.

1071. D'Orban, P.T., & O'Connor, A. (1989). Women who kill their parents. <u>British Journal of Psychiatry</u>, <u>154</u>, 27-33.

1072. Daniel, A.E., Robins, A.J., Reid, J.C., & Wilfley, D.E. (1988). Lifetime and six-month prevalence of psychiatric disorders among sentenced female offenders. <u>Bulletin of the American Academy of Psychiatry and the Law</u>, <u>16</u>, 333-342.
In a study of 100 women inmates, authors found high prevalence rates of schizophrenia, major depression, substance use disorders, psychosexual dysfunction,

and antisocial personality disorders. These prevalence rates were significantly higher than those of the general population.

1073. Dell, S., Robertson, G., James, K., & Grounds, A. (1993). Remands and psychiatric assessments in Holloway Prison. I: The psychotic population. British Journal of Psychiatry, 163, 634-640.

1074. Dell, S., Robertson, G., James, K., & Grounds, A. (1993). Remands and psychiatric assessments in Holloway. Prison II: The non- psychotic population. British Journal of Psychiatry, 163, 640-644.

1075. Edwall, G.E., Villanueva, M.R., Holigan, R.A., Buchanan, R.J., et al. (1989). Females incarcerated for assaultive crimes: Differential Personality and demographic variables. American Journal of Forensic Psychology, 7, 49-57.

1076. Epperson, D.L., Hannum, T.E., & Datwyler, M.L. (1982). Women incarcerated in 1960, 1970 and 1980: Implications of demographic, educational, and personality characteristics for earlier research. Criminal Justice and Behavior, 9, 352-363.
        Studied demographic, educational, personality and offense related characteristics of female offenders in an Iowa prison for a twenty year period and found that, although there was a an increase in the proportion of violent offenders incarcerated over the time period assessed, few differences in demographic characteristics, educational level, educational achievement, or personality factors as measured by the MMPI were found. The authors conclude that because the female prison population had remained fairly stable, earlier research with female offenders remains relevant and useful.

1077. Fehrenbach, P.A., & Monastersky, C. (1988). Characteristics of female sexual offenders. American Journal of Orthopsychiatry, 58, 148-151.

1078. Felthous, A.R., & Yudowitz, B. (1977). Approaching a comparative typology of assaultive female offenders. Psychiatry, 40, 270-276.

1079. Fogel, C.I. (1993). Hard time: the stressful nature of incarceration for women. Issues in Mental Health Nursing, 14, 367-377.

1080. Fogel, C.I., & Martin, S.L. (1992). The mental health of incarcerated women. Western Journal of Nursing Research, 14, 30-47.

1081. Hufft, A.G. (1992). Psychosocial adaption to pregnancy in prison. Journal of Psychosocial Nursing and Mental Health Services, 30, 19-22.
        Childbearing for incarcerated women is complicated by characteristics of special needs associated with psychosocial adaptation to increased stress, a restrictive physical environment, alteration of social support systems, and the displacement of the maternal role functions after birth. Psychiatric nurses are in a unique position to affect the health care provided for pregnant inmates by virtue of their knowledge and expertise in assessing and treating problems in psychosocial adaptation. Assessment of pregnant inmates is based on identification of the presence and magnitude of

dimensions of stress, environmental restrictiveness, social support systems, and maternal role displacement.

1082. Hurley, W., & Dunne, M.P. (1991). Psychological distress and psychiatric morbidity in women prisoners. Australian and New Zealand Journal of Psychiatry, 25, 461-470.
In a study of 92 women inmates screened for psychiatric disorder, it was found that distress was associated with recent stressful life events and was more severe in women awaiting trial. Fifty-three percent of the prisoners were diagnosed as current cases of a psychiatric disorder. The most frequent diagnoses were adjustment disorder with depressed mood and personality disorders. Lifetime prevalence of psychoactive substance use disorders was 54 percent. Aboriginal women were over-represented in this prison population. A follow-up survey after 4 months showed no fall in the prevalence of psychological distress and psychiatric morbidity.

1083. Kuhns, J.B., Heide, K.M., & Silverman, I. (1992). Substance use/misuse among female arrestees. International Journal of the Addictions, 27, 1283-1292.
This study compared the demographics, drug use histories, and past experiences with drug use treatment of 53 female prostitutes and 47 female arrestees. Prostitutes were more likely to have dropped out of school, to have ever tried drugs, to use drugs more frequently, and to have begun drug use at an earlier age than the female offender group. The authors conclude that early drug use may lead to vulnerability for prostitution among young females and that drug treatment and intervention needs to begin at a young age.

1084. Lamb, H.R., and Grant, R.W. (1983). Mentally ill women in a county jail. Archives of General Psychiatry, 40, 363-368.
Studied 101 inmates of a county jail for women who had been referred for psychiatric evaluation and found that 86% had a history of psychiatric hospitalization, and 94% had prior arrest records. Seventy percent had a history of serious physical violence and 84% of those who had children failed to demonstrate the ability to care for them. More than half met criteria for involuntary hospitalization, suggesting a need for mandatory aftercare and involuntary hospitalization.

1085. Long, C.K., Lenoir C., Phung, T., & Witherspoon, A.D. (1995). A partial replication of Lippin (1990) using the Myers-Briggs type indicator with a sample of female prisoners. Psychological Reports, 77, 467-472.

1086. Long, G.T., Sultan, F.E., Kiefer, S.A., & Schrum, D.M. (1984). The psychological profile of the female first offender and the recidivist: A comparison. Special Issue: Gender issues, sex offenses, and criminal justice: Current trends. Journal of Offender Counseling, Services and Rehabilitation, 9, 119-123.

1087. MacMillan, J., & Baldwin, S. (1993). A pilot study of an alcohol education course for young women offenders: What's good for the goose? Alcohol and Alcoholism, 28, 499-504.

Treatment interventions for women continue to be neglected and under-researched. This paper describes an alcohol education course designed for women offenders in prison, outlining course content and the rationale for its development.

1088. Maden, A., Swinton, M., & Gunn, J. (1992). The ethnic origin of women serving a prison sentence. British Journal of Criminology, 32, 218-221.

1089. Maden, A., Swinton, M., & Gunn, J. (1994). Psychiatric disorder in women serving a prison sentence. British Journal of Psychiatry, 164, 44-54.

1090. Maden, A., Swinton, M., & Gunn, J. (1994). A criminological and psychiatric survey of women serving a prison sentence. British Journal of Criminology, 34, 172-191.

1091. Magura, S., Kang, S., Shapiro, J., & O'Day, J. (1993). HIV risk among women injecting drug users who are in jail. Addiction, 88, 1351-1360.

1092. McGaha, G.S. (1987). Health care issues of incarcerated women. Annual Meeting of the Academy of Criminal Justice Sciences (1986, Orlando, Florida). Journal of Offender Counseling, Services and Rehabilitation, 12, 53-59.
Presents data on the physical and mental health status of incarcerated women, the prison health-care-delivery system, and the medical needs of female prisoners. Potential solutions to the problems identified include increased communication and education, better utilization of nursing personnel, and greater community resources.

1093. O'Connor, A., & O'Neill, H. (1991). Female prison transfers to the Central Mental Hospital, a special hospital (1983-1988). Irish Journal of Psychological Medicine, 8, 122-123.
Studied 99 female offenders transferred to the Central Mental Hospital in Ireland and found that the primary diagnoses were schizophrenia, mania, depression and stress, personality disorder, mental handicap, and drug addiction. The longest average stay at the hospital was for personality disorders (5 weeks). The longest sentences were for drug offenses. There were no cases of homicide or sex offenses. The authors conclude that many of these cases could be handled in their catchment area hospital rather than in a high security special hospital.

1094. Pendergrass, V.E. (1974). Innovative programs for women in jail and prisons: Trick or treatment. Criminal Justice and Behavior, 1, 359-368.

1095. Richie, D.E., & Johnson, C. (1996). Abuse histories among newly incarcerated women in a New York City jail. Journal of the American Medical Womens Associateiom, 51, 111-114, 117.

1096. Sherman, L.G., & Morschauser, P.C. (1989). Screening for suicide risk in inmates. Psychiatric Quarterly, 60, 119-138.

1097. Singer, M.I., Bussey, J., Song, L.Y., & Lunghofer, L. (1995). The psychosocial issues of women serving time in jail. Social Work, 40, 103-113.

1098. Southwell, M. (1981). Counseling the young prison prostitute. Journal of Psychiatric Nursing, 19, 25-26.

1099. Stewart, L.A. (1993). Profile of female firesetters. Implications for treatment. British Journal of Psychiatry, 163, 248-256.

1100. Strick, S.E. (1989). A demographic study of 100 admissions to a female forensic center: Incidences of multiple charges and multiple diagnoses. Journal of Psychiatry and Law, 17, 435-448.
Examined the characteristics of 81 female offenders admitted to a female forensics center over a 3-year period. On admission each woman was administered nursing, physical, and psychiatric evaluations and diagnosed according to the Diagnostic and Statistical Manual of Mental Disorders (DSM-III). Seventy-nine percent of all Ss were psychotic on admission. Combinations of more than one personality disorder were found in 61% of the sample diagnosed with Axis II disorders. Specialized services need to be made available to female forensic patients within the milieu of the holding facility, and prevention and outreach services are needed to serve this population after release.

1101. Teplin, L.A., Abram, K.M., & McClelland, G.M. (1996). Prevalence of psychiatric disorders among incarcerated women: Pretrial jail detainees. Archives of General Psychiatry, 53, 505-512.
The prevalence of 10 psychiatric disorders based on the Diagnostic Interview Schedule Version III-R was assessed in a sample of 1272 women awaiting trial in a correctional facility in Chicago. Results show that over 80% of the sample met criteria for one or more lifetime DSM-III-R disorders. Substance abuse or dependence, most often drug abuse or dependence, was the most prevalent disorder.

1102. Travin, S., Cullen, K., & Protter, B. (1990). Female sex offenders: Severe victims and victimizers. Journal of Forensic Sciences, 35, 140-150.

1103. Turner, T.H., & Tofler, D.S. (1986). Indicators of psychiatric disorder among women admitted to prison. British Medical Journal of Clinical Research and Education, 292, 651-653.
In a study of a random sample of 708 women inmates, it was found that 195 had a history of self harm, 125 had a history of psychiatric illness, 99 were opiate dependent, and 89 were regular users of other psychoactive drugs.

1104. Velimesis, M.I. (1981). Sex roles and mental health of women in prison. Professional Psychology, 12, 128-135.

1105. Wellisch, J., Anglin, M.D., & Prendergast, M.L. (1993). Numbers and characteristics of drug-using women in the criminal justice system: Implications for treatment. Journal of Drug Issues, 23, 7-30.

1106. Widom, C.S. (1978) An empirical classification of female offenders. Criminal Justice and Behavior, 5, 35-52.

1107. Wilfley, D.E., Rodon, C.J., & Anderson, W.P. (1986). Angry women offenders: Case study of a group. International Journal of Offender Therapy and Comparative Criminology, 30, 41-51.

Describes a therapy group for women offenders in a maximum security prison directed at facilitating learning to acknowledge, accept and constructively express their anger. The authors suggest that the group therapy increased participants' personal control, sense of responsibility, and the ability to formulate and use alternatives in dealing with anger-provoking situations, as well as providing a constructive mutual support system.

1108. Wilson, J. (1993). Childbearing within the prison system. Nursing Standards, 7, 25-28.

14

Professional and Ethical Issues

1109. Alexander, R. (1989). The right to treatment in mental and correctional institutions. Social Work, 34, 109-112.

1110. American Bar Association (1989). ABA criminal justice mental health standards. Washington, DC: Author.

1111. American Bar Association. (1984). Criminal justice mental health standards. Washington, DC: Author.

1112. American Psychiatric Association. (1984). Issues in forensic psychiatry. Washington, DC: Author.

1113. American Psychological Association. (1978). Report of the task force on the role of psychology in the criminal justice system. American Psychologist, 33, 1099-1113.

1114. Anonymous. (1980). The patient as offender: Panel discussion. Annals of the New York Academy of Sciences, 347, 209-212.

1115. Appelbaum, P.B., & Gutheil, T.G. (1991). Clinical handbook of psychiatry and the law (2nd ed.). Williamsburg, VA: William and Mary College.

1116. Appelbaum, P.S. (1986). Competence to be executed: Another conundrum for mental health professionals. Hospital and Community Psychiatry, 37, 682-684. Discusses ethical issues surrounding professional involvement in determinations of competency to be executed and in treatment of those found incompetent to be executed who, upon restoration to competency, will be executed.

1117. Arcaya, J. (1987). Role conflicts in coercive assessments: Evaluation and recommendations. Professional Psychology: Research and Practice, 18, 422-428.

1118. Aubrey, M., & Dougher, M.J. (1990). Ethical issues in outpatient group therapy with sex offenders. Journal for Specialists in Group Work, 15, 75-82.

1119. Aviram, U., & Segal, S. (1973). Exclusion of the mentally ill. Archives of General Psychiatry, 29, 126-131.

1120. Barnes, D.M. (1992). Prison care plan: sowing seeds of hope. Journal of Christian Nursing, 9, 28-31.

1121. Beck, J.C. (1995). Forensic psychiatry in Britain. Bulletin of the American Academy of Psychiatry and Law, 23, 249-260.

1122. Bernheim, J. (1993). Medical ethics in prison. Criminal Behaviour and Mental Health, 3, 85-96.

1123. Bernier, S.L. (1986). Corrections and mental health. Journal of Psychosocial Nursing and Mental Health Services, 24, 20-25.

1124. Bowden, P. (1976). Medical practice: Defendants and prisoners. Journal of Medical Ethics, 2, 163-172.

1125. Bowden, P. (1991). Treatment: Use, abuse and consent. Criminal Behaviour and Mental Health, 1, 130-136.
Reviews different treatments for sex abuse offenders including drug therapies such as cyproterone acetate and medroxyprogesterone acetate, hormonal ablation, and castration. It is recommended that drugs be used in combination with other intensive therapies such as sex therapy, sex education, family therapy, cognitive therapy, and covert sensitization. However, there is a substantial amount of evidence testifying to the failure of psychotherapy and behavioral methods to treat serious or dangerous sexual deviants.

1126. Brakel, S.J., Parry, J., & Weiner, B.A. (1985). The mentally disabled and the law (rev. ed.). Chicago, IL: American Bar Association.

1127. Brakel, S.J., Rock, R.S. (1971). The mentally disabled and the law. Chicago, IL: University of Chicago Press.

1128. Brodsky, S. (1973). Psychologists in the criminal justice system. Urbana, IL: University of Illinois Press.

1129. Burrows, R. (1995). Captive care: changes in prison nursing. Nursing Standards, 9, 29-31.
Discusses how the major developments in mental health provision and changing health patterns in inmate populations have influenced the evolution of specialist roles for nurses in correctional settings. Unresolved issues include training and salaries of

nurses who work in prisons remain and the complex ethical and legal conflicts associated with the prison environment.

1130. Calsin, J.B., Jr. (1992). Prison nursing: Rising above fear to care. Journal of Christian Nursing, 9, 22-26.

1131. Carroll, J. (1995). Attitude of prison nurse officers to drug misusers. Nursing Times, 91, 36-37.
Nurses are the key service providers to drug misusing inmates. The literature, however, suggests that the skills and knowledge base of the nursing profession has received very little attention. This study reports on the attitudes of nurses towards intravenous drug misusers in a Scottish prison. Age, sex, and grade appeared to affect attitudes, but the results were not clear cut. Some stereotyping of drug misusers was evident among respondents. Drug misusers, however, are a marginalised group in terms of health care, making it all the more important to address their needs while in prison. However, the skills of such staff are often not being used appropriately.

1132. Chalke, F.C.R., Roberts, C.A., Turner, R.E. (1995). Forensic psychiatry in Canada, 1945-1980. Canadian Journal of Psychiatry, 40, 120-124.

1133. Clements, C.B. (1987). Psychologists in adult correctional institutions: Getting off the treadmill. In E.K. Morris, & C.J. Braukmann (Eds.), Behavioral approaches to crime and delinquency: A handbook of application. New York: Plenum.

1134. Convit, A., Levine, S., Berns, S., & Evangelista, C. (1991). Type of symptomatology as a form of volunteer bias. Bulletin of the American Academy of Psychiatry and the Law, 19, 185-191.

1135. Cooke, D.J., Baldwin, P.J., & Howison, J. (1990). Psychology in prisons. London: Routledge.

1136. Crespi, T.D. (1990). School psychologists in forensic psychology: Converging and diverging issues. Professional Psychology: Research and Practice, 21, 83-87.

1137. Crossley, T., & Guzman, R. (1986). Psychologists and psychiatrists: Colleagues or rivals? American Journal of Forensic Psychology, 4, 3-9.

1138. Curran, W.J., & Harding, T.W. (1978). The law and mental health: Harmonizing objectives. Geneva: World Health Organization.

1139. Droes, N.S. (1994). Correctional nursing practice. Journal of Community Health Nursing, 11, 201-210.

1140. Dushkind, D.S. (1984). Forensic psychology: A proposed definition. American Journal of Forensic Psychology, 2, 171-172.
Offers a definition of the subdiscipline of forensic psychology which focuses on the application of scientific methods to subject matter relevant to law and the administration of justice including such functions as providing evaluations and

testimony in administrative proceedings, consultation to legal actors, alternative methods of dispute resolution, and performing individual, group, and marital therapy.

1141. Eisenmann, R. (1995). Cruel treatment of learning disabled, emotionally disturbed prisoners: The dilemma of a humanistic psychologist in an inhumane setting. International Journal of Adolescence and Youth, 5, 189-194.

1142. Emory, E. (1972). Problems encountered in a federal prison. American Journal of Psychiatry, 128, 1466.

1143. Fink, L., & Martin, J.P. (1973). Psychiatry and the crisis of the prison system. American Journal of Psychotherapy, 27, 579-584.

1144. Freeman, R.J., & Roesch, R. (1989).Mental disorder and the criminal justice system: A review. International Journal of Law and Psychiatry, 12, 105-115.
The problems of mentally ill offenders are due in part to their position at the inter of the mental health and legal systems. Differences in the meaning mental illness between these systems have led to growth of a largely unstudied population that falls between the cracks of these definitions. The law formally recognizes the existence of the mentally ill offender only in the context of fitness and insanity issues. Thus, those offenders who are diagnosable, in terms of the mental health framework who do not fit into the legal framework are often overlooked in research.

1145. French, L.A. (1983). The mentally retarded and pseudo retarded offender: A clinical/legal dilemma. Federal Probation, 46, 55-61.
Deinstitutionalization has led to great increases in the number of mentally ill and mentally retarded persons on the streets without adequate follow-up and aftercare who are at increased risk for incarceration and subsequent victimization in jails and prisons. These institutions are generally ill-equipped to address their special needs. Proneness of mentally deficient offenders to crime and clinical factors in the treatment of these offenders from both a mental health and legal perspective are discussed.

1146. Gibbons, F.X., Gibbons, B.N., & Kassin, S.M. (1981). Reactions to the criminal behavior of mentally retarded and nonretarded offenders. American Journal of Mental Deficiency, 86, 235-242.
A study of college students reactions to differing types of crimes committed by either a mentally retarded or nonretarded person found that subjects chose lighter sentences for the retarded person regardless of the type of offense. Results indicated that the subjects believed that the retarded offender was more likely to have coerced into committing the offense and in confessing to it, accounting for the lighter suggested sentences.

1147. Goldstein, N. (1983). Psychiatry in prisons. Psychiatric Clinics of North America, 6, 751-765.

1148. Goldstein, N. (1987). An overview of the elderly in the criminal justice system: Mental health perspectives. In R. Rosner & H.I. Schwartz (Eds.), Geriatric psychiatry and the law. Critical issues in American psychiatry and the law, Vol. 3. New York: Plenum.

1149.   Green, C., Menzies, R.P., & Naismith, L.J. (1991). Psychiatry in the Canadian Correctional Service. Canadian Journal of Psychiatry, 36, 290-295.
The history and current status of provision psychiatric services for mentally ill offenders in the Canadian are discussed, including current difficulties, including inadequate psychiatric staffing, lack of autonomy of medical and clinical staff, and inadequate communication with local universities.

1150.   Green, K. (1984). Psychological intervention. In K. Green, & A Schaefer (Eds), Forensic psychology: A primer for legal and mental health professionals. Springfield, IL: Thomas.

1151.   Greenberg, W.M., Shah, P.J., & Seide, M. (1993). Recidivism on an acute psychiatric forensic service. Hospital and Community Psychiatry, 44, 583-585.
A study of 150 acute forensic unit patients found that about half were recidivists to the forensic unit within 2 years. Further, those with the most severe conditions were the most likely to be readmitted. The authors conclude that the chronic mentally ill population is entrenched in a fragmented system of treatment and incarceration.

1152.   Greenspan, J. (1988). Comment: AIDS/ARC support group. Journal of Prison and Jail Health, 7, 76-79.
Addresses issues of segregation, discrimination, and stigmatization that may arise for members of AIDS/ARC support groups in a prison environment.

1153.   Grekin, P.M., Jemelka, R., & Trupin, E.W. (1994). Racial differences in the criminalization of the mentally ill. Bulletin of the American Academy of Psychiatry and the Law, 22, 411-420.

1154.   Grisso, J.T. (1974). On the role of mental health workers in the criminal justice system. American Psychologist, 29, 917-919.

1155.   Guze, S.B. (1976). Criminality and psychiatric disorders. New York: Oxford University Press.

1156.   Halleck, N.H., & Petrila, J. (1988). Risk management in forensic services. International Journal of Law and Psychiatry, 11, 347-358.
Discusses common situations that may give rise to liability in a psychiatric facility. To prevail in a malpractice action, a plaintiff must prove (1) the existence of a therapist-patient relationship, (2) a violation of that duty by the therapist's failure to conform to required care standards, (3) a causal connection between the violation of the care standard and patient harm or injury, and (4) proof of patient harm. The author discusses some frequently litigated issues and suggests risk management measures for forensic facilities.

1157.   Halleck, S. (1986). The mentally disordered offender. Rockville, MD: National Institute of Mental Health.

1158. Halleck, S.L. (1974). A troubled view of current trends in forensic psychiatry. Journal of Psychiatry and the Law, 2, 135-139.

1159. Halpern, A.L. (1979). Editor's introduction: Symposium on psychiatry and the criminal offender. Bulletin of the American Academy of Psychiatry and the Law, 7, vii-ix.

1160. Harmon, R.B. (1989). Administration and management of an urban forensic psychiatry clinic. In R. Rosner, & R.B. Harmon (Eds.), Criminal court consultation: Critical issues in American psychiatry and the law, Vol. 5. New York: Plenum.

1161. Heilbrun, K.S., Radelet, M.L., & Dvoskin, J. (1992). The debate on treating individuals incompetent for execution. American Journal of Psychiatry, 149, 596-605.
Arguments for and against provision of mental health treatment to persons judged incompetent for execution are presented in terms of the nature of the disorder being treated, the type of treatment provided, goals of treatment, and of the standards for judging competency for execution. Treatment of persons incompetent for execution may not violate ethical standards in some cases, however, treatment relevant to establishing competency requires the informed consent of the prisoner.

1162. Heilbrun, K., Radelet, M.L., & Dvoskin, J. (1993). "The debate on treating individuals incompetent for execution": Reply. American Journal of Psychiatry, 150, 678.

1163. Hodgins, S. (1993). Mental disorder and crime. Newbury Park, CA: Sage.

1164. Hollingsworth, J.B. (1985). Overview of correctional psychiatry. American Journal of Forensic Psychiatry, 6, 23-28.

1165. Hufft, A.G., & Fawkes, L.S. (1994). Federal inmates. A unique psychiatric nursing challenge. Nursing Clinics of North America, 29, 35-42.

1166. Kaufman, E. (1980). The violation of psychiatric standards of care in prisons. American Journal of Psychiatry, 137, 566-570.

1167. Kermani, E.J. (1989). Handbook of psychiatry and the law. Chicago, IL: Year Book Medical Publishers.

1168. Ketai, R. (1974). Role conflicts of the prison psychiatrist. Bulletin of the American Academy of Psychiatry and Law, 2, 246-250.

1169. Kleinman, S.B. (1990). Liberty and tardive dyskinesia: Informed consent to Antipsychotic medications in the forensic psychiatric hospital. Journal of Forensic Sciences, 35, 1155-1162.

1170. Krizek, G.O. (1993). [Memories of psychiatric practice in a North American prison]. Ceskoslovenska Psyciatrie, 89, 183-186.

1171. Kury, H., & Fenn, R. (1977). Problems and tasks for the psychologist in treatment-oriented penal institutions. Psychologische Rundschau, 28, 190-203.

1172. Lamb, H.R., Sorkin, A.P., & Zusman, J. (1981). Legislating social control of the mentally ill in California. American Journal of Psychiatry, 138, 334-339.

1173. Langton, J., & Torpy, D. (1988). Confidentiality and a "future" sadistic sex offender. Medicine, Sciences and the Law, 28, 195-199.

1174. Leong, G.B., & Silva, J.A. (1988). The right to refuse treatment: An uncertain future. Psychiatric Quarterly, 59, 284-292.
Discusses 3 court cases involving the right to refuse treatment (1) in psychiatric hospitals, (2) among convicted prisoners, and (3) in other criminal justice settings. The cases illustrate potential consequences that threaten the refusing patient, the integrity of the legal system, and society in general.

1175. Leong, G.B., & Silva, J.A. (1989). Asian American forensic psychiatrists. Psychiatric Annals, 19, 629-632.

1176. Maier, G.J., Bernstein, M.J., Musholt, E.A. (1989). Personal coping mechanisms for prison clinicians: Toward transformation. Journal of Prison and Jail Health, 8, 29-39.

1177. McLean, E.K. (1975). Prison and humanity. Lancet, 1(7905), 507-511.

1178. Meehl, P.E. (1971). Law and the fireside inductions: Some reflections of a clinical psychologist. Journal of Social Issues, 27, 65-100.

1179. Menninger, K. (1983). Observations on the present relations of our profession to the care and treatment of offenders. Bulletin of the Menninger Clinic, 47, 295-301.

1180. Mieville, C. (1979). Institutional therapy. Psychiatry and penitentiary problems, Schweizer Archiv Fur Neurologie, Neurochirurgie und Psyciatrie, 124, 191-195.

1181. Miller, R.D., Doren, D.M., Van-Rybroek, G.J., & Maier, G.J. (1988). Emerging problems for staff associated with the release of potentially dangerous forensic patients. Bulletin of the American Academy of Psychiatry and the Law, 16, 309-320.
Presents three cases that illustrate the dilemmas involved in the release of potentially dangerous forensic patients. Clinicians are viewed as being largely responsible for their current plight because they often overstate their ability to predict and treat aggressive behavior.

1182. Miller, R.D., Maier, G.J., Van Rybroek, G.J., & Weidemann, J.A. (1989). Treating patients "doing time": A forensic perspective. Hospital and Community Psychiatry, 40, 960-962.

1183. Miller, M.O., & Sales, B.D. (1986). Law and mental health professionals: Arizona. Washington, DC: American Psychological Association Press.

1184. Modlin, H.C., Porter, L., & Benson, R.E. (1976). Mental health centers and the criminal justice system. Hospital and Community Psychiatry, 27, 716-719.
Data from a study of 26 Kansas community mental health centers showed that in all large communities some reciprocal programs had developed between the mental health centers and the criminal justice system, but meaningful collaboration was rare in small communities. Juvenile courts, urban law enforcement agencies, and county probation officers were most receptive to collaborative programs. Based on data from some of the most effective collaborative ventures revealed 3 basic conditions that contributed to their success: an urban community setting, individual initiative by staff from each system, and location of the program within the criminal justice system.

1185. Monahan, J. (Ed.) (1980). Who is the client? The ethics of psychological intervention in the criminal justice system. Washington, DC: American Psychological Association.

1186. Monahan, J., & Monahan, L. (1977). Prediction research and the role of psychologists in correctional institutions. San Diego Law Review, 14, 1028-1038.

1187. Monahan, J., & Ruggiero, M. (1980). Psychological and psychiatric aspects of determinate criminal sentencing. International Journal of Law and Psychiatry, 3, 105-116.

1188. Morse, S.J. (1978). Law and mental health professionals: The limits of expertise. Professional Psychology, 9, 389-399.

1189. Murray, R.B., & Huelskoetter, M.M.W. (Eds.) (1991). Psychiatric mental health nursing: Giving emotional care (3rd. ed.). East Norwalk, CT: Appleton & Lange.

1190. Nelson, S.H., & Berger, V.F. (1988). Current issues in state mental health forensic programs. Bulletin of the American Academy of Psychiatry and the Law, 16, 67-75.

1191. Padberg, J. (1972). Nursing and forensic psychiatry. Perspectives in Psychiatric Care, 10, 163-167.

1192. Pearson, V. (1992). Law, rights, and psychiatry in the People's Republic of China. International Journal of Law and Psychiatry, 15, 409-423.

1193. Peternelj-Taylor, C.A., & Johnson, R. (1995). Serving time: Psychiatric mental health nursing in corrections. Journal of Psychosocial Nursing and Mental Health Services, 33, 12-19.

1194. Peterson, M., Stephens, J., Dickey, R., & Lewis, W. (1996). Transsexuals within the prison system: An international survey of correctional services policies. Behavioral Sciences and the Law, 14, 219-229.

1195. Pinta, E.R. (1993). "The debate on treating individuals incompetent for execution": Comment. American Journal of Psychiatry, 150, 677-678.

1196. Pogrebin, M.R., & Poole, E.D. (1987). Deinstitutionalization and increased arrest rates among the mentally disordered. Journal of Psychiatry and Law, 15, 117-127.

1197. Radelet, M.L., & Barnard, G.W. (1988). Treating those found incompetent for execution: Ethical chaos with only one solution. Bulletin of the American Academy of Psychiatry and the Law, 16, 297-308.
       Uses the case of Gary Alvord, the only inmate in modern times found incompetent to be executed, in order to illustrate the medical/ethical dilemma created by the demand to treat mentally incompetent prisoners so that they can be executed.

1198. Rappeport, J.R. (1978). The psychiatrist and criminal justice. In J.P. Brady, & H.K.H. Brodie (Eds.), Controversy in psychiatry. Philadelphia, PA: W.B. Saunders.

1199. Resnick, P.J. (1978). The political offender: Forensic psychiatric considerations. Bulletin of the American Academy of Psychiatry and the Law, 6, 388-397.

1200. Rogers, J.L. (1985). What is the client's best interest? Professional roles in the criminal justice system. Journal of Personality Assessment, 49, 665-668.

1201. Rogers, R., & Bagby, R.M. (1992). Diversion of mentally disordered offenders: A legitimate role for clinicians? Behavioral Sciences and the Law, 10, 407-418.
       Arguments for diversion are based on humanitarian interests and treatment needs. Arguments opposing diversion recommendations emphasize the variability of opinions regarding treatability, the lack of sufficient outcome data, and the potential for negative consequences in offering unsolicited opinions on diversion. Initial data from 271 pretrial evaluations underscore the range in psychiatric use of diversion recommendations, although inpatient referrals appear to be based on clinical status.

1202. Rollin, H.R. (1976). The care of the mentally abnormal offender and the protection of the public. Journal of Medical Ethics, 2, 157-160.

1203. Roth, L.H. (1978). Clinical and legal considerations in the therapy of violence-prone patients. In J. Masserman (Ed.), Current psychiatric therapies. New York: Grune & Stratton.

1204. Roth, L.H. (1980). Correctional psychiatry. In W.S. Curran, A.L. McGarry, & C.S. Perry (Eds.), Modern legal medicine, psychiatry, and forensic science. Philadelphia, PA: Davis.

1205. Roth, L.H. (1986). Correctional psychiatry. In W.J. Curran, L. McGarry, & S.A. Shah (Eds.), Forensic psychiatry and psychology: Perspectives and standards for interdisciplinary practice. Philadelphia, PA: F.A. Davis.

1206. Roy, C. (1976). Dilemmas of medical ethics in the Canadian Penitentiary Service. Journal of Medical Ethics, 2, 180-184.

1207. Sadler, C. (1992). Prison support. Nursing Times, 88, 21.

1208. Sadoff, R.L. (1988). Forensic psychiatry: A practical guide for lawyers and psychiatrists (2nd ed.). Springfield, IL: Charles C. Thomas.

1209. Saxton, G.H. (1986). Confidentiality dilemmas for psychologists and psychiatrists in the criminal justice system. American Journal of Forensic Psychology, 4, 25-32.

1210. Schilit, J. (1979). The mentally retarded offender and criminal justice personnel. Exceptional Child, 46, 16-22.

1211. Silber, D.E. (1974). Controversy concerning the criminal justice system and its implications for the role of mental health workers. American Psychologist, 29, 239-244.

1212. Slater, R.G. (1986). Abuses of psychiatry in a correction setting. American Journal of Forensic Psychiatry, 7, 41-47.

1213. Slovenko, R. (1973). Psychiatry and law. Boston, MA: Little, Brown.

1214. Smith, C.E. (1987). Prison psychiatry and professional responsibility. Journal of Forensic Sciences, 32, 717-724.

1215. Smith, S.R., & Meyer, R.G. (1987). Law, behavior, and mental health: Policy and practice. New York: New York University Press.

1216. Sommers, I., & Baskin, D.R. (1991). Assessing the appropriateness of the prescription of psychiatric medications in prison. Journal of Nervous and Mental Disease, 179, 267-273.

1217. Standing Committee on Association Standards for Criminal Justice, American Bar Association. (1982). ABA Provisional Criminal Justice Mental Health Standards: An executive summary. Mental Disability Law Reporter, 6, 269-295.

1218. Steadman, H.J. (1972). The psychiatrist as a conservative agent of social control. Social Problems, 20, 263-271.

1219. Stelovich, S. (1979). From the hospital to the prison: A step forward in deinstitutionalization? Hospital and Community Psychiatry, 30, 618-620.

1220. Stevens, R. (1993). When your clients are in jail. Nursing Forum, 28, 5-8.

1221. Szasz, T. (1989). Psychiatric justice. British Journal of Psychiatry, 154, 864-869.

1222. Szasz, T.S. (1972). Ideology and insanity. Garden City, NY: Doubleday.

1223. Szasz, T.S. (1977). Psychiatric slavery. New York: Free Press.

1224. Tanay, E. (1982). Psychiatry in the prison system. Journal of Forensic Sciences, 27, 385-392.

1225. Teplin, L.A. (1983). The criminalization of the mentally ill: Speculation in search of data. Psychological Bulletin, 94, 54-67.

1226. Teplin, L.A. (1984). Criminalizing mental disorder: The comparative arrest rate of the mentally ill. American Psychologist, 39, 794-803.
Reports findings of a study of 1,382 police-citizen encounters that demonstrate that, for comparable offenses, mentally disordered citizens had a significantly greater chance of being arrested the non-mentally disordered persons. The implications for mental health and criminal justice policy making are discussed.

1227. Teplin, L.A. (1984). Mental health and criminal justice. Beverly Hills, CA: Sage Publications.

1228. Teplin, L.A. (1986). Dr. Teplin replies. American Journal of Psychiatry, 143, 676-677.

1229. Teplin, L.A. (1991). The criminalization hypothesis: Myth, misnomer or management strategy. In S.A. Shah & B.D. Sales (Eds.), Law and mental health: Major developments and research needs. Rockville, MD: NIMH.

1230. Toch, H. (Ed.) (1986). Psychology and criminal justice, 2nd ed. Prospect Heights, IL: Waveland Press.

1231. Torrey, E.F. (1992). Criminalizing the seriously mentally ill. Washington, DC: Public Citizen.

1232. Waithe, M.E., Rappeport, J.R., & Weinstein, H.C. (1982). Ethical issues in the practice of forensic psychiatry. Journal of Psychiatry and Law, 10, 7-43.

1233. Warren, M.Q. (1977). Correctional treatment and coercion: The differential effectiveness hypothesis. Criminal Justice and Behavior, 4, 355-376.

1234. Weinberger, L.E., & Sreenivasan, S. (1994). Ethical and professional conflicts in correctional psychology. Professional Psychology Research and Practice, 25, 161-167.
The role of the mental health professional in a prison setting has changed to reflect the prevailing ideology of the correctional administration that de-emphasizes treatment and emphasizes security and custodial concerns. As a consequence, mental health professionals who work in corrections have experienced unique ethical and professional conflicts. Standards were developed to address the conflicts and provide guidelines for professional conduct, but dilemmas continue to exist. The authors indicate this can be attributed to (1) the standards being vague and (2) correctional personnel not understanding or supporting the standards or the psychologist's role as a mental health professional. This article examines these propositions in more detail, using vignettes and discussion, and offers other approaches to resolving the dilemmas and improving the delivery of mental health services to incarcerated individuals.

1235. Weinstein, H.C. (1984). How should forensic psychiatry police itself? Guidelines and grievances: The AAPL Committee on Ethics. Bulletin of the American Academy of Psychiatry and the Law, 12, 289-302.

1236. Weisstub, D.N. (1988). Law and mental health: International perspectives. New York: Pergamon.

1237. Wells, J.A., & Zonana, H. (1986). "The criminality of the mentally ill: A dangerous misconception": Comment. American Journal of Psychiatry, 143, 675-676.

1238. West, D.J. (1989). Szasz on psychiatric justice. British Journal of Psychiatry, 154, 870-871.

1239. Wexler, D.B. (1981). Mental health law: Major issues. New York: Plenum Press.

1240. Williams, P. (1983). The rights of prisoners to psychiatric care. Journal of Prison and Jail Health, 3, 112-118.

1241. Williams, R. (1986). Psychologists participating on or chairing prison disciplinary boards: Comments. Psychological Reports, 59, 57-58.
        Discusses some practical and ethical dilemmas posed for psychologists and other mental health professionals asked to participate in the punitive process of a prison's disciplinary boards.

1242. Wright, F., Bahn, C., & Rieber, R.W. (1980). Forensic psychology and psychiatry. Annals of the New York Academy of Sciences, 347, 364.
        Topics discussed in this article include competency to stand trial, issues of psychological evidence, crisis intervention and hostage negotiation, the patient as offender, violence and the family, media and crime, and human nature, crime, and society.

15

Education and Training

1243. Bender, S.L., et al., (1985). The teaching of psychiatry in the correctional institution at the third year level: A new dimension in the medical school curriculum at New York Medical College. Psychiatric Journal of the University of Ottawa, 10, 139-146.

1244. Ben-David, S. (1992). Staff-to-inmates relations in a total institution: A model of five modes of association. International Journal of Offender Therapy and Comparative Criminology, 36, 209-219.
Contrary to E. Goffman's (1961) description of staff-inmate relations in total institutions, results of this study indicate that the social relations between prison staff members and prisoners are quite diverse and not necessarily fixed and/or hostile. Five types of staff-inmate relations are described.

1245. Coleman, C.R. (1988). The clinical effectiveness of correctional staff in prison health units. Psychiatric Annals, 18, 684-687, 691.

1246. Dietz, P.E. (1987). The forensic psychiatrist of the future. Bulletin of the American Academy of Psychiatry and the Law, 15, 217-227.

1247. Felthous, A.R., & Miller, R.D. (1989). Teaching forensic psychiatry to medical students. Journal of Forensic Sciences, 34, 871-880.
Conducted a survey of 127 U.S. medical schools to identify course work or practica in forensic psychiatry and compared findings to earlier surveys.

1248. Fry, L.J. (1989). Counselor reactions to work in prison settings. Journal of Offender Counseling, Services and Rehabilitation, 14, 121-132.

1249. Goldmeier, J., & Silver, S.B. (1988). Women staff members and ward atmospheres in a forensic hospital. International Journal of Offender Therapy and Comparative Criminology, 32, 257-265.
Discusses efforts to employ more women staff on secure wards in a forensic hospital. There were 2 goals: (1) creating equal employment opportunities, and (2) enhancing the resocialization of patients through more positive ward atmospheres. Presents results of a study of ward atmosphere in two wards including one with high numbers of women staff and one with low numbers of women staff. Patients in the ward with more women staff rated their ward atmosphere higher on several relationship and system maintenance dimensions of the Ward Atmosphere scale and lower on aggression permitted than did patients in the ward with fewer women staff.

1250. Gormally, J., & Brodsky, S.L. (1973). Utilization and training of psychologists for the criminal justice system. American Psychologist, 28, 926-928.
Surveyed manpower patterns in 31 state correctional systems and found that large numbers of professional mental health workers are needed to meet standards set by corrections administrators.

1251. Johnson, S.C. (1988). The prison forensic unit: Training ground. Psychiatric Annals, 18, 680-683.
Discusses the advantages of the prison psychiatric facility in developing the skills and experience needed to practice criminal forensic psychiatry.

1252. Jones, H.V. (1973). Staff training for group work in a local prison. Medicine, Science and the Law, 13, 61-73.

1253. Kropp, P.R., Cox, D.N., Roesch, R., & Eaves, D. (1989). The perceptions of correctional officers toward mentally disordered offenders. International Journal of Law and Psychiatry, 12, 181-188.
Studied the perceptions of mentally ill offenders in a sample of 78 correctional officers and found that the officers perceived mentally ill less favorably than other prisoners. However, the officers wanted at least some additional training in working the mentally ill prisoners.

1254. Lombardo, L.X. (1985). Mental health work in prisons and jails: Inmate adjustment and indigenous correctional personnel. Criminal Justice and Behavior, 12, 17-27.

1255. Lomis, M.J., & Baker, L.L. (1985). Microtraining of forensic psychiatric patients for empathic counseling skills. Journal of Counseling Psychology, 32, 84-93.

1256. Marrocco, M.K., Uecker, J.C., & Ciccone, J.R. (1995). Teaching forensic psychiatry to psychiatric residents. Bulletin of the American Academy of Psychiatry and the Law, 23, 83-91.

1257. Murphy, G. (1989). Managing persons with mental disabilities: A curriculum guide for police trainers. Washington, DC: Police Executive Research Forum.

1258. Norton, S.C. (1990). Supervision needs of correctional mental health counselors. Journal of Addictions and Offender Counseling, 11, 13-19.

Describes a model for supervision of correctional mental health staff in which supervisees pass through a 3 level training process. The supervisor can help the trainee in the early stages to become acclimated to the prison environment and develop therapeutic techniques and, later on, to refine those techniques and learn to generalize their application to different aspects of correctional psychology.

1259.   Nuehring, E.M., & Raybin, L. (1986). Mentally ill offenders in community based programs: Attitudes of service providers. Journal of Offender Counseling, Services and Rehabilitation, 11, 19-37.
Findings from a key informant survey of criminal justice professionals, mental health and forensic professionals, and social service agency representatives in Miami Florida indicate that mentally ill offenders and defendants are seen as manageable within the community, although high levels of structure, security, and control are recommended.

1260.   Otto, R.K., & Ogloff, J.R.P. (1988). A manual for mental health professionals working with jails. Lincoln, NE: Nebraska Department of Public Institutions.

1261.   Otto, R.K., Heilbrun, K., Grisso, T. (1990). Training and credentialing in forensic psychology. Behavioral Sciences and the Law, 8, 217-231.

1262.   Rodenhauser, P., & Khamis, H.J. (1988). Relationships between legal and clinical factors among forensic hospital patients. Bulletin of the American Academy of Psychiatry and the Law, 16, 321-332.
A study of 380 patients involuntarily admitted to a maximum-security forensic hospital found a significant relationship between previous incarceration and substance abuse. Length of hospitalization was significantly related with the whether the charge was a felony or misdemeanor. The highest proportion of patients diagnosed as psychotic occurred among those charged with kidnapping/coercion and assault.

1263.   Shah, S.A., & McGarry, A.L. (1986). Legal psychiatry and psychology: Review of programs, training, and qualifications. In W.J. Curran, A.L. McGarry, & S.A. Shah (Eds.), Forensic Psychiatry and Psychology. Philadelphia, PA: F.A. Davis.

1264.   Young, T.J. (1989). Treatment of multicultural counseling in correctional psychology textbooks. Psychological Reports, 65, 521-522.

Author Index

(Entries are citation numbers rather than page numbers)

Aadland, R.L. 164
Aarkrog, T. 1033
Abram, K.M. 1, 100, 480, 481, 581, 1101
Abrams, A.I. 589
Abramson, M.F. 482
Adams, J.J. 483, 734
Adams, K. 101, 269, 380, 393, 472, 858
Adams, N. 774
Adams, S. 270
Adler, C. 875
Adshead, G. 930
Ahr, P.R. 23
Aks, S.E. 666
al-Jabally, M. 14
Albers, D. 505
Alcabes, P. 527, 717
Alexander, R. 272, 1109
Allebeck, P. 46
Allen, D. 590
Allen, J.F. 994
Alves, E. 391
Ambtman, R. 231, 823
American Bar Association 1110, 1111, 1126, 1217
American Medical Association 484, 520
American Psychiatric Association 5, 273, 736, 1112
American Psychological Association 450, 1113, 1183, 1185
Amerikaner, M. 1046
Anderson, W.P. 1107
Andrasik, F. 342
Andreou, C. 928
Andrew, J.M. 737, 995, 996
Andrews, B.P. 202
Andrews, D.A. 166
Anechiarico, B. 876
Anglin, M.D. 305, 1105
Annis, H.M. 167
Anno, B.J. 274
Ansbacher, H.L. 591
Anthony, D. 874
Antonowicz, D.H. 613, 987
Appelbaum, P.B. 1115
Appelbaum, P.S. 1116
Appleby, L. 108
Apter, A. 168, 998
Arboleda-Florez, J. 276, 485, 512
Arbuthnot, J. 1024
Arcaya, J. 394, 1117
Archer, R.P. 999
Arms, T.S. 2
Arthur Bolton Associates 487
Arvidson, B. 490
Ashford, J.B. 488, 738

Ashley, M.C. 395
Atkinson, B.J. 1000
Atkinson, D.R. 277
Atwater, J.D. 1038
Aubrey, M. 877, 1118
Austin, R.L. 169
Aviram, U. 1119
Awad, G.A. 1052
Ax, R.K. 624

Bagby, R.M. 461, 1201
Bahn, C. 1242
Bailey, J. 281
Bain, K.P. 179
Baker, K.L. 1026
Baker, L.L. 337, 1255
Baldwin, L.J. 2, 345
Baldwin, P.J. 1135
Baldwin, S. 1087
Balier, C. 592
Balla, D.A. 1037
Bancroft, J. 947
Banerjee, S. 278
Barbaree, H.E. 952, 953
Barbera-Sharon, S.S. 466
Barbour-McMullen, J. 109
Barbur, P. 401
Bard, J.S. 45
Baridon, P.C. 1062
Barker, E.T. 279
Barker, J.G. 878
Barlow, D. 871
Barnard, G.W. 193, 739, 854, 986,
    1197
Barnes, D.M. 1120
Barnett, R.W. 207, 222
Barte, H.N. 280
Barthwell, A.G. 281
Baskin, D.R. 1216
Bassett, J.E. 112
Bassin, A. 464
Batter, T.E. 615
Baxter, D. 1069
Beal, D. 1001
Beck, J.C. 1121
Beck, N.C. 2, 345
Becker, J.V. 872, 873, 880
Beckerman, A. 3
Beidleman, W.B. 616

Belcher, J.R. 489
Belfrage, H. 282, 283, 333, 740
Bell, R.A. 761
Ben-Aron, M. 199
Ben-David, S. 617, 669, 881, 1244
Bender, S.L. 1243
Benezech, M. 284
Benson, R.E. 1184
Beran, N.J. 741
Berger, P. 883
Berger, R.H. 188
Berger, V.F. 1190
Bergman, B. 742
Berlin, F.S. 285, 882
Berlin, L. 612
Bernasco, W. 710
Berner, W. 883, 884
Bernheim, J. 1122
Bernier, S.L. 1123
Berns, S. 1134
Bernstein, M.J. 1176
Bigelow, D.A. 400, 406
Birecree, E.A. 1063
Blackburn, R. 110
Blanchard, E. 871
Blanchard, R. 243
Bland, R.C. 670
Blankstein, H. 743
Blaske, D.M. 885, 1002
Bloom, J.D. 51, 286, 287, 392,
    397-401, 490, 1063
Blount, W.R. 1064
Bockting, W.O. 903
Boddis, S. 793
Bohn, M.J. 257
Bokos, P. 281
Bonovitz, J.C. 402, 403, 491, 492
Bonovitz, J.S. 402, 491
Bonta, J. 166, 170, 493
Borduin, C.M. 885, 1002, 1003, 1029,
    1058
Borgman, R.D. 404
Borzecki, M. 171, 992
Boss, M.W. 172
Boucher, R. 781, 782
Boulet, J. 172
Boulton, A.A. 180, 181
Bourget, D. 744, 1065
Bowden, P. 288, 886, 1124, 1125

Bradford, J. 113, 1004
Brakel, S.J. 1126, 1127
Brannon, J.M. 1005
Braslow, C.A. 527
Breteler, M.H. 165
Briar, K.H. 562
Bricout, J. 584
Brismar, B. 742
Brodsky, S. 494, 1128
Brondino, M.J. 1054
Brooks, P.W. 1067
Brooner, R.K. 500
Brosch, W. 593
Brown, C. 54
Brown, D.R. 618
Brown, G.C. 106
Brown, J.D. 654
Brownstein, H. 762, 1018
Brownstone, D.Y. 1068
Brownstone, G. 884
Bruce-Jones, W.D. 115
Bruhn, A.R. 256, 855
Buchan, T. 405
Buchanan, B.D. 1053
Buchele, B.J. 914
Buchsbaum, M.S. 766
Buck, M.H. 279
Buckley, R. 406
Bullock, S. 509
Burdock, E.I. 869
Burdsal, C. 1006
Burger, G. 994
Burgess, A.M. 1007
Burgess, A.W. 916
Burrows, R. 1129
Bussey, J. 1097
Butka, G.J. 504, 681
Byrne, P.H. 145

Caddell, J.M. 142
Caffaro, J.V. 619, 890
Caldeira, L. 529
Calsin, J.B., Jr. 1130
Camp, B.H. 1008
Cannon, W.G. 252
Carbonell, J.L. 173, 214
Card, R.D. 891
Carey, R.J. 174
Carlesso, M.L. 359

Carlisle, A.L. 245
Carmel, H. 776
Carnes, P.J. 892
Carney, F.L. 407
Carr, K. 495
Carrera, F. 739
Carroll, J. 1131
Carroll, K.R. 582
Carson, D. 116
Cavanaugh, J.L. 239, 408, 476
Cavior, H.E. 176
Cebula, C.M. 1055
Cedeck, M. 607
Cervantes, N.N. 409
Cesnik, J. 894
Chalke, F.C.R. 1132
Chamberlain, T.J. 747
Chan, D. 167
Chandler, S.M. 28
Chapel, J.L. 897
Chaplow, D. 271, 667
Chato, F. 275
Chen, P. 518
Cheraskin, E. 446
Chiles, J.A. 5, 6, 326
Chlumsky, M.L. 161
Churchill, C.M. 89
Churgin, M. 410
Ciccone, J.R. 1256
Cimino, A.T. 496
Clannon, T.L. 748
Clare, I.C. 597
Clark, D.C. 672
Clarke, J.W. 411, 749
Cleckley, H. 117
Clements, C.B. 1133
Cocozza, J. 750, 751
Coffler, D.B. 497
Coffman, J.A. 915
Cohen, F. 290
Cohen, M. 752
Coid, J. 109, 115
Colaizzi, J. 753
Cole, W. 893
Coleman, C.R. 1245
Coleman, E. 894
Coles, C.J. 767
Collins, D. 1050
Collins, J.J. 119

Conacher, G.N. 291
Condelli, W.S. 292
Cone, L.T. 1003
Connor, D.G. 1009
Conrad, J. 770, 859, 1028
Contreras, C.M. 926
Convit, A. 75, 709, 860, 1134
Cook, D.A. 895
Cooke, D.J. 412, 1135
Cooke, G. 177, 293
Cooke, M.K. 293
Cooper, A.J. 1069
Copeland, A.R. 673
Copello, A.G. 754
Corder, B.F. 1010
Cordess, C. 648
Cordoba, O.A. 897
Cormier, B.M. 294
Cormier, C.A. 132, 133, 356
Cornell, D.G. 8, 178
Cornwall, T. 1010
Corrigan, P.W. 295
Corsini, R.J. 594
Cotton, A. 458
Courtless, T.F. 329
Cowburn, M. 898
Cowden, J.E. 963
Cox, B. 724
Cox, D.N. 1253
Cox, J.F. 675, 676
Cox, M. 458, 595, 596
Coyne, J.C. 621
Craig, T.J. 498
Craissati, J. 899
Cravens, J.M. 746
Crespi, T.D. 1136
Cronin, K. 523
Crossley, T. 296, 1137
Cullen, K. 900, 954, 1102
Cummings, L. 809
Curran, W.J. 1138
Cyr, M. 73

D'Orban, P.T. 1070, 1071
Dabbs, J.M. 756
Dahlstrom, L.E. 179
Dahlstrom, W.G. 179
Dalby, J.T. 244
Dalton, E. 662

Dan, D. 622
Daniel, A.E. 1072
Daniel, C. 757, 1011
Daniel, D.A. 623
Dank, N.R. 413
Danner, T.A. 1064
Danto, B.L. 677-679, 715
Datwyler, M.L. 1076
Davies, W. 120
Davis, B.A. 180
Davis, D.L. 182, 297
Davis, G.L. 183
Davis, J. 973
Davis, R.W. 184
Davis, S. 414, 499, 957
Davison, F.M. 597
Day, A. 598, 1012
Day, D.M. 949
Day, K. 298, 299
de Rios, M.D. 1044
de St.Croix, S. 415
Deisher, R.W. 1017
Deitchman, M.A. 319
Dell, S. 77, 78, 460, 1073, 1074
Demone, H.W. 416
Denkowski, G.C. 9
Denkowski, K.M 9
Dennis, D.L. 466, 467
Derks, F. 389
Devereux, J. 281
Devonshire, P.A. 121
Diamond, R.J. 373, 500
DiCataldo, F. 186
Dickens, S.E. 82, 154, 240, 241
Dickey, R. 199, 912, 1194
Dies, R.R. 641
Dietz, P.E. 792, 1246
DiFrancesca, K.R. 187
Dimock, J. 113, 1004
Dinitz, S. 122, 770, 859, 1028
Divall, J. 597
Dix, G. 417, 901
Djenderedijian, A. 872
Dodd, C. 1011
Dodd, D. 1034
Doidge, G. 21
Dolente, A.S. 548, 549
Dollard, N. 447
Doren, D.M. 1181

Dorman, A. 10
Dougher, M.J. 877, 1118
Dougherty, A.M. 1013
Draine, J. 501, 502, 563-565
Driscoll, R. 648
Drob, S.L. 188
Droes, N.S. 1139
Dry, R. 415
Duckro, P. 1001
Duclos, C.W. 680
Dudley, H.K. 233, 812
Dunn, C.S. 503
Dunne, M.P. 1082
DuRand, C.J. 504, 681
Durbin, J.R. 505
Durden, D.A. 180, 181
Dushkind, D.S. 1140
Duthie, B. 189
Dvoskin, J. 290, 372, 1161, 1162
Dwyer, S.M. 894, 902-904
Dyck, R.J. 670

Earls, C.M. 905, 906
Eaves, D. 80, 539, 560, 1253
Ebbeson, E. 936
Eccles, A. 953
Eckerman, W.C. 300
Edelmann, R.J. 849
Edinger, J.D. 190, 301
Edwall, G.E. 1075
Edwards, A.C. 60, 302
Egan, M.J. 375, 656
Eisenman, R. 11, 907, 1014
Elliot, F. 758
Ellis, M.J. 1015
Ellison, T.K. 430
Emory, E. 1142
Emory, L.E. 908
Enos, T. 19
Epperson, D.L. 1076
Ernst, K. 956
Ervin, F. 360, 820
Esparza, R.E. 682
Evangelista, C. 1134
Evans, A. 304
Evans, B. 303
Exworthy, T. 278
Eysenck, H. 191

Fabricatore, J.M. 621
Fagan, T.J. 624, 786
Faison, K. 722
Falck, Z.A. 981
Falkin, G.P. 305
Faltico, G.J. 1016
Farley, G. 759
Farrall, W. 891
Faubert, M. 368
Faulk, M. 13
Faulkner, L.R. 51, 60, 287, 302, 392
Fawkes, L.S. 1165
Feder, L. 418, 419
Federman, E.J. 504, 681
Fedora, O. 909
Fedora, S.K. 909
Fehr, R.C. 244
Fehrenbach, P.A. 1017, 1077
Feigenbaum, K.D. 506
Feldbrugge, J.T. 123
Feldman, C.A. 652
Feldman, M. 760
Feldman, P. 120
Feldman, T.B. 761
Felthous, A.R. 683, 1078, 1247
Fendrich, M. 762, 1018
Fenn, R. 1171
Ferguson, M.G. 523
Ferguson, R. 523
Fields, J. 1049
Filson, C.R. 90
Fine, E.W. 15
Fink, L. 1143
Fiqia, N.A. 938
Fishbein, D.H. 507
Fisher, R. 763
Flaherty, M.G. 1019
Fliedl, R. 85
Fogel, C.I. 1079, 1080
Foldes, P. 85
Fontana, L. 3
Forbes, M.R. 624
Force, R.C. 1006
Forth, A.E. 128-130
Fosen, R.H. 896
Foster, D.V. 306
Foster, H. 927
Fox, C.A. 895
Foxman, J. 684

Frady, R.L. 756
Frager, S. 625
Fraley, S.E. 307
Frances, A. 441
Frances, R.J. 1020
Frankiewicz, R.G. 1046
Franklin, R.K. 685
Freedman, B.J. 626
Freeman, R.J. 1144
Freeman-Longo, R.E. 910
French, A.P. 189
French, L.A. 686, 1145
Freund, K. 911, 912
Freyne, A. 10
Friedt, L.R. 192
Fry, L.J. 1248
Fuller, D. 1035
Fuller, J.R. 308
Furac, C.J. 987

Gaa, J.P. 1046
Gabel, S. 1020
Gabrielsen, G. 765
Galbraith, D. 436
Gallemore, J.L. 349
Ganzarain, R. 913, 914
Gardos, P. 874
Garofolo, R. 781, 782
Garske, J.P. 174
Garwick, G.B. 985
Gaston, L. 22
Gauthier, R. 924
Geis, G. 810
Geist, C. 614
Gelder, M. 947
Gelkopf, M. 844
Geller, E.S. 309
Genoves, V.G. 1021
Georgiades, S. 597
Gerard, H. 284
Gerbing, D.W. 83
Giacinti, T.A. 587
Gibbons, B.N. 1146
Gibbons, F.X. 1146
Gibbs, J.C. 1035
Gibbs, J.L. 508
Gillis, J.R. 82, 154, 240, 241
Glancy, G.D. 16
Godson, D. 458

Goertzel, V. 439
Gold, M. 1022
Golden, C.J. 915
Goldenberg, E.F. 599
Goldmeier, J. 310, 420, 421, 1249
Goldstein, N. 1147, 1148
Goldstein, P. 762, 1018
Goldstrom, I. 348, 376
Gomes, A.A. 600
Good, M.I. 17
Gordon, A. 180, 181
Gordon, D.A. 1024
Gordon, R. 764
Gorecki, M. 607
Gormally, J. 1250
Gottlieb, P. 765
Gottschalk, L.A. 766
Gouvier, W.D. 192
Graber, B. 915
Graber, S. 1026
Graham, J.R. 922
Graham, S.A. 601
Grant, J.D. 380
Grant, R.W. 517, 1084
Green, C. 180, 181, 1149
Green, K. 1150
Green, R.H. 1043
Greenberg, W.M. 1151
Greene, A.F. 767
Greene, R. 101
Greenspan, J. 1152
Greer, A. 186
Gregory, D. 25, 325
Grekin, P.M. 1153
Griffiths, A.W. 18
Grisso, J.T. 1154
Grisso, T. 1261
Grochowski, S. 707
Groder, M.G. 312
Groh, T.R. 602
Gross, B.H. 440
Gross, M. 19
Grossman, L.S. 476
Groth, A. 752
Groth, N. 917, 918
Grounds, A. 77, 78, 422, 460, 1073, 1074
Grubin, D. 919, 920
Gruenke, C. 609

Grumet, B.R. 768
Grunberg, F. 768
Guarner, J. 687
Gudjonsson, G.H. 313
Guerra, F. 335
Guest, R. 614
Guild, D. 871
Guitierrez, K. 883
Gumz, E.J. 64, 65
Gunn, J. 20, 47, 48, 96, 124, 204, 339,
    1088-1090
Gustafson, D. 319
Gustafson, K.E. 1024
Gutheil, T.G. 1115
Guy, E.R. 403, 492
Guzman, R. 296, 1137

Haapala, D.A. 1025
Haddock, B.D. 423
Hadley, R.G. 497
Hains, A.A. 1026
Hakstian, A.R. 129
Haley, M.W. 510
Hall, G.C. 921, 922
Hall, J.N. 923
Hallaux, R.J. 51
Halleck, N.H. 1156
Halleck, S. 603, 1157
Halliwell, S. 242
Halpern, A.L. 1027, 1159
Halton, A. 92
Hambridge, J.A. 425, 769
Hamlin, P.H. 309
Hamm, M.B. 426
Hamm, M.S. 314
Hammett, E. 511
Hamparian, D. 770, 1028
Handy, L. 199, 939
Hankins, G.C. 193
Hannum, T.E. 1076
Hanson, R.K. 924
Hanzlick, R. 687
Hardesty, A.S. 869
Hardiman, E. 10
Harding, T.W. 1138
Hare, R.D. 125-131, 135, 137
Harmon, R.B. 315, 427, 1160
Harpur, T.J. 129, 131
Harris, G.T. 132-134, 235, 316, 356,

    829
Hart, D.S. 1041
Hart, S.D. 135, 137, 771
Hartl, A.J. 582
Hartman, C.R. 1007
Hartmann, K. 915
Hartstone, E. 317
Haskell, M.R. 627
Hawk, G.L. 8, 178
Haycock, J. 688-691
Haycox, J.A. 504, 681
Hayes, L.M. 692-701
Hayman, P.M. 318, 628
Hedlund, E. 925
Heide, K.M. 1083
Heilbrun, A.B. 136
Heilbrun, K. 319, 1162, 1261
Heilbrun, M.R. 136
Hemphill, J.F. 137
Hemphill, L. 102
Henderson, M.C. 138
Henggeler, S.W. 885, 1002, 1003,
    1029-1031, 1054, 1058
Herranz-Bellido, J. 702
Herrera-Hernandez, E. 926
Herrman, H. 21
Herrman, L.P. 1026
Hess, A.K. 227, 703
Heyne, B. 727
Hilkey, J.H. 320, 629
Hillbrand, M. 704, 772, 927
Hinkle, B. 495
Hirt, M. 772, 927
Hiscock, C.K. 194
Hiscock, M. 194
Hivert, P. 139
Hobart, S.C. 889
Hochstedler, E. 428
Hodes, P. 899
Hodges, E.L. 766
Hodges, J. 928
Hodgins, S. 22, 321, 773, 1163
Hoffman, B.F. 429
Hoffman, R.G. 183
Hoge, R.D. 166
Holanchock, H. 292
Holcomb, W.R. 23, 774
Holigan, R.A. 1075
Holiman, M. 652

Holland, A.J. 597
Holley, H.L. 485, 486, 512
Hollingsworth, J.B. 1164
Holmen, M.L. 943
Holmes, R.M. 929
Holohan, E.J. 372
Homant, R.J. 630, 631
Hood, G. 811
Hoover, J.O. 327
Horne, A.M. 629, 1013
Horton-Deutsch, S.L. 672
Hosford, R.E. 203, 219
Hotz, A.M. 396, 741
Houston, J. 930
Howard, R. 109
Howard, R.C. 121, 140, 141
Howell, R.J. 12, 245, 878
Howells, K. 775
Howison, J. 1135
Hoyer, G. 322
Hryhorczuk, D.O. 666
Hucker, S. 983
Huckle, P.L. 931
Hudson, S.M. 933
Huelskoetter, M.M.W. 1189
Huey, C.J. 915
Hufft, A.G. 1081, 1165
Hultquist, A. 445, 1040
Humphrey, J.A. 817
Hundley, J. 195
Hunter, G.C. 323
Hunter, M. 776
Hurley, W. 777, 1082

Iancu, I. 168, 998
Inciardi, J.A. 431
Ingersoll, S.L. 932
Ingram, B. 495
Ingram, G.L. 432
Ishikawa, Y. 324
Israelson, L. 1033
Issac, C. 973
Ivanoff, A. 705-707
Jackson, M. 24
Jackson, P.A. 255
Jacobson, R. 610
Jacoby, J. 157
James, J.F. 25, 325
James, K. 77, 78, 460, 1073, 1074

Jang, S.J. 706, 707
Jemelka, R. 326, 513, 1153
Jew, C. 748
Johnson, C. 1095
Johnson, D.F. 309
Johnson, E.H. 767
Johnson, G.M. 1038
Johnson, J. 515
Johnson, M.E. 219
Johnson, R. 708, 1193
Johnson, S.C. 327, 1251
Johnson, T.F. 1032
Johnson, W.E. 90
Johnston, P. 933
Jones, B.E. 26
Jones, E.J. 632
Jones, G.H. 931
Jones, H.V. 1252
Jones, R.K. 25
Jordan, B. 883
Joseph, H. 522
Joseph, P. 108
Joukamaa, M. 27
Jurkovic, G.J. 756
Justice, B. 778
Justice, R. 778

Kaiser, G. 98
Kal, E.F. 516
Kalichman, S.C. 138
Kang, S. 1091
Karp, J.G. 709
Karp, S.A. 247
Kassebaum, G. 28
Kassin, S.M. 1146
Katsampes, P.L. 587
Katz, N.D. 26
Kauffmen, H. 409
Kaufman, E. 328, 633, 1166
Kearns, A. 29
Kearns, W.D. 546, 548-550
Keilitz, I. 196
Kellener, R. 970
Kennedy, T.D. 197, 309
Kerkhof, A.J. 710
Kermani, E.J. 1167
Kerr, C.A. 329
Ketai, R. 1168
Keveles, C. 93

Khamis, H.J. 79, 236, 1262
Kiefer, S.A. 1086
Kilburn, H. 533
Kilmann, P.R. 934
Kindred, M. 30
Kinney, J.M. 1025
Klabucar, L. 634, 779
Klein, G.A. 421
Klein, K.E. 707
Kleinsasser, D. 217
Klinger, B.I. 768
Knight, R.A. 935
Kofoed, L. 286
Kohlmeyer, W.A. 330
Kokkevi, A. 31
Komer, B. 436
Konecni, V. 936
Kopelman, M.D. 32
Koshland, E. 112
Kozol, H. 780-782
Kraft, J. 778
Kramp, P. 1033
Krizek, G.O. 1170
Krop, H. 959
Kropp, P.R. 135, 771, 1253
Kuhlman, T. 783
Kuhns, J.B. 1083
Kulishoff, M. 413
Kunjukrishnan, R. 33-35, 437
Kury, H. 1171
Kutch, J.M 331

Labelle, A. 744
Laben, J.K. 438, 1034
LaCalle, J.J 937
Lamb, D. 19
Lamb, H.R. 439, 440, 517, 518, 1084,
    1172
Landsberg, G. 519, 674-676, 711
Lane, J. 870
Lane, S. 973
Lang, R.A. 938
Langevin, R. 199, 939
Langton, J. 1173
Lanyado, M. 928
Larkin, E.P. 36
Lau, B.W. 37
Launay, G. 940
Lavallee, Y.J. 73

Lavergne, M.P. 784
Lavergne, T. 784
LaWall, J.S. 200
Lawrence, S. 201, 941
Laws, D.R. 942-944, 958, 967, 970
Layman, L.B. 194
LeBeau, W. 680
Lee, S.R. 38
Lee-Evans, J.M. 111
Leeman, L.W. 1035
Lees-Haley, P.R. 39-41
Leong, G.B. 1174, 1175
Leschied, A.W. 234
Lester, D. 712-715
Letourneau, E. 962
Leuchter, A.F. 42
Leukefeld, C.G. 43
Leverette, M.D. 1063
Levine, D. 44, 785
Levine, S. 1134
Levinson, R. 332
Levinson, T. 454
Lewis, C. 522
Lewis, D.A. 787
Lewis, D.O. 45, 760, 1036, 1037
Lewis, J. 663, 1060
Lewis, W. 1194
Liberman, D. 1046
Library Information Specialists, Inc.
    716
Lidberg, L. 144, 333, 740
Linde, P.R. 520
Lindqvist, P. 46
Lindsey, M.L. 533
Link, N.F. 145
Lipper, S. 511
Lira, F. 645
Liska, F.J. 64, 65, 543, 544
Liss, R. 441
Lloyd, C. 334, 335
Locke, T.P. 1038
Loeber, R. 1056
Loeffelholz, P.L. 89
Logue, P.E. 190
Lombardo, L.X. 336, 521, 1254
Lomis, M.J. 337, 1255
Long, C.K. 1085
Long, G.T. 1086
Losada-Paisey, G. 338

Louscher, P.K. 203
Lowe, D. 500
Lozes, J. 663, 1060
Lucore, P. 462
Lunghofer, L. 1097
Lurigio, A.J. 787

Mabil, J. 374, 655
Mabli, J. 442
MacAskill, R.L. 94
MacDevitt, J.W. 635
Mackesy-Amiti, M.E. 762, 1018
MacMillan, J. 1087
Maddicks, R. 598, 1012
Maden, A. 20, 47, 48, 96, 204, 339,
    1088-1090
Madry, M.A. 833
Magargal, L.E. 106
Magura, S. 522, 1091
Mahorney, S.L. 511
Maier, G.J. 303, 340, 788, 801, 1176,
    1181, 1182
Malin, H.M. 285
Mallouh, K. 760
Malouff, J.M. 462
Mandelzys, N. 789
Manderscheid, R.W. 94, 348, 376
Mann, B.J. 1003, 1029
Mann, M.F. 102
Manson, S.M. 398, 399
Mansour, M. 666
Marceau, R. 789
Marchenko, M.O. 566
Marciniak, R.D. 49
Marcus, P. 717
Margolin, L. 1039
Mark, V.H. 790
Marks, I. 947
Marlow, G.A. 103
Marques, J.K. 948, 949
Marrocco, M.K. 1256
Marshall, W.L. 933, 950-953
Martin, S.L. 1080
Martin, S.S. 431
Martin-Escudero, R. 702
Marvan, L. 926
Mason, P. 341
Mason, T. 19
Mathias, R.E. 205, 637

Matthews, A. 444
Mattlin, J. 1022
Mattocks, A.L. 638
May, J. 91
May, R.L. 550
Maynard, P.E. 445, 1040
McCabe, S. 226
McCartney, J.L. 206
McCarty, D.W. 571, 572, 676
McColl, M.A. 632
McCormack, A. 1007
McCormack, J.K. 207
McCoy, E.C. 498
McDonagh, E.W. 446
McDonough, L. 528
McDougall, C. 793
McFarland, B.H. 51
McGaha, G.S. 1092
McGarry, A.L. 1263
McGrath, P.G. 52
McGreevy, M.A. 447
McGuire, J. 794
McIntosh, J.W. 265
McLean, D. 887, 888
McLean, E.K. 1177
McMahon, D. 598, 1012
McMain, S. 208
McNamara, J.R. 342
McNeil, K. 209
McNiff, M.A. 343
McPherson, L.M. 127, 130
McShane, M.D. 344
Medella, J.T. 954
Megargee, E. 795
Meine, D. 604
Meldman, L. 557
Melick, M.E. 570
Meloy, J.R. 53, 187, 215, 483, 524,
    525, 734
Melton, G.B. 1029, 1031, 1054
Melville, C. 54
Mendelson, E.F. 216, 448, 955
Menditto, A.A. 2, 345
Menghini, P. 956
Menninger, K. 1179
Menuck, M. 798
Menzies, R. 180, 181
Merritt, L.C. 620
Mertell, D. 860

Metzner, J.L. 217
Meyer, C.K. 800
Meyer, R.G. 209, 1215
Meyer, W. 989
Meyers, C.J. 526
Meyerson, A. 502, 565
Michaels, D. 527
Michaels, K.W. 1043
Mieville, C. 1180
Mikkelsen, E.J. 218
Milgram, D. 639
Miller, H.R. 252
Miller, K. 867
Miller, M.O. 450, 1183
Miller, M.P. 102
Miller, R. 340
Miller, R.D. 217, 451, 801, 1181, 1182, 1247
Mills, J. 21
Milner, J.S. 346
Miner, M.H. 903
Minervini, M.G. 185
Mio, J.S. 1044
Mirchandani, H.G. 679
Mitchell, G. 1067
Mitchison, S. 55
Mittelman, M.S. 873
Modlin, H.C. 1184
Moffitt, T.E. 56
Moglia, R. 642
Moituk, L.L. 170
Mollerstrom, W.W. 346
Monahan, J. 57-59, 452, 453, 529, 802-811, 957, 1185-1187
Monahan, L. 1186
Monastersky, C. 1017, 1077
Monroe, R. 720
Moore, A.M. 894
Moore, H.D. 833
Morgan, C. 530, 531
Morgan, D.W. 60, 302
Moritz, M.S. 483, 734
Morris, S.M. 467
Morrison, E.F. 347
Morrison, J.W. 909
Morrissey, J.P. 348, 376, 532, 533, 571, 572
Morrow, B.R. 340
Morschauser, P.C. 246, 1096

Morse, S.J. 1188
Mortimer, D.B. 61
Moser, A.L. 454
Moss, C.S. 203, 219
Motiuk, L.L. 71
Mulcahy, E. 936
Mullen, J.M. 812
Mullen, P.E. 62
Mulvey, E.P. 1045
Murdoch, D. 813
Murphy, G. 1257
Murray, R.B. 1189
Murrin, M.R. 548, 958
Murring, M.R. 549
Musante, G. 349
Musholt, E.A. 1176
Mutch, P.J. 814
Myers, W.C. 814
Myrick, R.D. 223

Naismith, L.J. 1149
Nanjundappa, G. 1044
National Coalition for Jail Reform 534-536
National Council on Crime and Delinquency 815
National Institute of Mental Health 94, 300, 329, 350, 351, 363, 475, 494, 503, 561, 571, 576, 807, 856, 864, 1157
National Institute on Drug Abuse 1
Neidigh, L. 959
Neighbors, H.W. 63
Nelson, C. 949
Nelson, S.H. 1190
New York University Symposium 718
Newman, G. 739, 854, 986
Newman, S.C. 670
Nielsen, E.D. 537
Ninzy, N.M. 538
Nisenbaum, M. 281
Nolan, P. 640
Norton, K. 146, 352
Norton, S.C. 816, 1258
Novy, D.M. 1046
Noyes, R. 89
Nuehring, E.M. 1259
Nunez, C.E. 319
Nussbaum, D. 237

O'Connell, B.A. 1047
O'Connell, M.A. 960
O'Connor, A. 10, 29, 961, 1071, 1093
O'Day, J. 1091
O'Donohue, W.T. 962
O'Neill, H. 10, 1093
Oberkirch, A. 605
Ogloff, J.R. 539
Oldroyd, R.J. 147, 221
Oleski, M.S. 541
Oreland, L. 740
Orn, H. 670
Osborn, C.A. 874
Osgood, D.W. 1022
Otto, R.K. 540, 542, 1260, 1261
Ownby, R.L. 222

Pacht, A. 896
Padberg, J. 1191
Page, R.C. 223
Paisey, T.J. 338
Palermo, G.B. 64, 65, 543, 544
Palmer, S. 817
Palsson, A. 66
Panton, J.H. 67, 68, 179, 224, 225,
    606
Paravati, M.P. 674, 676
Parker, N. 148
Parloff, M.B. 641
Parrott, J.M. 97
Parry, J. 1126
Pascoe, H. 909
Pasewark, R.A. 505
Patchner, M.A. 346
Patterson, E.F. 310
Patton, S.D. 932
Pavelka, F.L. 149, 455
Pawlak, A. 992
Payne, C. 226
Pearson, M.A. 1048
Pearson, V. 1192
Pease, K. 180, 181
Peay, J. 150
Pelissier, B.M. 353
Pendergrass, V.E. 1094
Peretti, P.G. 607
Perkins, D. 818, 964
Perr, I.N. 69
Peternelj-Taylor, C.A. 1193

Peters, J. 271, 667
Peters, R.H. 354, 545-550
Peterson, M. 1194
Petrich, J. 366, 551-554
Petrila, J. 1156
Pfohl, S. 819
Phillips, S.L. 1049
Phung, T. 1085
Piazza, N.J. 659
Pihl, R.D. 813
Pinta, E.R. 1195
Pithers, W.D. 965
Platt, J.J. 509
Polischuk, D. 1050
Pollock, H.M. 456
Pollock, N.L. 966
Pols, J. 70
Poole, E.D. 1196
Porporino, F.J. 71
Porter, L. 1184
Porter, S. 1051
Posey, C.D. 227
Potter, M. 433, 434
Poulin, C. 1069
Poulson, J. 409
Prandoni, J.R. 228, 457
Prendergast, M.L. 1105
Priedlander, A. 529
Prins, H. 821, 822
Pritchard, C. 458
Profit, W.E. 186
Protter, B. 1102
Proulx, J. 906
Pruett, N.S. 471
Pueschel, J. 642
Pugh, D.N. 229

Quinsey, V.L. 72, 73, 134, 230, 231,
    823, 967

Raba, J. 666
Rabiner, C.J. 824
Rada, R.T. 968-970
Radelet, M.L. 1161, 1162, 1197
Raine, A. 151, 152, 825
Rakis, J. 719, 720
Rappaport, R.G. 643, 644
Rappeport, J.R. 826, 981, 1198, 1232
Ratzoni, G. 168, 998

Rautio, E.A. 375, 656
Raybin, L. 1259
Rayburn, C.A. 608
Reali, M. 459
Rebello, T. 766
Rector, M. 827
Reddon, J.R. 909
Reeder, D. 557
Regehr, C. 16
Regoli, R.M. 556
Reich, J. 153, 232
Reid, J.C. 1072
Reinehr, R.C. 233
Reitsma-Street, M. 234
Remington, B. 355
Remington, M. 355
Rennie, Y. 828
Renvoize, E.B. 55
Repucci, N.D. 1045
Resnick, P.J. 74, 1199
Resnick, R.J. 645
Reuland, M. 507
Reynolds, R.M. 252
Rice, A.H. 375, 656
Rice, D.G. 626
Rice, M.E. 132-134, 235, 356, 829
Rich, A.R. 671
Richie, D.E. 1095
Richman, B.J. 75
Rideau, W. 76
Rieber, R.W. 1242
Rieger, W. 646, 721
Rikard-Bell, C. 558
Ringel, N.B. 559
Ritz, G.H. 163
Rix, K.J. 55
Rizzo, N.D. 830
Robbins, L. 193, 739, 854, 986
Robbins, P.C. 317
Roberts, C.A. 1132
Robertson, G. 77, 78, 460, 1073, 1074
Robertson, J.M. 647
Robins, A.J. 1072
Robinson, B. 903
Robinson, S. 648
Robison, J. 863
Robles, I.N. 357
Rock, R.S. 1127
Rodenhauser, P. 79, 236, 1262

Rodon, C.J. 1107
Roe, A.V. 245
Roesch, R. 80, 539, 560, 771, 1144, 1253
Rogers, J.L. 287, 1200
Rogers, R. 81, 82, 154, 237-241, 461, 1201
Rokach, A. 649
Rold, W.J. 358
Rollin, H.R. 1202
Roman, D. 259
Romero, J.J. 971
Romig, C.A. 609
Rood, L.R. 722
Rooth, F.G. 895
Rosenblum, A. 522
Rosenstein, M.J. 94
Rosner, K. 1062
Ross, D. 813
Ross, R.R. 359
Rosser, B.S. 904
Roth, J.A. 329
Rowan, J.R. 701
Roy, C. 1206
Roys, D.T. 972
Rubin, B. 832
Rubin, J.S. 639
Ruggiero, M. 1187
Rummele, W. 650
Rundell, O.H. 25
Ryan, G. 973

Saavedra, M. 926
Sadler, C 1207
Sadoff, R.L. 84, 1208
Sagatun, I.J. 974
Sales, B. 30
Salive, M.E. 723
Saltstone, R. 242
Samenow, S. 266
Sanislow, C. 635
Sauer, R.H. 310, 420
Saunders, E. 1052
Savage, C. 500, 651
Saxton, G.H. 1209
Scannell, T.D. 361
Scapinello, K.F. 243
Scarnati, R. 833
Scarpitti, F.R. 431

Scavo, R. 1053
Schag, D.S. 164
Schanda, H. 85
Scheela, R.A. 975
Scherer, D.G. 1054
Scherer, S.E. 145
Schilit, J. 1210
Schippers, G.M. 165
Schlenger, W.E. 119, 142
Schmalz, B.J. 244
Schmidt, A. 176
Schock, R. 518
Schonfeld, L. 547
Schramski, T.G. 652
Schrink, J.L. 314
Schrum, D.M. 1086
Schuerger, J.M. 163
Schulte, J.L. 86, 362
Schultz-Ross, R.A. 87
Schuster, R. 770, 1028
Schutte, N.S. 462
Schwartz, B.K. 976
Schweiger, M. 55
Schwenkner, C.E. 236
Schwitzgebel, R.K. 363
Scogin, F.R. 289
Scott, E.M. 653
Scott, P. 836
Scott, W. 977
Scrapansky, T.A. 103
Scull, A. 463
Seager, M. 610
Seamons, D.T. 245
Segal, A.C. 559
Segal, S. 1119
Seide, M. 1151
Seigel, R. 752
Sellars, C. 121
Senay, E.C. 281
Sepejak, D.S. 799
Serber, M. 978
Serin, N. 284
Serin, R.C. 155, 837
Severson, M.M. 364
Shaffer, C.E. 838
Shah, P.J. 1151
Shah, S. 365
Shanok, S.S. 1037
Shapiro, I. 726

Shapiro, J. 1091
Shapland, J. 391, 459
Sharma, K.K. 870
Shaw, D.M. 89
Shepherd, J.R. 922
Sherman, L.G. 246, 1096
Shern, D. 462
Shively, D. 366
Shore, J.H. 287, 490
Sibelman, M. 416
Sidley, N.T. 367
Siegel, L.M. 589
Sigal, M. 844
Sikorski, C. 759
Silber, D.E. 247, 1211
Silberman, C.E. 845
Silfen, P. 669, 881
Silva, J.A. 1174, 1175
Silver, S.B. 1249
Silver, S.N. 979
Silverman, I. 1083
Sinclair, B. 76
Singer, M.I. 1097
Singer, R.G. 561
Singh, B. 21
Siscoe, K. 98
Skegg, K. 724
Slater, R.G. 1212
Sloane, B.C. 725
Slovenko, R. 1213
Sluga, W. 884
Small, M.A. 980
Smets, A.C. 1055
Smith, A.B. 464, 612
Smith, C.E. 1214
Smith, G. 863
Smith, J. 504, 681
Smith, L.A. 1031
Smith, L.B. 247
Smith, L.D. 369
Smith, M.B. 65, 543, 544
Smith, S.R. 1215
Smith, W. 1017
Smyth, N.J. 707
Sneed, L. 1034
Snow, W.H. 562
Solomon, P. 501, 502, 563-565
Sommers, I. 1216
Song, L.Y. 1097

Sorkin, A.P. 1172
Sosowsky, L. 567, 847
Souma, A. 303
Southwell, M. 1098
Sovronsky, H.R. 726
Spellman, A. 727
Spencer, L.D. 438
Spodak, M.K. 981
Sprull, J. 91
Sreenivasan, S. 1234
Standing Committee on Association
        Standards 1217
Steadman, H. 57, 58
Steffy, R.A. 924
Stein, E. 654
Stein, L.I. 373
Stein, R.J. 885, 1002
Steinberg, A. 248
Steinbock, E.A. 95
Steinfeld, G.J. 374, 375, 655, 656
Stelovich, S. 1219
Stephens, J. 1194
Sterling, S. 849
Stermac, L.E. 850, 982, 983, 990
Stevens, R. 1220
Stewart, S.D. 249, 468
Stober, W.C. 498
Stokman, C.L. 851
Stone, D. 202
Stone, W.E. 728
Stone, W.N. 620
Stone-Romero, E.F. 202
Stouthamer-Loeber, M. 1056
Strachan, K.E. 128
Streiner, D.L. 252
Strick, S.E. 1100
Sturup, G. 984
Sultan, F.E. 1086
Sutker, P.B. 251
Swaminath, R.S. 1068
Swaminath, S. 1069
Swank, G.E. 573, 574
Swanson, C.K. 985
Swanson, J.W. 348, 376
Swanson, S.C. 252
Swartz, C.P. 228
Swartz, J.D. 233
Swartzfager, A.K. 432
Swett, C. 253, 469

Swinton, M. 20, 48, 96, 339,
        1088-1090
Szasz, T. 1221

Taff, M.L. 679
Tanay, E. 377, 1224
Tardiff, K. 852
Task Force on Psychiatric Services
        378, 575
Tata, P.R. 754
Taylor, P.J. 97
Templeman, R. 180, 181
Templer, D.I. 98, 252, 254, 255
Teplin, L.A. 1, 99, 100, 471, 481,
        576-581, 1101, 1225-1229
Thaut, M.H. 658
Thomas, J.N. 1057
Thomas-Dobson, S. 252
Thompson, W.D. 153, 232
Thorburn, K.M. 729
Thornberry, T. 157
Thornton, D. 920
Thorwarth, C. 177
Thyer, B.A. 1008
Tien, G. 539
Tingle, D. 854, 986
Tobey, L.H. 256, 855
Toch, H. 101, 379, 380, 472, 856-858,
        1230
Tofler, D.S. 1103
Topitz, A. 85
Torpy, D. 1173
Torrey, E.F. 1231
Towberman, D.B. 657
Trasler, G. 473
Traub, G.S. 257
Travin, S. 900, 954, 1102
Troyer, R. 1005
Trupin, E. 326
Tucker, H.G. 766
Tuley, M.R. 259
Turner, R.E. 1132
Tyano, S. 168, 998

U.S. Government Accounting Office
        381
Uecker, J.C. 1256
Ulrich, C. 421
Urco, N. 994

Valdisseri, E.V. 582
Valliant, P.M. 613, 987
van den Hurk, A.A. 165
Van Deusen, J. 474
Van Dine, S. 859
Van Lankveld, J. 988
Van-Rybroek, G.J. 1181
Varan, L.R. 35
Vega, M. 1064
Velimesis, M.I. 1104
Verieur, D.E. 1044
Villanueva, M.R. 259, 1075
Virginia Department of Mental Health
    583
Virkkunen, M. 158
Vivian-Byrne, S. 648
Volavka, J. 860
Von Holden, M.H. 382, 383
von-Cleve, E. 6

Wagoner, J.L. 659
Waithe, M.E. 1232
Walker, N. 226, 861
Walker, P. 989
Wall, R.V. 910
Wallace, J.H. 645
Wallbrown, F.H. 207, 222
Walsh, J. 584
Walters, G.D. 102, 103, 159-161,
    260-262
Warren, M.Q. 475, 1233
Washington, P.A. 384, 585
Wasyliw, O.E. 408, 476
Waters, W.F. 838
Watson, R.J. 911, 990
Watson, S.M. 1058
Weaver, C.M. 895
Webster, C.D. 208, 238, 241, 263,
    385, 415, 449, 477, 799, 862
Weidemann, J.A. 1182
Weinberger, L.E. 440, 1234
Weiner, B.A. 1126
Weinstein, H.C. 586, 1232, 1235
Weiss-Cassady, D.M. 628
Weissman, J.C. 587
Weisstub, D.N. 1236
Weizman, R. 168, 998
Welldon, E.V. 661
Weller, B.G. 386

Weller, M.P. 386
Wellisch, J. 1105
Wenk, E. 863
West, D.J. 1238
West, M.A. 949
Westmore, B. 865
White, E.V. 420, 421
White, G. 1052
White, S.L. 1059
Whiteford, H.A. 865
Whiteside, R. 1010
Whitman, L. 709
Whitmer, G.E. 588
Wideranders, M.R. 388
Widom, C.S. 1106
Wiederholt, I.C. 991
Wiertsema, H.L. 389
Wilcox, D.E. 866
Wilfley, D.E. 1072, 1107
Wilhelm, C.L. 629
Williams, L.M. 971
Williams, M. 390, 1063
Williams, P. 1240
Williams, R. 1241
Williams, T. 391
Williams, W. 867
Wilson, J. 1108
Winer, D. 573, 574
Winfree, L.T. 731, 733
Winkler, G.E. 732
Winslow, W.W. 970
Wise, A. 833
Witherspoon, A.D. 1085
Wolpe, J. 978
Wong, S. 660
Wool, R. 478
Wooldredge, J.D. 733
World Health Organization 104, 1138
Wormith, J.S. 992
Wortzman, G. 199
Wright, F. 1242
Wright, P. 939
Wrobel, N.H. 265
Wrobel, T.A. 265
Wulach, J.S. 105, 162
Wunderlich, R.A. 663, 1060

Yang, H.K. 106
Yarbrough, J. 474

Yarvis, R.M. 107
Yelsma, J. 868
Yelsma, P. 868
Yeudall, L.T. 909
Yokelson, S. 266
Young, J.T. 392
Young, L.G. 945
Young, T.J. 1264
Yu, P.H. 180, 181
Yudowitz, B. 1078

Zager, L.D. 267
Zenoff, E.H. 329
Zimmerman, R.R. 614
Zimpfer, D.G. 664, 665, 1061
Ziskin, J. 268
Zitrin, A. 869
Zohar, A. 992
Zoloth, S.R. 527
Zona, M.A. 870
Zonana, H. 1237
Zusman, J. 1172
Zverina, J. 479, 993
Zwerling, I. 509

Subject Index

(Entries are citation numbers rather than page numbers)

Acting Out 669, 881

Addiction 18, 26, 165, 354, 501, 1029, 1091, 1093

Adjustment to Prison 102, 174

Adolescence 149, 455, 708, 1014, 1046, 1141

Adolescent Offenders 756, 1000, 1009, 1011, 1014, 1030, 1052, 1054

Adolescents 113, 663, 885, 999, 1002, 1004, 1007, 1009, 1026, 1030, 1041, 1050, 1060

Affective Disorders 17, 35, 99, 408, 578, 1063

Affective Disturbances 187

African Americans 142, 405, 875, 1037, 171, 233, 260, 774, 786, 1054, 1062, 579, 774

Aftercare 38, 489, 1084, 1145

Aggression 17, 128, 649, 739, 745, 775, 793, 837, 876, 949, 950, 985, 1249

Aggressive Behavior 2, 127, 425, 1035, 1041, 1181

AIDS 10, 19, 458, 691, 1034, 1091, 1152

Alcohol Abuse/Misuse 15, 23, 56, 89, 94, 167, 175, 200, 250, 253, 286, 384, 406, 426, 458, 469, 497, 546, 548, 762, 800, 813, 860, 992, 1009, 1011, 1018, 1087

Alcoholism 15, 113, 200, 242, 480, 553, 622, 887, 961, 970, 1004, 1087

Alternatives to Incarceration 579

American Indians 306

Anger 111, 220, 263, 624, 649, 652, 757, 767, 793, 837, 849, 850, 966, 1107

Anger Control 263, 624, 757, 850

Antisocial Behavior 6, 15, 31, 45, 64, 68, 89, 109, 110, 118, 119, 122, 126, 149, 154, 158, 159, 161, 240, 327, 455, 480, 507, 579, 606, 1003, 1029, 1072

Antisocial Personality 6, 31, 45, 64, 89, 109, 118, 119, 126, 149, 154, 158, 159, 161, 240, 327, 455, 480, 579, 1072

Anxiety 31, 67, 68, 108, 142, 225, 500, 541, 553, 554, 589, 606, 613, 637, 745, 849, 1030

Arrest 3, 23, 48, 75, 90, 184, 250, 305, 388, 413, 501, 505, 507, 511, 512, 517, 522, 527, 546, 567, 570, 581, 690, 1064, 1084, 1196, 1226

Arson 860
Assertive Case Management 431
Assertiveness Training 616, 962
Aversive Conditioning 910, 914

Beck Depression Inventory 2, 345,
    1121
Behavior Change 342, 424
Behavior Disorders 442
Behavior Modification 309, 355, 387,
    914
Behavior Therapy 295, 316, 323, 345,
    613, 874, 978
Benzodiazepines 745
Biofeedback 789
Biological Factors 882
Bipolar Disorder 17, 147, 221, 834
Borderline Personality 142, 685, 825,
    913
Brain Damage 199, 598, 915, 1012

Case Management 143, 431, 440, 467,
    501, 563, 565
Castration 106, 886, 981, 984, 993,
    1125
Child Abuse 962, 973, 1055
Childhood 132, 507, 854, 860, 912,
    986, 1007
Chronically Mentally Ill 2, 382, 400,
    534, 535, 620
Civil Commitment 350, 396, 403, 492,
    804, 839
Civil Rights 526
Classification of Offenders 53, 118,
    160, 166, 169, 170, 173, 174,
    197, 206, 210, 212, 215, 235,
    258, 264, 267, 525, 878, 1106
Cocaine 507, 546, 548, 830
Coercion 1233, 1262
Cognitive Restructuring 962
Cognitive Therapy 886, 1125
Community Mental Health 24, 26,
    290, 310, 311, 325, 349, 406,
    438, 452, 453, 459, 462, 467,
    482, 489, 519, 528, 532, 537,
    565, 732, 803, 1045, 1184
Community Mental Health Centers 26,
    467, 1184
Community Mental Health Services
    482, 528, 537, 565
Community Treatment 287, 339, 400,
    463, 476, 554, 579
Community-Based Services 467, 546
Competence to be Executed 1116
Competence to Stand Trial 1242
Conditional Release 135, 388, 398,
    400, 743, 1173, 1209
Conjugal Visits 646
Consultation Services 290
Coping 332, 366, 380, 472, 500, 547,
    549, 850, 1006, 1176
Correctional Institutions 300, 368,
    599, 875, 1109, 1133, 1139,
    1186
Correctional Psychiatry 1164, 1204,
    1205
Correctional Psychology 1234, 1258,
    1264
Corrections 217, 234, 274, 314, 353,
    406, 423, 427, 442, 513, 515,
    523, 568, 577, 583, 621, 716,
    726, 1123, 1193, 1234, 1250
Counseling 36, 54, 68, 223, 293, 337,
    368, 384, 416, 423, 442, 457,
    464, 562, 585, 606, 608, 609,
    611, 616, 623, 628, 631, 636,
    637, 645, 647, 657, 665, 925,
    990, 1001, 1005, 1011, 1013,
    1026, 1029, 1039, 1050, 1086,
    1092, 1098, 1248, 1255, 1258,
    1259, 1264
Countertransference 407
Court Mandated Treatment 359
Covert Sensitization 375, 656, 886,
    910, 1011, 1125
CPI 109, 183
Creativity 11
Crime 16, 32, 35, 46, 57, 59, 69, 90,
    100, 105, 128, 175, 185, 191,
    200, 220, 244, 250, 282, 283,
    354, 386, 477, 531, 581, 733,
    737, 751, 752, 756, 781, 782,
    802, 806, 813, 815, 847, 860,
    863, 869, 910, 996, 1068,
    1133, 1145, 1163, 1242
Criminal Activity 3, 93, 522
Criminal Careers 130
Criminal History 488, 499, 738

Criminal Responsibility 35, 72, 230
Criminality 17, 56, 161, 261, 505, 587,
    773, 1003, 1064, 1155, 1237
Criminalization 429, 482, 485, 489,
    499, 506, 512, 526, 544, 1153,
    1225, 1229
Crisis Intervention 290, 413, 495, 676,
    683, 684, 1242

Dangerousness 122, 136, 230, 231,
    420, 438, 741, 743, 752, 763,
    764, 780-782, 785, 809, 811,
    812, 818, 819, 823, 832, 836,
    838-843, 848, 851, 862, 867,
    901
Death Row 179, 205, 760
Deinsitutionalization 482, 562
Delay of Gratification 112
Delusions 178, 870
Demographic Characteristics 1076
Denial 654, 940, 951, 962, 1053
Depression 6, 12, 68, 108, 480, 576,
    579, 606, 926, 1072, 1093
Detoxification 522
Development 252, 284, 331, 341, 349,
    366, 580, 609, 620, 632, 654,
    683, 703, 973, 1026, 1036,
    1046, 1053, 1087
Diversion 80, 402, 404, 412, 414, 433,
    434, 451, 461, 465, 466, 467,
    470, 472, 482, 491, 560, 579,
    1201
Domestic Violence 250
Driving Under the Influence 622
Drug Abuse 1, 6, 18, 19, 31, 56, 89,
    106, 242, 250, 426, 546, 860,
    1007, 1044, 1101
Drug Abusers 104, 207, 623
Drug Addiction 31, 1093
Drug Therapy 108
Drug Treatment 79, 236, 249, 305,
    406, 468, 522, 547, 550, 910,
    1083
Drug Use 48, 305, 431, 474, 507, 522,
    547, 548, 1029, 1083
Dual Diagnosis 5, 31, 43, 480, 1063
Dysthymia 6, 887

Education 19, 28, 54, 281, 307, 364,

638, 811, 886, 959, 962, 993,
    1009, 1011, 1026, 1038, 1053,
    1087, 1092, 1103, 1125
Elderly Offenders 67, 68, 97, 225,
    606, 1007, 1017, 1148
Emotionally Disturbed 102, 103, 269,
    653, 1141
Empathy 962, 965, 1053
Employment 298, 303, 474, 548,
    1064, 1249
Ethical Issues 665, 877, 954, 1116,
    1118, 1129, 1161, 1197, 1232,
    1234, 1241
Ethics 1122, 1124, 1185, 1202, 1206,
    1235
Ethnic Differences 26, 233, 426, 771,
    1088
Ethnic Minorities 26
Etiology 882, 944, 949, 950
Exhibitionism 876, 887, 902

Faking 943
Family Dynamics 1029
Family Therapy 423, 424, 430, 443,
    625, 646, 648, 886, 908, 937,
    974, 1000, 1024, 1045, 1058,
    1125
Fathers 619, 890
Female Offenders 657, 1068, 1072,
    1076, 1078, 1093, 1100, 1106
Followup Studies 157, 418, 1011
Forensic Hospitals 79, 236, 440, 772,
    776, 1249, 1262
Forensic Psychiatry 15, 30, 35, 49, 62,
    86, 124, 200, 271, 276, 296,
    303, 315, 342, 362, 486, 596,
    679, 711, 747, 866, 1112,
    1121, 1132, 1158, 1160, 1164,
    1191, 1205, 1208, 1212, 1232,
    1235, 1247, 1251, 1256, 1263
Forensic Psychology 39, 41, 189, 201,
    244, 259, 335, 425, 799, 816,
    937, 941, 1051, 1075, 1136,
    1137, 1140, 1150, 1209, 1242,
    1261
Frontal Lobe 121, 860

Geriatric Psychiatry 1148
Grief Therapy 611, 769

Group Counseling 645, 647, 657, 665, 990, 1005
Group Dynamics 424, 654
Group Psychotherapy 495, 599, 602, 615, 617, 621, 627, 634, 638, 641, 643, 644, 650, 652, 657, 662, 779, 907, 910, 959, 971, 1010
Group Therapy 167, 374, 500, 620, 623, 629-631, 633, 635, 636, 637, 639, 652-655, 659, 660, 663, 665, 877, 908, 914, 925, 939, 955, 965, 976, 977, 985, 1034, 1053, 1060, 1107, 1118

Halfway Houses 170, 424
Hallucinations 15, 90, 178
Health Care Services 26, 143, 274, 311, 328, 347, 378, 481, 523, 552, 555, 575, 1081, 1092, 1131
Heroin 830
Homelessness 43, 75, 143, 473, 489, 501, 527, 565, 566, 791
Homicide 504, 681, 712, 713, 744, 762, 765, 768, 769, 817, 860, 1018, 1064, 1093
Hormonal Treatment 756, 981
Hostility 220, 233, 237, 259, 507, 589, 745, 754
Hypersexuality 897
Hypnosis 591

I-Level 169
Imprisonment 21, 42, 124, 184, 418, 472, 584, 1021
Impulse Control 1065
Impulsivity 151, 507, 850
Incest 893, 913, 914, 924, 937, 951, 960, 974, 975, 983
Incidence 18, 34, 42, 49, 185, 710, 739, 915, 961, 973, 1019, 1063
Individual Counseling 657, 1029
Individual Differences 109, 121, 125, 141, 152
Individual Psychotherapy 243, 293, 602, 939
Infanticide 217, 744, 1161, 1169
Inpatient Treatment 325

Insanity 35, 45, 94, 286, 321, 371, 397, 398, 400, 401, 408, 440, 447, 462, 470, 605, 654, 753, 1144, 1222
Insomnia 589
Intelligence 29, 91, 136, 774, 985, 992, 1052
Intensive Case Management 501
Interpersonal Relations 657, 885, 1002

Jail Detainees 99, 480, 481, 513, 568, 576-579, 581, 1101
Jail Environment 508
Jails 43, 64, 76, 80, 99, 273, 274, 281, 336, 354, 358, 378, 384, 409, 413, 439, 466, 467, 480, 481, 483, 484, 487-489, 493-495, 497-504, 507-510, 513, 515 524, 526, 528, 530-557, 559-563, 565, 566, 568, 569, 575-588, 666, 671, 673-677, 681-683, 688-697, 701, 703, 705, 710, 714, 716, 717, 719, 723, 727-729, 731-734, 738, 1019, 1084, 1091, 1094, 1095, 1097, 1101, 1145, 1152, 1176, 1220, 1240, 1254, 1260
Juvenile Delinquency 1007, 1024, 1035, 1061

Life Sentence 757
Lithium Carbonate 834
Locus of Control 229, 323
Longitudinal Studies 46, 180, 181, 485, 581, 733
LSD 651

Major Depression 12, 1072
Malingering 40, 41, 45, 178, 188, 268
Mania 6, 7, 105, 1093
MAO Inhibitors 144, 740
Marijuana 830
Marital Therapy 626, 911, 955, 1140
MCMI 163, 209
Measurement 233, 638, 750
Medical Personnel 284
Mental Health Services 23, 217, 248, 287, 290, 292, 320, 321, 327, 348, 364, 372, 376, 384, 438,

465, 482, 487, 494, 496, 498,
    503, 510, 515, 519, 528,
    530-533, 537, 539, 555-557,
    561, 565, 571, 611, 1063,
    1081, 1123, 1193, 1234
Mental Health Standards 515, 1110,
    1111, 1217
Mental Health Training 703
Mental Retardation 9, 76, 91, 113,
    338, 583, 746, 923, 961, 985,
    1004, 1145, 1146, 1210
Methadone Treatment 359, 522
Milieu Therapy 279
Military Offenders 49, 89, 102, 103,
    159, 160, 185, 346
Minor Tranquilizers 500
MMPI 40, 41, 67, 68, 83, 102, 103,
    109, 147, 149, 154, 159, 160,
    163, 170-172, 174, 177, 179,
    183, 187, 189, 190, 209-212,
    214, 220-222, 224, 225, 227,
    237, 239, 240, 243, 244, 247,
    252, 257, 259, 260, 265, 267,
    455, 548, 606, 637, 767, 774,
    797, 922, 999, 1076
Mood Disorders 142
Multiple Personality Disorder 45, 69,
    115
Multisystemic Therapy 885, 1002,
    1003, 1029-1031, 1054
Murder 90, 762, 774, 830, 1018
Music Therapy 7, 293, 640, 658
Myers-Briggs 1085

Narcissism 162
Needs Assessment 325
Neuroleptic Drugs 440
Neurological Factors 758
Neurosis 553
Neuroticism 589
Nursing Practice 343, 347, 557, 611,
    1034, 1048, 1079-1081, 1092,
    1098, 1100, 1108, 1120, 1123,
    1129-1131, 1139, 1165, 1189,
    1191, 1193, 1207, 1220

OBS 50
Occupational Therapy 304, 334, 335,
    632

Opiate 31, 587, 1103
Outpatient Treatment 401, 407, 408,
    440, 443, 462, 479, 885, 908,
    979, 985, 1002
Overcrowding 544, 713

Paranoia 108
Paranoid Schizophrenia 90
Paraphilias 934, 981, 1069
Parole 23, 136, 161, 175, 393, 394,
    430, 457, 474, 501, 612, 756,
    771
Parricide 747
Pastoral Counseling 608
Pathological Gambling 98
Patricide 755
Pedophilia 912
Personality Assessment 159, 163, 184,
    187, 207, 227, 228, 239, 245,
    256, 260, 855, 922, 1200
Personality Characteristics 67, 103,
    149, 175, 225, 455, 654, 772,
    1076
Personality Disorders 15, 56, 79, 108,
    113, 123, 124, 137, 146, 147,
    154, 221, 236, 240, 303, 384,
    554, 579, 883, 913, 1004,
    1067, 1072, 1082, 1093
Physical Abuse 113, 1004
Physiological Measures 967
Plethysmograph 878
Police 373, 399, 402, 406, 444, 471,
    485, 491, 512, 519, 529, 674,
    677, 800, 856, 870, 1226,
    1235, 1257
Policy Making 1226
Polydrug Use 28
Pornography 896, 955, 958
Post-Release Adjustment 60, 393
Poverty 458, 501
Pregnancy 1081
Pretrial Assessment 208, 449, 539,
    541, 799, 939, 1101, 1201
Prevalence of Mental Disorder 3, 9,
    12, 17, 31, 36, 49, 50, 63, 80,
    91, 99, 102, 142, 200, 209,
    362, 372, 499, 527, 560, 562,
    578, 579, 670, 691, 704, 771,
    1072, 1082, 1101

Prevention 42, 675, 683, 694, 695,
        697-700, 710, 711, 714, 715,
        719, 726, 744, 803, 874, 942,
        948, 953, 976, 1003, 1100
Prison Adjustment 174, 186, 214, 264
Prison Environment 290, 327, 592,
        1129, 1152, 1258
Probation 23, 249, 305, 355, 364, 394,
        426, 429, 430, 458, 464, 468,
        474, 498, 612, 615, 635, 647,
        659, 771, 971, 1024, 1145,
        1184
Professional Roles 1200
Prognosis 480, 927
Program Evaluation 170, 338
Psychiatric Assessment 144, 433, 819
Psychiatric Diagnosis 164, 1068
Psychiatric Services 21, 43, 94, 273,
        287, 378, 502, 575, 586, 724,
        997, 1149
Psychiatric Symptoms 6, 15, 108, 119,
        165, 168, 178, 188, 354, 508,
        545, 566, 576, 592, 870, 998
Psychoanalysis 604
Psychodrama 617, 627, 652, 657
Psychodynamics 874, 914, 925, 991
Psychological Assessment 129, 172,
        212, 213, 217, 220
Psychological Autopsy 672, 727
Psychopathology 113, 132, 144, 172,
        188, 260, 508, 517, 548, 767,
        813, 837, 1004, 1036
Psychopathy 109, 112, 120, 125, 128,
        129, 131, 132, 136, 137, 141,
        144, 151, 152, 155, 919
Psychopathy Checklist 129, 131, 132,
        141, 151, 155
Psychosis 740, 746
Psychosocial Rehabilitation 303
Psychotherapy 68, 134, 243, 293, 407,
        445, 479, 495, 593, 595, 596,
        598-600, 602, 603, 605, 606,
        610, 612, 614, 615, 617, 619,
        621, 627, 634, 638, 641, 643,
        644, 649, 650, 652, 657,
        661-663, 761, 767, 779, 876,
        886, 890, 892, 907, 910, 914,
        925, 928, 939, 959, 971, 977,
        981, 1010, 1012, 1014, 1026,

        1040, 1060, 1125, 1143
Psychosis 2, 38, 42, 53, 56, 77, 147,
        178, 215, 221, 228, 236, 245,
        295, 429, 449, 498, 525, 554,
        558, 582, 899, 966, 1063,
        1068, 1073, 1074, 1100, 1262
PTSD 3, 49, 89
Public Policy 481, 839, 840, 843
Punishment 42, 106, 269, 366, 428

Race Bias 1037
Rape 669, 881, 887, 916, 917, 926,
        1017
Recidivism 22, 132, 149, 167, 170,
        272, 285, 342, 356, 359, 370,
        388, 408, 419, 420, 436, 455,
        501, 563, 565, 663, 764, 885,
        924, 953, 974, 980, 985, 1002,
        1008, 1024, 1035, 1060, 1151
Referral Decision Scale 186, 580
Rehabilitation 9, 54, 67, 86, 95, 123,
        166, 175, 183, 225, 259, 270,
        272, 280, 285, 303, 307, 335,
        340, 359, 362, 368, 384, 416,
        424, 426, 435, 442, 457, 464,
        497, 549, 562, 584, 585, 589,
        616, 623, 628, 630, 631, 636,
        637, 659, 704, 757, 883, 894,
        908, 953, 975, 991, 1021,
        1026, 1032, 1039, 1086, 1092,
        1248, 1259
Relapse Prevention 874, 942, 948,
        953, 976
Religious Beliefs 833
Role Conflicts 1117, 1168
Rorschach 228, 245
Rural Offenders 505, 510, 1054

Sadistic Personality 883
Schizophrenia 2, 4, 6, 16, 33, 46, 60,
        64, 79, 85, 90, 94, 99, 102,
        106, 113, 280, 303, 327, 384,
        408, 553, 576, 578, 579, 595,
        634, 779, 899, 1004, 1062,
        1067, 1072, 1093
Schizotypal Personality 825
SCL-90 408, 508
Screening 161, 172, 186, 192, 195,
        196, 198, 217, 242, 246, 253,

260, 261, 290, 354, 469, 527,
    539, 543, 545, 555, 562, 576,
    580, 683, 703, 1096
Self-Concept 167, 614, 1051
Self-Help 426, 974
Self-Injurious Behavior 685, 704
Self-Mutilation 158, 729
Sex Offenders 94, 276, 443, 613, 669,
    854, 874-879, 881, 883, 887,
    894, 895, 899-902, 904, 907,
    908, 910, 911, 915, 920, 930,
    931, 936, 939, 940, 942, 948,
    951, 953-955, 957, 961-963,
    965, 971, 973, 976, 977,
    985-991, 993, 1005, 1008,
    1017, 1026, 1051, 1052, 1053,
    1055, 1086, 1093, 1102, 1118
Sexual Abuse 669, 760, 881, 912,
    932, 962, 965, 972, 1007, 1014
Sexual Arousal 871, 878, 905, 921,
    967, 976, 992, 1069
Sexual Assault 944, 958, 966, 1052
Sexual Deviation 916, 993
Social Climate 652
Social Control 1172, 1218
Social Isolation 289
Social Learning 345
Social Skills Training 29, 110, 295,
    423, 613, 874, 880, 910, 939,
    961, 962
Social Support 1081
Social Withdrawal 136
Solitary Confinement 280
Stress 3, 40, 42, 49, 89, 423, 442, 671,
    748, 850, 1081, 1093
Stress Management 423
Substance Abuse 5, 6, 26, 31, 75, 94,
    100, 119, 142, 195, 199, 281,
    323, 339, 354, 406, 423, 454,
    467, 481, 495, 502, 512,
    545-550, 562, 579, 581, 639,
    659, 746, 1063, 1064, 1101,
    1262
Substance Abuse Treatment 281, 323,
    354, 423, 454, 545, 546, 548,
    549, 550
Suicide 108, 246, 292, 504, 554, 666,
    667, 670-675, 677, 678, 680
    683, 685, 687-700, 702, 703,

705, 706, 710-722, 724-727,
    730, 732, 733, 817, 1019, 1096
Suicide Prevention 675, 683, 714,
    719, 726
Support Groups 1152

Tardive Dyskinesia 1169
Taxonomies 922
Testosterone 756, 887, 888, 981
Therapeutic Communities 133, 146,
    293, 301, 325, 339, 356, 374,
    655, 887, 981
Token Economy 316
Torture 280
Training 86, 110, 277, 281, 293, 295,
    298, 303, 362, 423, 458, 495,
    613, 616, 623, 624, 645, 649,
    703, 717, 726, 789, 874, 910,
    939, 985, 1129, 1250-1253,
    1258, 1261, 1263
Transcendental Meditation 589
Transsexuals 1194
Treatment Compliance 939
Treatment Effectiveness 79, 176, 230,
    272, 293, 298, 406, 424, 457,
    467, 522, 533, 549, 623,
    629-631, 645, 895, 1006,
    1010, 1233, 1245
Treatment Planning 182, 297, 354,
    366

Validity 160, 165, 169, 172, 174, 193,
    209, 229, 247, 258, 262, 851,
    967
Veterans 3, 49, 89, 207
Videotape 19, 629, 726
Vietnam Veterans 3, 89, 207
Violence 1, 46, 128, 136, 211, 219,
    220, 250, 346, 483, 488, 523,
    581, 734, 738, 739, 741, 756,
    758-761, 767, 772, 776, 778,
    780, 788-790, 797, 799, 803,
    804, 808, 813, 825, 829, 831,
    834, 837, 843, 845, 847, 850,
    851, 852, 854, 856, 857, 863,
    869, 887, 888, 928, 960, 986,
    988, 989, 1003, 1052, 1084,
    1203, 1242
Violent Offenders 199, 654, 740, 748,

754, 766, 795, 825, 860, 875,
    1062, 1076
Vocational 86, 293, 303, 323, 335,
    623
Voyeurism 876, 902

WAIS 786

About the Compilers

RODNEY VAN WHITLOCK is a community psychologist in private practice. He was a co-compiler with Bernard Lubin for *Family Therapy: A Bibliography* and *Homelessness in America, 1893–1992: An Annotated Bibliography*.

BERNARD LUBIN is Professor of Psychology and Medicine at the University of Missouri-Kansas City. He is the compiler of numerous bibliographies for Greenwood Press, including *Family Therapy: A Bibliography* and *Homelessness in America, 1893–1992: An Annotated Bibliography* with Rodney Van Whitlock.

ISBN 0-313-30186-7

90000>

9 780313 301865

HARDCOVER BAR CODE

EAN